HARVEY S. FIRESTONE

THE FIRESTONE STORY

THE
Firestone Story

A HISTORY OF THE
FIRESTONE TIRE & RUBBER COMPANY

by Alfred Lief

WHITTLESEY HOUSE

McGraw-Hill Book Company, Inc.
New York · Toronto · London

THE FIRESTONE STORY

PUBLISHED BY THE MCGRAW-HILL BOOK COMPANY, INC.

PRINTED IN THE UNITED STATES OF AMERICA

Contents

APPENDIX

THE FIRESTONE STORY

An institution is the lengthened shadow of one man.—EMERSON

THE energy of the American people swept through the years in pursuit of fullness of living. Our freedom for growth enabled the nation to grow great. On the threshold of the twentieth century we were fired afresh with the spirit of venture and adventure. New enterprises were planned and launched and tested in the marketplace. They made contributions to society, to the ever-rising standard of American well-being. Industry marched with the buoyancy of self-confidence and the steady drive of faith in one's product. The year was 1900.

Background

THE year was 1900 and Harvey S. Firestone, already experienced in the rubber business, left Chicago for the rubber center of Akron, Ohio. He was thirty-one years old. He arrived with his wife and infant son in a January snowstorm. Harvey jr. snug in his arm, the couple went afoot from the depot to the Windsor Hotel, about four blocks away. This would be their quarters till they found a suitable house. From this day, Akron was home.

Akron was a bustling city with less than 43,000 population, formerly important for the manufacture of harvesting machinery. That industry had shifted to Illinois and Wisconsin, closer to the newer grain sources. The rubber-goods industry, however, having gained a foothold here in competition with New England, was in readiness when the bicycle vogue engulfed the country in the 1890s, and a vast production of tires to keep millions of eager cyclists happy was turned out in Akron. Virtually every bicycle factory had its own brand of tire, built under contract.

Next came a demand for solid rubber tires on carriages, a demand awakened by persistent salesmanship. Liverymen, doctors, undertakers, and soon a wider public took to the innovation of comfort in riding. The cushioning effect of rubber spared both the vehicles and the occupants from a jolting. Rubber City simmered with awareness of opportunity. People engaged in other businesses branched out—men already active in mowers and

3

reapers, in street railways, in building construction—they saw a future in rubber. A firm that manufactured twist drills, Whitman & Barnes, produced a line of carriage tires and rubber horseshoe pads.

Harvey Firestone came to Akron to join Whitman & Barnes. As an early enthusiast he had sported the first rubber-tired carriage in Detroit in 1893. In those days this youthful state manager for the Columbus Buggy Company and member of the Gentlemen's Riding Club of Highland Park, Michigan, was riding high—before the depression of 1896 caused the buggy works to collapse like the fabled shay and spurred him to go into business for himself. With two financial partners, he bought out a shop in busy Chicago, and in a wagon he traversed the cobbled streets to pick up wheels at livery stables.

This was a retail business, with service. Firestone bought the tires from a manufacturer. They came in lengths, with two longitudinal wires in them to secure them in the channel, a new improvement on the method of clinching the rubber between converging rim flanges. Firestone thought he had obtained the use of a welding machine with the shop, but it developed that the machine had been leased to his predecessor by a company which now took it back; and he had to manage by brazing the wire ends together. The difficulties of a beginner were his lot; the overcoming of them, his success. "He was one of the hardest working men I ever met," said a Chicago contemporary.

By 1898, the Firestone Rubber Tire Company on Wabash Avenue was in a position to buy out a rival down the street, the Imperial Rubber Tire Company, and between the two of them these separately run concerns did the largest carriage-tire business in the city. As they thrived, they caught the eye of a promoter who held a good grip on the patent situation, and when they were invited to sell out, an attractive price was offered and accepted. Thus the two firms went into the hands of the Rubber Tire Wheel Company, of Springfield, Ohio, which in turn became part of a huge combination, the Consolidated Rubber Tire Company, organized by a New York syndicate. It was an era of mergers and big money.

The big money paid off Firestone and his partners but retained him as manager of its Chicago wholesale-retail business. In this capacity, he placed large contracts with Akron tire factories, dividing the orders among them. Disagreement over policy arose between Firestone and the Springfield home office; he was restless, and a few months later he left for Akron, with about $42,000 capital.

Owning a patent on a device for applying tires to carriage wheel channels, he proposed to take over Whitman & Barnes' tire department. Their "Easy" tires did not fit standard channels; Firestone's did. The great problem of the day was how to keep tires from slipping off, and competition tended to concentrate upon mechanical features, for the rubber compound itself was rather standardized. His patent, instead of following the common practice of springing the tire into place after joining the ends, applied even tension to the retaining wires, prior to the joining, and thus held the tire firmly and evenly in the channeled rim.

Prior commitments by Whitman & Barnes forestalled the deal the two parties had in mind. Yet the company wanted to handle the "Firestone Tire" in some way, without covenanting to manufacture standard-channel tires exclusively for him. They had not been making much headway with the "Easy." On the other hand, Firestone needed action. The result was that he went along with them in their Buchtel Avenue factory down by the railroad tracks, as manager of tire sales. He would be paid a royalty on tires made and sold under his patent.

But soon Firestone realized that Whitman & Barnes was taking the path of least resistance, pushing the shoe pad for fire-truck and ambulance horses in New York and other cities and not giving him proper support in tire manufacturing. By the summer of 1900, the company offered him an option on the tire department.

At this point, several Akron men, sharing a patent for a sidewire device that would free tires of the danger of wire cutting and prevent creeping on the rim, sought him out. These drawbacks had persisted despite progress in the art. At first, tires had been compressed so deep in the rim that their surface possessed little resilience. When a shallower channel with diverging flanges was introduced (controlled by the Springfield company), more of the rubber was exposed; also, the internal wires did a better job of holding the tire in place. This was what gave the carriage-tire business its real boom. Moreover, the Consolidated began to operate a factory in Akron, acquired in the merger, and threatened to bring infringement suits against its former suppliers there who were manufacturing similar tires for their own customers.

But strain in use caused these solid tires to tear away from their anchorage, and in the case of heavier commercial vehicles creeping was inevitable. Naturally, Firestone was interested when Dr. Louis E. Sisler, the county auditor and a retired physician, asked him to look at the sidewire invention. If it could do all that it promised, a large market would be opened.

They met in the home of James Christy jr., on East Buchtel Avenue, near the college campus. Christy was in the leather business. Present also were James A. Swinehart, the originator of the invention, and W. D. Buckman, one of Sisler's deputies. Swinehart was a building contractor with a yearning for rubber, and he had helped put up a factory to produce under a Springfield license; but the license was eventually withheld, and the idea for the sidewire came to him in his necessitous state. Fire destroyed the plant before he could manufacture. He assigned part ownership to his friends Sisler and Christy, and together they went in quest of a man who had capital and experience and dependability.

That July night Firestone examined the new tire: instead of longitudinal wires it had cross bars embedded near the base of the rubber and two endless retaining wires sprung over the channel edges to engage the projecting ends of the cross bars. That night The Firestone Tire & Rubber Company was conceived.

I

The Beginning

THE Firestone Tire & Rubber Company of Akron, Ohio, received its charter as a corporation under the laws of West Virginia on August 3, 1900, eight days after Harvey S. Firestone signed an agreement with his associates.* By the terms of the agreement he put up $10,000, half the cash investment, they the other half; he contributed his patent and his Whitman & Barnes option, while they assigned the sidewire patent to the corporation. The capital stock consisted of 400 shares of common at $100 par (increased by 100 shares before the end of the year) and Firestone received fifty percent of the total.

At the first meeting of the board of directors he was named general manager, to serve at a salary of $3,000 a year and receive a $600 bonus if profits justified it. James Christy jr. was elected president, James A. Swinehart vice president, Harvey S. Firestone treasurer, and Louis E. Sisler secretary. The officers' titles were nominal. The work fell to the general manager.

He took over the unexpired leases of Whitman & Barnes' stores in three cities, arranged with that company to manufacture the tires, and rented a small one-room building on its grounds to house the new corporation. The room was partitioned off into a shipping department

* Ohio's corporation laws at this time imposed double liability upon stockholders. This provision no longer obtained when the company expanded and reorganized under an Ohio charter in 1910.

and three tiny offices. From his cramped corner Harvey
Firestone launched a sales campaign.

Duplicated letters, individually addressed to owners of
livery stables in each of the cities, notified them of the
change:

The Whitman & Barnes Mfg. Co. deciding to discontinue the sale
of rubber tires to the carriage trade have turned over their branches
to us in New York, Chicago, and Boston, and we will use our best
efforts to take care of their trade. We purchased their stock of Easy
tires, and will sell them at reduced prices, no guarantee. It is not
our intention to push the sale of Easy tires as we have another tire
superior to *any* tire ever placed on the market. In saying this we
realize that we must prove our statement. This we are prepared to
do, as our tire has been thoroughly tested in actual service for nearly
two years, and we have the endorsement of every carriage manufacturer that has tested the tire, and can refer you to them as well
as leading liverymen who have given them a severe test and cannot
recommend them too highly.

For the past four years the writer has endeavored to furnish the
best tire he could obtain, and now feels safe in saying he can furnish
you a tire that will give you one-half more to twice the amount of
service that can be obtained from any tire having retaining wires
passing through the tire. It is a well-known fact that *these wires cut*
the tire before they are half worn out. No wires *through* our tires to
cut—*they wear out*. Every carriage maker and liveryman is interested,
we *absolutely have* what we claim. Telephone us and we will have our
representative call and demonstrate the advantages of our tire—we
are prepared to give you quick service.*

Form letters went out also to lists of physicians—the
family doctor must have elegance in his horse and buggy.
New branches were opened in St. Louis, a carriage-build-
ing center, and Philadelphia. Franchises were extended
to agents in Pueblo, Colorado, Fond du Lac, Wisconsin,
and other promising communities. The network of a
sturdy sales organization began to stretch over the map.
In the first booklet that was issued, Firestone tires—

* First letter to the trade, Aug. 31, 1900.

described as "overcoming the faults of all the old-style tires"—were offered as ideal not only for horse-drawn vehicles but equally so for those new horseless, self-propelled pleasure cars that some folks preferred to call automobiles. "Absolutely solid, no holes." The comparison was an allusion to the type that had longitudinal tunnels in them to harbor internal wires, where uneven compression forced rubber up on the sides or away from the channel. Solids fastened the sidewire way stayed gripped. They kept sand and cinders and water from working in between channel and tire.

In the manufacturing process, warmed-up rubber was fed into a "tubing" machine and extruded through a die that determined the shape of the cross section. While the rubber was still in the "green" state, cross bars were plunged in at intervals of three-quarters of an inch. Thus, when the tire was vulcanized, the bars were an integral part.

Another feature was a cylinder mold. Firestone's Perfect Side-Wire Tire was molded in a coil—you could not do this with the internal-wire article—a coil twelve inches in diameter, and since this was smaller than the diameter of the wheel, it meant that when the tire was put around the wheel the rubber immediately clung to the surface.

"Easily and inexpensively applied by any mechanic." The company furnished liverymen and carriage makers with a machine that snapped the outside retaining hoops over the rim and onto the projecting bars. It was simpler than most other methods of application, and the public appreciated this. Prices ranged from $35 for a set of four tires with a three-quarter-inch tread to $135 a set for the two-inch size, steel channels included.

In a few months, the company was overloaded with orders. It had to apologize to the trade and invoke their patience. Whitman & Barnes' facilities being taxed to the limit, Firestone needed another licensee and gave Goodrich a contract.

The sales volume for the first year was $110,000. But there were no profits. Harvey Firestone received no bonus. This did not bother him, for he was building an enterprise. As more capital was needed to finance the orders, the board voted to increase the capital stock from $50,000 to $150,000; many a time Firestone had been obliged personally to endorse a bank loan. Half of the increase was distributed, as a 100 percent stock dividend, to the stockholders in proportion to their current holdings. He became a stock salesman as well as a tire salesman, buttonholing friends and business acquaintances and buying more shares himself.

"I must manufacture my own tires," he said. That would be the road to profits. He met a banker who was eager to dispose of several old iron foundry buildings in South Akron, and he decided to take one of them, with six lots, for $4,500. This was in September, 1901. The banker accepted notes and told him that payment could be made any time the company could afford it. More than a year elapsed before manufacturing actually began.

Meanwhile sales had totaled $150,000 in the company's second year, again without yield to the investors, and Swinehart divested himself of most of his shares. Swinehart organized a new firm, to sell European rights to the sidewire patent, and went abroad on a successful trip. Shortly afterward, Christy resigned and moved to Washington. For a brief period, Firestone was president in his place, Sisler serving temporarily as treasurer. (It may be noted here that Sisler remained as a director until his death in 1925.)

Firestone had sunk all his money into the venture that claimed his convictions and energetic ardor. He held 750 of the 1,500 shares and was living modestly in a rented house for $40 a month on a pleasant street called Fir Hill. Other entrepreneurs cutting a figure in Akron business life had homes of their own, but he could not spare a cent for any investment other than in his company.

The virtues of the Firestone tire made it especially desirable for service in transport, and this was the field he particularly plowed despite timid souls who looked askance at heavy freight on rubber. Rubber tires had come in as a touch of luxury. Their first appearance on business wagons had lent a bit of advertising glamour. But to use them in trucking seemed like dressing up a drayman in fauntleroys—or so the critics snickered, for the pace of horse-drawn trucks was too slow to require absorption of vibration. Such experts lacked imagination. They failed to see that the resilience of rubber would enable heavy vehicles to take the shocks of the road while going fast; that a rubber tread could give traction and therefore greater speed with safety.

In other words, rubber tires made hauling more economical.

Firestone sold them for baggage transfer wagons, busses, trucks, and fire engines. A customer in St. Louis, the Interstate Transit Company, using four-inch tires, jubilantly reported that one of them had run 5,000 miles.

Advertising hailed "the only practical solid tire" for this purpose. For automobiles too: the electrics, steamers, and gasoline cars. As the driving power of a motor car had to be transmitted through the wheels, it became obvious that rubber tires really were means of making automobiles feasible.

Firestone tires were advertised as "constructed to withstand the severe strain on propelling wheels without cutting out at the base or becoming loose . . . desirable for light automobiles with delicate mechanisms, as well as for the heavier machines where endurance is the great requisite."

As business in Chicago grew, the branch moved into a building of its own. Letters to the trade there gave this reminder: "Chicago streets are hard on rubber tires." Hence, nothing less than the best was needed. Firestones "look neater, ride easier, turn out of car tracks easier."

Vigilance! The company warned its agencies against defective tires which Firestone had rejected from Whitman & Barnes, who were offering them to the trade (at cut prices) although not authorized to sell them. The contract with Whitman & Barnes had expired, having run only a year.

Plans were projected for the factory. They required more cash and a stronger foundation for credit. One of Harvey Firestone's prospects for the purchase of stock was James Christy's brother Will, a leader in the expanding industrial community. Will Christy had pioneered Akron's horsecar line and later organized the interurban electric to Cleveland; he was the head of the telephone company, of a building company, of a bank. His name would bring prestige, Firestone figured, as he sold him $10,000 worth of stock and induced him to assume the presidency.

The next step was to make a further increase in the capitalization—to $200,000—at a board meeting in 1902. While Firestone was busy selling stock, he was also busy equipping a plant. The one-story foundry building acquired for the company was built of tile and afforded 75- by 100-foot floor space. In it he installed an engine bought secondhand for $1,135, two boilers costing $1,800, a machine for washing rubber $850, two mills for mixing it (one of them new) $2,500, two tubing machines, two pumps, a vulcanizer (secondhand), and several used molds. There was no money to spend on a calender, essential for rubber-coating the strip of fabric applied to the base of a tire; for the first year they would have the fabric calendered outside. A well was dug in the yard to furnish the water.

On December 27 everything was ready. With an eye for the dramatic—and for the prophetic—Firestone held up his boy Harvey, who was scarcely five years old, and told him to pull the engine switch. His son started the factory in operation.

From the supply of capable workers in Akron, Firestone selected a foreman and eleven other good men. The foreman was engineer, pipefitter, plumber, and general utility man, but had no time to repair the roof that leaked; nor could the company afford to call in a tinsmith, not for a while. The prevailing hourly rates ranged from 16½ cents to 27½ cents. Although a workday was generally twelve hours long, there was no fixed number of hours in a Firestone day: work did not stop till it was done. Firestone himself took charge as superintendent, thereby adding another duty to his list.

The first tires made in the factory were a three-quarter-inch tread and a four-inch tread, on January 3, 1903. From that time, the plant was never to be idle a single day.

Among the orders coming in from the branches were some for Springfield internal-wire tires; the patent on them had been invalidated recently by the United States Circuit Court of Appeals in Cincinnati. These tires were cheaper than Firestone's and, although inferior, the company did not hesitate to produce them as well, for the demand was strong and nobody wanted to let sales go by default. Such was the nature of the industry. Goodrich, for example, once Firestone became self-sustaining as a manufacturer, did not stop making sidewires but continued for its own account and guaranteed Firestone a $25,000 minimum annual royalty.

Removal of the patent barrier to the production of Springfield tires had been acclaimed in Akron by the ringing of bells and the tooting of whistles. Freed of quota restrictions, the rubber companies made a race for the markets. Freed of the fixed prices that had been imposed on licensees, they underbid each other. The resultant condition in the industry was characterized as "demoralized" by the advocates of a pool, and such a pool was formed, each of eighteen tire makers contracting with the Rubber Tire Wheel Company to maintain prices and provide a fund for crushing outside competitors. Firestone did not join. The Consolidated, holder of the patent, eventually proceeded against Firestone in the New York jurisdiction.

While these conspiratorial moves were getting under way, the Firestone firm occupied itself with hard work. Its first export business was done this year. An order came through from José Alvarez y Cía., of Havana, for special-shape inch-and-a-half sidewire tires, and it was almost lost. Harvey Firestone guessed that novice workmen had made a mess of applying them and failed to follow the instructions, so he dispatched his bookkeeper, Stacy G. Carkhuff, to Havana to show them how. After this effort, not only was the customer kept, but Alvarez obtained an exclusive agency for Cuba and for a time was the company's largest single outlet.

The Boston branch made especially good progress. Ninety percent of the commercial motor cars in that city were equipped with Firestone tires. The company's total sales for the fiscal year reached $230,000.

It was not surprising then, at the annual meeting in August, 1903, that a profit should be reported after a little more than half a year's manufacturing—only $8,503 to be sure, but it proved a point. No dividend, however, was declared. The money must be conserved for growth.

Now the factory, which had started with a daily output of forty tires, was running a night shift in the busy season and had a full-time superintendent. With all these orders, the company needed funds for the purchase of large quantities of crude rubber, payable one-third in cash, the balance in sixty and ninety days. Both Will Christy and Harvey Firestone endorsed notes. Problems of financing always kept the general manager stepping lively, dashing to out-of-town banks (Akron banking capital was insufficient to meet the demands of all the rubber manufacturers) and paying off obligations as they matured.

At this point it was decided that Christy should step down to the vice presidency and Firestone should become the head of the firm again in name as well as in fact.*

Foresight in anticipating an increased demand for large-size tires was ascribed to the company by the *India Rubber World*, which said it had been "able to make preparations and keep abreast of the times." More than foresight, it was faith. For Firestone knew that with such tires available, more trucks, more fire engines, and other heavy vehicles would roll on rubber.

The company could point—and did—to the fact that twenty-two of the biggest baggage transfer organizations in the country were using Firestone tires exclusively. In the words of the Frank Parmelee Company, which conducted a horse-drawn cab and transfer business in Chicago:

In 1898 we had forty of our heavy coaches equipped with rubber tires, and thereafter gradually equipped the balance. Our work is very hard on rubber tires, part of the coaches running twenty-four hours a day. We have tried a number of different tires upon the market and regret to say that we had considerable trouble until we

* Aug. 15, 1903.

adopted your tire, about a year and a half ago. Since that time we have noted a marked decrease in loss of time to our vehicles caused by delays for repairs to the tires, and have found that your tires do not cut out at the base, and it is our common experience to have them wear to the channel without repairs.

On account of the service we have received from your tire and the courteous and fair treatment we have received at your hands, we feel justified in giving you our experience as above, and so long as you continue to give us the service and treatment that you have we will continue to favor you with our business.*

The fire department of New York City placed an order. Promptly after a writeup appeared in the *Fireman's Herald,* reproductions of it were sent to fire chiefs in many cities. Soon the company was able to issue a special catalog showing photographs of fire apparatus equipped with Firestone tires and to make the claim that they had been adopted almost exclusively by the engine manufacturers and by more than a hundred municipalities. Safety and protection to the men and the horses; greater ease in making a run. These were the persuasive talking points. No other tire could stand the severity of fire department work.

Another important customer was the Anheuser-Busch Brewery, in St. Louis, for its fleet of electric trucks, some of them five-ton. A stream of letters and other literature poured out to the trade. Firestone was alert to every advertising opportunity. A booklet entitled "Tire Record" was issued to users, enabling them to determine which of their tires lasted longest and required the least repairs. A letter to the Chicago Automobile Club pointed out that the Firestone tire had "almost as great resiliency as any properly inflated pneumatic tire but none of the annoying weaknesses." Those early pneumatics fell easy prey to punctures, tube pinching, sidewall strains, and

* Testimonial letter from Frank Parmelee Co., July 8, 1903.

blowouts. They were not yet good enough to meet the Firestone standard of service for heavy vehicles.

Until the Firestone sidewire came upon the scene, solid tires had given only forty percent of their expected life, the company declared; they were thought to use up more power, they were not of sound mechanical construction, were not built with regard for the load. At the New York Automobile Show, Firestone exhibited specimens of sidewires still holding in place with less than a third of the rubber remaining.

New avenues of distribution kept opening up. Detroit carriage and wagon manufacturers were notified that arrangements had been made with the Fisk Rubber Company to handle the Firestone tire in Michigan. Studebaker Bros. of California took on the representation in San Francisco.

A letter to the general trade urged them to make contracts at once because the crude-rubber market was advancing, and if it continued to do so the current quotations on tires might not hold. Prices for sets of two-and-a-half-inch tires on twenty-five-inch wheels were $32, on sixty-inch wheels $68, including steel channels; for four-inch tires, $72 in the smaller wheel size, $160 in the larger. Other tire widths were five, six, and seven inches. A sensation at the show were Firestone's eight-inch solids; they sold for $734 the set, $50 extra for the rims. Cushion tires—solids with a soft core—were becoming "increasingly popular for light vehicles" in widths of one inch, one and a half, one and five-eighths.

Another source of business—because it was another service to the trade—was the development of live-steam vulcanization of tires in continuous lengths. They were sold in reels, and not an inch needed to be wasted. The trade would not be obliged to carry inventory in ten separate diameters for ten different wheels. This news was announced with customary cheer:

Among the good things we have to offer the coming season is both the Firestone Side-Wire Tire and the Firestone Internal Wire Tire in any length desired up to 500 feet. This method of construction has three strong points of advantage to the trade:

First. You always have the right length.

Second. It eliminates waste.

Third. Reduces to a minimum the necessary investments in stock.

We have devoted a great deal of time and expended a large amount in perfecting a process of manufacturing tires in long lengths and have it adaptable to the live steam process of curing, which is the only successful method of curing high grade rubber. It has always been our policy to produce the best tires possible and to use the most improved methods, and we take pride in being the first to offer this great improvement to the trade.

Our proposition for 1904 is interesting. If you have not secured it we would be glad to furnish you full particulars upon request, and will also send you a copy of the handsomest souvenir catalogue ever issued by a rubber tire company. Write us today.*

In the summer of 1904, the Louisiana Purchase Exposition, held in St. Louis, awarded Firestone a gold medal for its products, exhibited in Transportation Hall. Every rubber tire in service on the fair grounds—on electric busses, delivery trucks—was a Firestone.

The same summer the first dividend was declared. It was four percent. Profits of $71,043 had been earned on sales of $456,773. To produce this volume of business, the company had bought the two-story building next to it (not available at a bargain price this time), and by using the lower floor for shipping and the upper one for offices, it was able to devote the original foundry entirely to manufacturing.

The company was now the largest maker of solid-rubber tires in the world. It claimed that the sidewire

---

* Letter, March, 1904.

motor tire "has made possible the success of commercial automobiles today and is used on 85 percent of all such vehicles operated in this country."

Expansion meant that the perennial problem of obtaining adequate operating cash persisted. Firestone gave his personal notes, secured by his own stock, to small banks in Ohio and Michigan. R. G. Dun & Company issued this credit report on him:

> Character and habits are good and personal standing and business ability quite good . . . lives in a rented house and has all his means invested in the Firestone Tire & Rubber Company in which his holdings are placed at about $100,000 or half the entire capital stock. He may have borrowed money indebtedness individually but the amount is not believed over moderate. Receives $5,500 annual salary . . . and a royalty besides. Has the name of meeting his obligations to the letter and is deemed worthy of confidence and credit.*

Actually he held 937 shares, but in 1905, after the declaration of a six percent dividend (production 22,000 tires, sales $769,982, profits $122,361), the board voted to increase its capitalization to $500,000. Of the $300,000 new stock, the present holders were given the privilege of subscribing for $100,000 at par proportionately. The president and general manager manifested his confidence in the future by enlarging his investment to 1,143 shares.

The old capital had been insufficient to swing the large volume that the company had achieved with 130 employees. The new money would provide for additional plant capacity.

"Very successful and cleaned up a handsome profit on their business," R. G. Dun reported at the beginning of 1906. "Doing even better so far this fiscal year, and their outlook . . . quite favorable." A very profitable business, steadily expanded, "well managed in all respects." The company was discounting all bills, except for giving notes

* Dun report, Apr. 5, 1904.

for some of the rubber. "Their credit in the eastern rubber market is high. Local purchases are large and reported invariably discounted." Harvey Firestone was "well regarded in all respects." Will Christy, prominent electric railway builder and owner, "devotes some time to the company in an advisory capacity." Sisler was now living at Port Huron, Michigan, "comfortably well off." *

The big news reflected in Dun's report was Firestone's pneumatic tire. The trade had seen it at the New York Automobile Show. It had won "favorable recognition"— the company "booked large orders."

* Dun report, Jan. 27, 1906.

2

Enter, the Pneumatic

WHEN the Firestone Company brought out its first pneumatic tire, the earnest tinkering in many a Middle Western and Eastern workshop was just beginning to hammer out an automobile industry. Only a few years back, the *Carriage Monthly* had made smiling mention of "the present horseless vehicle furore" and expressed a loyal belief that there would be "no immediate progress in horseless pleasure carriages."

By the beginning of the century, 8,000 automobiles were registered: steam, electric, and gasoline. They had emerged from an imitation of a buggy without whip-socket or shafts. They had reduced the high wheels and lowered the center of gravity, considering the greater weight, and adopted a bonnet to cover the motor between the front wheels. Prices were high, for individual production of each maker was small; hence cars appealed primarily to the wealthy class, and popular interest had to be stirred up by staging racing events.

But by 1905 registration had reached 77,000, the first mass production (5,000 one-cylinder cars) had been started by Ransom E. Olds, Henry Ford was abandoning expensive touring cars for low-priced runabouts, and close to 200 establishments were manufacturing cars, delivery wagons, bodies, or parts. The automotive era had noisily begun.

The same year the Glidden Tours were started. Charles J. Glidden, of Brookline, Massachusetts, was an enthusiast for the machine age. He had made a fortune in the telephone business and, after selling out consolidated companies to the Bell system, he decided to spend his leisure promoting automobile touring for the family as "the best health-giving recreation." Speed did not concern him. He offered a trophy for the car making the best performance on a trip from New York to the White Mountains in New Hampshire and back, scheduling twelve nightly stops. The thirty-odd contestants themselves were the judges. As a result, automobiling won much publicity, and incidentally attention was called to the poor condition of the roads. Glidden and the American Automobile Association chose a new route each year.

The possibility of speed, though, fascinated the public along with freedom of movement, and car manufacturers responded by stepping up the horsepower of their machines. This put the burden on the tire makers—literally, for theirs was the task of supporting both the automobiles and the claims made for them.

Threadlike solids, an inch and a half wide, such as Elwood Haynes and Charles E. Duryea had used on their first "buggyauts," had long been abandoned. Bigger cars required more resiliency and wider treads. The first pneumatics for automobiles were single-tube bicycle tires. The cross sections were narrow, the casings composed of a few plies of calendered fabric laid straight along the circumference.

Double-tube tires, which had attained greater popularity among cyclists in Europe, were now adopted. The highly inflated inner tube provided a sturdy yet elastic body of compressed air to sustain the outer casing and cushion the car against shocks. Just as new engineering principles had been applied in the construction of these modern vehicles, so the functioning of tires in their new capacity had to be studied. The location of the driving force was different than in a buggy. An automobile imposed strains upon tires that tended to separate plies from each other and the tread from the plies. It was seen that the square-woven fabric threads broke by offering resistance to the strain; therefore the fabric was cut to lie on a bias, putting the threads in the line of the strain, as well as enabling the tire builder to stretch the fabric around the building core without leaving a wrinkle.

The clincher type, with rubber beads hooking into turned-in rims, was held in place by the air pressure. The clincher bead was given harder rubber. This pinched the tube, it didn't solve the problem of rim cutting and afforded no certain protection against slipping, but the clincher clung.

These were the "shoes" that the bicycle tire manufacturers were producing for the new motor trade. Treads were made wider and thicker, but tire life was not long. Determined, hardy drivers endured punctures, blowouts, and exasperating tire changes. However blasphemously a motorist might swear of a Sunday, he knew that a pneumatic yielded somewhat to the bumps on the road instead of running on top of them and giving him an unmerciful jolt.

In mitigation of one of the current hardships, tire manufacturers had come to an agreement in 1903 to standardize the shapes of clinchers and clincher rims. Previously each one had had his own design; now the different brands were interchangeable on most cars. This harmony had not been difficult to achieve, for the manufacturers were licensees of patent holders who had formed them into the G. & J. Clincher Tire Association.

Clincher patents dated back to the hectic bicycle period of the early nineties and were not due to expire until 1909. They had passed from Gormully & Jeffery to the American Bicycle Company trust and in turn to the combine known as the Rubber Goods Manufacturing Company; and now the latter became a subsidiary of a huger combination, the United States Rubber Company, by virtue of stock control.

Harvey Firestone was enjoying good business with the automobile industry for his solid tires. Maxwell, Premier, Stanley, and White were some of his customers. His solids were infinitely better for commercial vehicles than any pneumatic extant, but in order to make pneumatics for the pleasure-car trade that wanted them he had to obtain a license from the association. So he applied. But he was refused.

Only eight tire companies were permitted to share, in varying percentages, the available business; and they were bound to sell at a fixed price. Three of them, subsidiaries of U.S. Rubber, got a third of the total. Any association members who sold in excess of their quotas were obliged to pay penalties—a tax on popularity. When the pool "commissioner" in New York rejected his application in 1904, this intrepid Akronite purposed to develop a substitute for the clincher.

While bidding for additional automobile trade with solids made of a more resilient compound, he put an engineer to work on the task of avoiding the clincher principle in pneumatics. A wire cable was inserted in the bead, and the tire was clamped to the wheel by bolted rim flanges, the inextensible wire keeping it from expanding and loosening. The pinching hook was eliminated.

There were trials and there were errors. Firestone negotiated early in 1905 with an inventor for an exclusive license on a method that improved upon this mechanical fastening device. The novel element was a small triangular plate, riveted to the tire, just above the bead, with the bolt penetrating the rim side, the plate, and the wheel felloe. All in all, a revolutionary departure in pneumatics.

Although the inner tube was safe from pinching, the mounting needed refinement to make it more secure. Months, costly months, passed before the construction was acceptable to the Firestone staff. Then the manufacturing technique had to be perfected and made cheaper to bring the price into competitive range. By late summer, Firestone had the first practical straightside pneumatic tire.

He did not own a car—this lover of horses still drove to work in a rig (sometimes a surrey). He must test the product. Deciding on a Maxwell, he went to Tarrytown, New York, where the plant of the Maxwell-Briscoe Motor Company was situated, purchased their latest touring model, and shipped it to Akron. Here the wheels had to be refitted with new rims. It was easy to slip the new shoes on; crowbars could now be discarded from motorists' standard equipment.

The test run was made to Firestone's birthplace near Columbiana, Ohio, sixty dusty miles away, he and Carkhuff taking turns at the wheel, their wives in the back seat. Mother Firestone, waiting for them at the homestead farm, was obviously relieved when they arrived; her son's satisfaction was keener.

He could soon point with proof to the efficacy of his new tire. His confidence in high key, Firestone expanded the company's facilities both to accommodate the increasing volume of solid-tire sales and to manufacture pneumatics. The original structure was razed, a three-story brick building erected in its place in 1905; an 800-horsepower engine was purchased and installed in a new power house; air compressors and other machinery were bought, along with equipment for making the new line. Plant capacity trebled. The company now had 130 employees.

After putting the pneumatics on the market and making good at rival automobile shows held in New York at Madison Square Garden and the Sixty-ninth Regiment Armory, as well as shows in Chicago and Boston, Harvey Firestone heard that the Ford Motor Company in Detroit was planning to produce four-cylinder runabouts to sell at $500. He had once met Henry Ford. Ten years before, back in the days of selling carriages in that city for the Columbus Buggy Company, Ford, a machinist experimenting with gasoline engines, had stepped into his store; and Firestone sold him a set of rubber carriage tires. Now the acquaintance would be renewed.

Visiting Ford in Detroit, he found three circumstances in his favor. First, clincher tire manufacturers seeking the business all had made uniform bids of $70 a set of four tires (two-and-a-half-inch tread), the association price. Ford was irked, for he was determined to buy equipment in the open market and keep his costs down. Second, Ford had been crowded out by the Association of Licensed Automobile Manufacturers, controlling the Selden patent, who refused him the right to turn out a cheap car. For this reason he sympathized with Firestone over the rebuff given by the clincher tire ring. And third, Firestone had a product to be proud of.

"He tested tire after tire on the car before he became satisfied as to its quality and gave us the order," Firestone related to his associates in Akron.

The *India Rubber World* reported that this was the largest single order for tires ever placed by an automobile manufacturer.* It was for 2,000 sets. Ford had the vision of a mass market for cars. Firestone was on the ground floor of a coming great American industry.

* March, 1906.

This was also the first original-equipment order for straightside pneumatics. The delivery schedule called for 2,000 tires in April, 1906, to be followed by 4,000 in May, and 2,000 in June. Firestone had given Ford a price of $55 a set—a rather close price, but one based on the consideration that owners of Ford cars would have to come to him for replacement tires, since no other makes could be applied to the special rims.

To fill this $110,000 order, heavy commitments must be made for rubber, fabric, rims, and metal parts. A serious undertaking—but Firestone knew he must get used to doing things in a big way. From this point forward, he could see only giant strides in growth.

Letters acclaiming Firestone Mechanically Fastened Pneumatics were sent out by the company to garage keepers, auto manufacturers, auto owners. Users and Ford agents were informed that, as some Ford car purchasers would want three-inch tires after receiving their automobiles, it would be more practical for them to specify this size at the time of purchase; Firestone could make changes (no exchanges), but Ford was ready to supply cars with the larger tires at extra cost ($50).

The company advertised extensively in periodicals. It took the back cover of a trade journal to deliver this message:

You have read of Automobile Tires coming off while in service and the occupants of the car being either killed or injured. Only a small percentage of such accidents are recorded.

You have never heard of Firestone Pneumatics coming off while in service and you never will. They could not GET off if they were alive.

They are mechanically fastened—held firm in rim by wire cables and securely bolted through flanges and felloe. Can be removed in two minutes, no matter where you are, and a wrench is the only tool you need. No muscular effort is required—they slide off and on easily.

The highest grades of material and workmanship are there; the possibility of pinching the inner tube, rim cutting or creeping is left out.

The Firestone Pneumatic is not a substitute for the clincher but its superior.

Our Solid Rubber Tires are the World's Standard—our Pneumatics have won a reputation on their own merits.

QUALITY   SECURITY   SIMPLICITY*

One repercussion of the company's invasion of the pneumatic field was the disruption of the clincher association. The members saw Firestone break into their domain without being bound by quotas and subjected to fines. Two of them gave notice that they would withdraw from the combination. The Ford order hurt. The agreement expired and was not renewed. Commenting on the likely consequences, *Motor Way* said:

We may look for increased quality at the same price, for the keen competition will compel a resort to quality while the cost of replacements of unsatisfactory tires has proven a serious loss heretofore. In self-protection the tire makers will still compel car manufacturers to equip with sufficiently heavy tires to obtain the best results. †

Although the association ended, licensing of the tire makers was not affected.

But there was an unexpected development. After Ford had begun to accept deliveries, came the realization in Detroit that adoption of mechanically fastened tires at this stage was detrimental. Neither Ford nor Firestone had distributing centers on a wide enough scale to enable motorists to obtain replacements speedily. (Firestone had branches in New York, Chicago, Boston, Philadelphia, Detroit, and St. Louis, and agencies in a number of other areas but not "everywhere.") The Ford company wanted

* *Motor Way,* June 28, 1906.
† *Ibid.*

to avoid any cause for dissatisfaction and was eager to remove any barrier to new sales. Firestone was informed that he must furnish clinchers to retain the order.

He hurried to New York to plead again for a license. He was refused again.

There was no recourse but to defiance, just as Henry Ford had stood his ground and had not been cowed by the claimants to a basic automobile patent. If Firestone did not make clinchers, he would lose not only Ford but the chance to participate in pneumatic replacement business. Acting at once, he instructed an engineer to make drawings for clincher tire specifications.

Fortunately, Ford delayed production of his runabouts. The postponement was, of course, onerous to Firestone inasmuch as heavy investments had been made in materials, but it afforded a breathing spell.

Meanwhile other tire manufacturers were experimenting with ideas for improving on the clincher, for they saw the technological handwriting on the wall. The wire bead was a certainty for the future. Various rings and locking devices were employed to perfect the straightsides. To accommodate the variety of wire-cable clincher and standard clincher tires, the tire factories brought out universal rims, and as a next step combined to standardize these rims.

By the end of the year, Firestone was offering a universal rim with removable flanges. "We furnish clincher flanges adapting the rim to receive any standard clincher tire. Flanges and tire are held in place by a simple and ingenious safety locking rim."

A trade letter in January, 1907, announced that the company was now making a complete line of clincher tires besides the mechanically fastened one. They comprised: a standard clincher, a detachable type for use on three of the rims on the market, and a quick-detachable cable-bead tire for other rims including the new Firestone Safety Universal rim with its reversible side rings.

Orders came in fast. Again there were insufficient manufacturing facilities, insufficient working capital. An extension added to the brick building filled in the gap to the adjacent structure and temporarily remedied one of these situations. But the heaviest borrowing season in the rubber industry (four months in spring and summer) lay ahead, and the company's needs had risen beyond its usual credits.

An Akron bank offered company notes personally endorsed by Harvey Firestone to other Ohio banks: "Owing to the tightness of the local money market, some of our best concerns have been compelled to go outside for loans." Firestone profits had averaged better than fifty percent on its capital—"which is more than any other local rubber company has earned." Its stock ($100 par value) sold readily at $200, but the bank observed that there was no possibility of obtaining any at this figure. "The notes are gilt-edge investment." This was tempting enough.

The enormous demand, sending the company into the million-dollar class (28,000 units sold in 1906, grossing $1,045,172, and 44,000 units in 1907, grossing $1,681,-191), was attributable in part to the spurt in automobile popularity, but equally to management's sound policies. In production, the company was insistent on quality; in service, it made aggressive effort toward improvements in order to overcome "that great bugbear of motoring, tire troubles." These policies provided a foundation for vigorous promotion and reaped rewards of $112,174 profits in 1906 and $214,287 in 1907.

But there was one result that transcended current gains: the rising fame of the name "Firestone," which

had become increasingly familiar in its black-letter type*
and was earning goodwill for future business life.

High quality of rubber, year after year. "No off years,"
the literature said. "No recognition of the demand for
cheap or medium grade tires; none but a rigid adherence
to the original Firestone policy of high grade tires only."
Motorists were given a hint: "Nearly all manufacturers
will honor specifications for tires preferred by their customers."

The rubber was Up-river fine Para (Para a port on
the Amazon River). The plies were made of "the stoutest weave of Sea Island cotton fabric" (long-staple cotton
grown on the coastline from South Carolina to northern
Florida); each roll was carefully tested and prepared to
receive "the coatings of rubber gum with such rigid adhesion that it is a practical impossibility to separate rubber from fabric." As the function of the casing was to
contain the tube of compressed air, the fabric must give
strength to the casing and prevent it from stretching and
bursting under pressure.

Every tire is of wrapped tread construction and cured in open
steam . . . which retains all the strength of the fabric and makes the
rubber tough and lively. The layers are thus combined in an
integral, inseparable whole.

An innovation was the "dual tread," an early step in
the direction of overcoming skidding. Somewhat thicker
than the ordinary tread, it consisted of two ridges five-
eighths of an inch high. This was Firestone's first answer
to the danger that had developed with the increased
horsepower of automobiles. Pneumatics, being softer than
solids, had a greater tendency to side-slip; rounded tires
were more prone to skid than flat treads. Some manu-

* This typography is based upon the lettering in medieval English manu-
scripts. Sometimes known as gothic, in contrast to roman, type, it has a variant
in Old English. The first appearance of the name of Firestone in black letter
was on advertising blotters in 1905.

facturers tried to produce an anti-skid effect by having
metal studs vulcanized in the tread, and others baked a
combination of rivets and leather onto it.*

While dual treads were offered on pneumatics, twin
tires mounted on a single rim presented something new
in solids. This feature afforded more traction and more
resilience. There was convenience too, in that each twin
had an independent fastening. Heavy trucks adopted
these tires at once for rear wheels, and sightseeing busses
also quickly recognized their usefulness.

Sidewire solid tires still accounted for the major part
of Firestone's volume. "We are today furnishing the
great bulk of motor tires [solids] now in use on this hemi-
sphere." Knox electrics, Packard trucks, "all the oldest
established manufacturers of motor buggies or high-
wheel automobiles," in this transitional period of transportation were using Firestones and consuming "twenty-
five percent less current." † Nor were carriage and wagon
makers neglected. On the contrary, they were notified of
an intensive campaign reaching out to liverymen in many
cities with letters, booklets, mailing cards, and hangers.

The Firestone line included inner tubes, usable in all
makes of pneumatic tires, and—hoof pads. No, the horse-
and-buggy age had not departed. Automobile registrations exceeded 140,000 in 1907, but there were still many
millions of dobbins in harness.

Time hung over the crossroads of overlapping eras.

* Weather hazards had confronted the first automobile race in America, set
for Thanksgiving Day, 1895, in Chicago. There had been a storm the day before,
and snow and slush covered the road. Two of the entrants hit on the idea of
twisting twine around their tires to secure a firmer grip.

† Among other customers there were Electric Vehicle Co., Baker Motor
Vehicle Co., Woods Motor Vehicle Co., Northern Motor Co., Chase Motor
Truck Co., Studebaker Automobile Co., Mack Bros. Motor Car Co., Hewit
Motor Co., Elwell-Parker Electric Co. of America, Bendix Co., Pope Motor Car
Co., and manufacturers of ninety percent of the rubber-tired fire apparatus then
in use.

Harvey Firestone rushed to the roadside the hot July day that the Glidden Tour passed his homestead. This year's cavalcade of fifty chugging mechanisms (with right-hand drives) was kicking up dust from Cleveland to New York, by way of South Bend, Columbus, Baltimore, and Philadelphia, and was going by Columbiana on the ninth day's hop from Canton to Pittsburgh. A big canvas sign strung between two poles told the tourists where they were. Mother Firestone and her son had baskets of food and drink ready for those who could afford to stop. Some of them, behind schedule, had time only to snatch a basket by the handle as groups of neighbors on both sides of the lane of traffic waved them on.

The year was not one of undiluted bliss. The Consolidated Rubber Tire Company, which had proceeded against Firestone in the New York jurisdiction for infringement of its internal-wire patent, had won a decree. On appeal, the Circuit Court of Appeals affirmed this, holding that the patent, while a combination of old elements, produced a new result and constituted an invention.* (In Ohio, as noted, the patent had been invalidated.) Firestone came to terms with the Consolidated. In liquidation of damages, the rights to the continuous-length tire were transferred to that company.

Firestone was not sued, however, by the clincher patent owners. In a test case brought in the name of the Gormully & Jeffery Tire Company against another tire manufacturer, the court held: "All the patents here involved antedated the automobile art and contemplated use on bicycles." † This freed everybody from the obligations of a license and royalty payments, and it removed the advantage Firestone had been enjoying over those competitors who had not been brave enough to defy the

* 151 Federal Reporter 237 (1907).
† 155 Federal Reporter 982 (1907).

old clincher association. Moreover, the patents would have had only a few years more to run, and the clincher was yielding to improved straightsides.

There was another menace this year. In the fall came a bank panic, tying up credit. Firestone was in the midst of putting up a four-story addition and had to suspend construction. He had already built a rubber-reclaiming unit and a vacuum dryer. It looked as though this time he had stepped into a pitfall of overconfidence. But the stringency was short-lived. Success, no less than optimism, was abounding.

The most serious issue of 1907 concerned rims and the united attempt of other tire manufacturers to keep the latest Firestone development off the market. Firestone's rim was superior—and so was his determination.

3

The Role of Rims

THE role of rims was vital. As in the evolution of the solid rubber tire, so with pneumatics, the means of secure attachment to the wheel dominated the early stages of tire history. Most of the tire manufacturers had their own rim designs and endeavored to induce the automobile maker to adopt them—until a Clincher Rim Association brought uniformity. In essence, a simple steel channel with inward curving flanges.

But as car development proceeded and heavier machines necessitated larger pneumatics, the evils of creeping and cutting became more pronounced. Tire firms worked out systems with lugs, brass cleats, and staybolts. There was a new multiplicity of rims, and a new annoyance. The complicated process of removing a clincher tire was laboriously described by a contemporary:

First . . . a jackscrew to lift the wheel. Then a forked bar to hold the wheel still while the various pinchbars are used to prize up the bead. A special tool is needed to disengage the bead from the clincher seat, where it often gets stuck. Special wrenches are made to unscrew the lugs, and thumbscrew clamps are put around the tire to hold back the bead when it is disengaged. A special lever, which fits the bead, lifts it up until the flat pinchbars can take hold.

Many a man has become disgusted at this stage of the game and pried the thing off with a pickaxe or crowbar. A crowbar is often found still more necessary in putting on a tire, though its use is apt to be attended with disastrous results.

There are special applying tools, generally made with two prongs. . . . These small levers are often inadequate, however, when it comes to shoving the last twelve or eighteen inches of bead over the rim. For this purpose a system of small jackscrews is made for lifting the last section of the bead. These jacks run from the hub to the rim, and several are needed to do the job properly, locking each while the other is being worked.*

Rigidity at the juncture of bead and rim was the prime objective, from a technical standpoint. Hence efforts to improve the rim went hand in hand with the devising of a better bead. One way to make life easier for the motorist who had been wrestling to stretch the bead of a large-size tire over the clincher rim was to split the rim longitudinally; while one flange gripped a bead whose core was made of twisted fabric strips (or wires) and gave little stretch (or was nonstretchable), the other flange was detachable. Removal of this flange was made possible by the loosening of a side locking ring. The twist of a turnbuckle tightened the ring, held the flange in place, and thus made the bead secure.

Lugs, however, interfered with the easy operation of this device, and a great variety of detachable flanges were introduced in the general striving for practicality. At the same time, experiments with inextensible wire cable beads brought the straightside tire more clearly into the picture. These wired-on tires had little use for hooking edges, hence both flanges could be made detachable. Now the automobile world had its choice—and confusion—of mechanical fastenings and of two main types: clincher or straightside. The car owner, in the capacity of innocent bystander, was rescued. Reversible flanges were brought out, so that he could use the same rim to fit either type of tire.

Quick-detachable tires having made their entree, the

* *Rubber Tires and All About Them*, Henry C. Pearson, India Rubber Publishing Co., 1906, pp. 116–17.

natural sequence was some method of simultaneously removing both the rim and the tire from the wheel to
enable a driver to mount an already inflated spare in a
jiffy. This would be the next development in rims. In
France, where auto racing had become a great pastime,
such rims had been brought into play—quick play—in
the 1905 James Gordon Bennett race. On Long Island
the next year they were seen again in action on foreign
car entries in the Vanderbilt Cup race. A good thing for
racers, it was thought. These rims weighed more, cost
more; they were not considered urgent for pleasure cars.
But Harvey Firestone saw the advantage and seized it.

His engineers made drawings. He sent them to the
Standard Welding Company, of Cleveland, a firm that
manufactured rims for most of the tire companies, and
the design went into experimental production.

A new movement for standardization was under way
—inspired by the automobile manufacturers. They
wanted the tire people to agree among themselves on a
uniform detachable rim. Firestone, convinced that his
own Safety Universal rim was better than the others,
was eager nevertheless to join with them. His competitors
did not share his convictions, so he submitted his case to
the nation's auto makers. In a letter to all of them—a
list of 207—he wrote:

> The automobile manufacturers, through their associations, have
> been demanding that a standard universal rim be adopted by the
> tire manufacturers. The tire manufacturers are equally anxious to
> have a standard rim, but there has been considerable difference in
> opinion as to the merits of the different rims which have been
> produced. These differences have been somewhat prejudiced on
> account of each manufacturer having a rim of his own and using it
> to help sell his tires.
>
> There is an honest difference in opinion as to which is the best
> construction of tire; the standard clincher, the quick-detachable
> clincher, or the quick-detachable cable type tire. Until this is settled,

if it ever is, it is to the advantage of both the automobile and tire manufacturers to have a standard rim which is practical and safe and will take any of the types mentioned.

We produced our Safety Universal Rim, which possesses all the features desired, about a year ago and have experimented with it ever since. As a manufacturer, you appreciate the length of time it takes to get special shapes from the steel mills. We now have completed rolls for hot stock, special machinery and rolls with the rim manufacturers, and can produce these rims in quantities at a price which makes them a commercial success.

We are not rim manufacturers, and if the automobile manufacturers, through their associations, approve of our rim, we will, in order to accomplish the desired results, turn it over to the rim manufacturers who, in our opinion, are the proper source for your rim supply. We know absolutely that our rim is the most practical and safest rim yet produced, and our object in writing you is to offer you a set of our rims without charge for examination and trial. If you do not care for a complete set for the test, will be glad to send you a single rim for examination, as we know you are interested in securing a standard rim.*

The automobile manufacturers were more interested in the certainty of a steady supply than in a conflict between one tire man and his rivals. Matters stood pretty much the same for two years before the latter banded together to pool their constructions and patents in the United Rim Company, which would select the best features of the four most prominent rims and become the sole source of supply.

But the spring 1907 catalog issued by Firestone included not only the Safety Universal, it introduced the Firestone Dismountable Rim.† Periodical advertising stressed this high point in easy tire changing. The "dismountable" had a channel attached to the felloe band by six bolts; beveled plates riveted to the band engaged plates on the rim. Removal of the bolts permitted the rim and its attached tire to slide off the wheel in one

* May 3, 1907.
† Advertised in *Motor Age*, May 30, 1907; *Horseless Age*, July 31, 1907.

motion. "Secure, cannot rust on, and is adjustable both to the standard clincher and the quick detachable clincher tires and their rims."

The auto industry was slow to welcome a fresh complication to its problem of standardization. Because of this resistance, Firestone did not press the issue with them. Changeovers made here and there on cars in service would exert their own eloquent pressure. The efficiency of the new rim—now called "demountable"—was tested at the Fairmount Park race at Philadelphia in the fall of 1908. It was an exciting event over a two-hundred-mile course. A time-saver would count! Two Locomobiles entered the race, equipped with Firestone demountables and Firestone tires. They won first and third places.

Enjoyment of this triumph was interrupted by difficulty in getting the rims manufactured. Standard Welding, licensed by the United Rim Company to produce two standard designs for United members, informed Firestone that it was obliged to cease working for him on pain of losing the United business. He cast about for another source and found a spring-wheel manufacturer with a small shop in Detroit, who had electric welding machinery and could turn out rims better and ten percent cheaper. They signed a two-year contract. The contract ended abruptly.

The new rim supplier, tracked down by the United, had received warning of infringement. The Detroiter said he was in no position to fight and asked to be released. Thus, Firestone was catapulted into rim manufacturing.

In a frame shed on the company's grounds, the beginning of 1909, machinery was assembled to roll flat sections of steel into rims. First deliveries—the output was small—were made in February. These were Safety Universals. By spring, after studying how to provide maximum strength with minimum weight and how to remove stresses caused by imperfect design, the engineers felt that they had developed a demountable rim that would assure longer life to tires.

June saw "Type A" demountables marketed. They had an inner flange set as a permanent clincher and an outer flange with a loose clincher ring and split locking ring. Six square beveled blocks were attached on the circumference to engage the felloe band and prevent creeping. A raised beveled flange on the inside edge of the band provided a seat for the rim, the area of contact between rim and band so reduced as to avoid rusting. Sidewise slipping was another hazard to guard against: bolts running through the felloe were clamped at both ends.

These mechanical preoccupations might seem like a far cry from the rubber business, but not really. The security of a tire was paramount. And hadn't the company begun its life with a fastening device? The new aspect was the discovery that one was also in the steel business.

Demounting the rim was accomplished by loosening the nuts, thus freeing the outside clamps, which were turned in the opposite direction, and by lightly drawing up the nuts to hold them in position. Now the lugs and the valve stem were flush with the inside of the rim: the rim came off. In mounting, the inflated spare tire and its own attached rim were lifted onto the wheel, the clamps were loosened and reversed, the nuts tightened. As simple as that.

A universal demountable, "Type B," was offered to the trade in the same month of June. This had two loose reversible side rings carried on a single endless base. A split locking ring held the outer ring in place, and by the same token made it readily removable. The locking ring rested securely in a groove along the outer edge of the rim base and also pressed in upon the side ring; its high upward projection supported the back of the side ring and kept the latter from being blown off. A clamping ring, clamps, bolts, and nuts held the rim to the felloe band. The motorist desiring to use straightside tires was, by these intricacies, made happy.

"My company began the manufacture of rims in order to provide the car owner with better tire service," Firestone announced. "We are not promoting them for the sake of profit in the rims themselves." After all, this was a *tire* company, but a tire "could not give satisfactory performance without a suitable rim."

It had taken about three years of unflagging purpose and concentration. Now the everyday driver became a quick-change artist.

Firestone Demountable Rim equipment includes a rim fitted to each wheel and an extra rim carried as a spare, equipped with an inflated tire. When overtaken by tire trouble, the motorist may instantly remove the damaged tire and its rim, substitute the spare rim with its already inflated tire, and resume his journey without further interruption. The deflated tire may then be attended to at the journey's end . . . no annoying exertion, no prying of damaged tires from their rims and then forcing them back on again, no tire pumping on the road. The temptation to run tires deflated for even a short distance and so damage them is removed. . . .

What if repeated punctures occur before the end of the ride? Herein lies one of the greatest points of superiority possessed by Firestone Demountable Rims, for additional tire changes *without limit* are practical while on the road. This feature is wholly lacking in other demountable rims. . . .

We have discarded as out-of-date demountable rims adapted exclusively to regular clincher tires and their rims. They are merely makeshifts when compared with the superior *working advantages* of the new quick detachable Firestone Demountable Rims . . . adaptable to *all* quick detachable and clincher tires. They may be fitted without changing the present tire equipment in any way on practically any car, new or old. No new cases of tubes to buy; not even a valve stem.*

* Booklet, *Demountable Rims*, August, 1909.

Despite this unwilling entry into the manufacture of rims, Firestone found that they were cheaper to make than they had been to buy. Besides, they were not encumbered with a two-dollar-a-set royalty which the United Rim Company decided to add to its price. Firestone quoted a set of three-and-a-half-inch and four-inch tires and rims at $65, including one spare rim. Next larger sizes, $75 and $85. Extra rims, $7.25 and $8.25 each.

Popularization of Firestone tires by way of racing events had already proved effective. Now Barney Oldfield, the idol of the track, began to break world speed records with these tires on demountable rims. At the inaugural meet on the Indianapolis Speedway in August, 1909, Oldfield captured one crown after another, capping the climax in a kilometer sprint in 26.2 seconds; only a few minutes before, the world record had been smashed by Walter Christie in 28.7 seconds. Finally came a fierce 300-mile race on the rutted, macadamized track —with accidents—and the race was halted. Oldfield, in a National, had covered 195 miles without having touched his tires. As Firestone's subsequent letter to the trade noted, "all other makes of tires required one or more stoppages for tire changes. AND—only regular Firestone stock tires were used."

In the first year of operating its rim manufacturing adjunct, the company consumed only twelve tons of steel for pneumatics. The next year brought an extension of this activity into the realm of rims for solid-rubber tires, the production of "Type C" rims for pneumatics, and the erection of a one-story plant, 250 feet long, wholly devoted to rim production. The progress of the company in an area which the United group had staked out for themselves gave promise of the day when Firestone would be in a position to solicit, and win, contracts from large automobile factories. As a matter of fact, to go ahead of the story a bit, Firestone's steel consumption in 1914 was 12,000 tons.

The sidewire solid, with plies of duck fabric cemented to the base, had been eminently satisfactory until heavier trucks were wanted, and then the trend went toward a base of hard rubber. To meet this demand—with an improvement—Firestone made the demountable rim for solids, the hard base being welded to the corrugated surface of the rim. The steel mills were not yet rolling special sections for the company, so Firestone's men had to cut down standard structural channel steel at the flanges, to proper height, and machine the surface.

The range of motor truck transport had been restricted before the advent of demountable rims for solids. Large sizes were difficult to apply. There were few service stations along the road. Now the remedy was "a few minutes and a wrench." Deliveries were kept going, layups were avoided. Truck operators no longer had the dead expense of a vehicle out of commission.

The company had discontinued the exclusive clincher pneumatic rim because of "the staybolt nuisance." The "Type C" rim came in response to the growing interest in straightside tires. Its inside flange was rolled outward, forming a straightside contour, and the outside ring was reversed to fit the bead. A new safety locking ring prevented the rim from coming apart and releasing the tire, despite the strain.

Alertness to market needs, and anticipation of them, carried Firestone into prominence as a dependable supplier, lifted the company beyond the reach of the United combination (in fact, undermined that monopoly), and laid the foundation for the Firestone Steel Products Company.

4

In Quest of Mileage

"CHEAP quality is always expensive in mileage cost." This reminder to the public was also Harvey Firestone's maxim for himself and his organization. If any of the men offered an excuse for failing to meet his standards, he had a private remark for them: "We can't sell alibis. We have tires to sell."

In the first few years of the century, pneumatic tires ran 3,000 to 4,000 miles, if they were that good, and although guarantees were not given, price adjustments were usually made to purchasers on a basis of 3,500 miles. Paralleling rim development, the steady concern of manufacturers to produce a better product inevitably brought progress and helped check the threat of a new national ailment, "tire trouble."

The public had to be educated on the hazards of overloading and underinflation; in short, they had to do their part. Here and there, wiseacres were saying in the midst of the efforts to perfect quick-detachables and demountables that what a motorist wanted was not a tire that could be removed easily but one that would not have to be removed. Automobile makers kept increasing the weight of their cars and stepping up speed capacity—and counting upon the tire producers to make this feasible.

Soon it became apparent that the most outstanding aspect of the tire industry was the continual improvement of its merchandise.

Lasting qualities. Tires made with this objective would spread satisfaction and stimulate automobile buying. Touring would be encouraged, distance no longer a bugaboo. Harvey Firestone's perception of the situation and his drive to become foremost in the industry led to a daring decision—so daring that he asked for the formal approval of the board of directors. It was the hiring of a chemist. The business, confining expenditures to essentials, had been faring well enough without one. A chemist and a laboratory were regarded in those days as luxuries because they did not seem directly productive. But Firestone believed that the extra expense would pay off in quality. Something better than twisting, pulling, and smelling rubber was needed.

Scientific testing, instead of cursory examination, must determine whether rubber and fabric supplies were up to grade. In place of guesswork at performance, let study of the properties of the materials reveal shortcomings and possibilities. Little was known of rubber chemistry. More knowledge would result in a better compound. Did science need an apology? The rubber could be toughened yet made more resilient. And as fabric failure was most responsible for curtailing tire life, the proper selection of fabric would lessen vulnerability to strains and internal heat.

In 1908, Firestone engaged a young man named John W. Thomas, who had received a degree in chemistry at Akron's Buchtel College four years before. After working in the laboratory of another tire firm, Thomas was eager for an opportunity to manage one all by himself. Unaware, in his first conversation with his prospective employer, that the questions Firestone put to him had a purpose beyond sizing him up as a chemist, Thomas was being measured as a man.

In a modest way, the company's first laboratory was

set up in a small room and testing instruments were installed. The room included a cot, for in addition to his technical duties Thomas administered first aid. He worked on the formula for the compound, with its specific parts of rubber, sulphur, lime, or magnesium to accelerate the fusion of the sulphur with the rubber, and zinc oxide and lampblack to endow the rubber with greater stamina in resisting abrasion.

The best rubber was *Hevea brasiliensis*, and this was the grade used for tires: Up-river Para. Collected in jungles along the upper reaches of the Amazon River, it was shipped from the port of Para to London, the rubber market of the world. The price kept mounting with the growing needs of the American auto industry. Tire prices either responded to the rise or were maintained by a sacrifice of quality. Firestone's policy was manifest in the phrasing and the overtones of a sales letter which at the same time set forth the company's ultimate goal:

> The recent financial panic and business depression have taught us all a great lesson—to be more economical—to seek small savings and guard against small losses—to use greater care in buying.
>
> Hereafter vehicle owners will seek the tire that will cost them the least—not in original price, but in cost per mile of service.
>
> The users who put their tires to the most severe test, such as the large livery companies, transfer companies, users of commercial trucks, etc., have adopted Firestone Tires because they have found that these tires give the greatest mileage with the least expense.*

In the surge of automobile production, the Ford Motor Company leaped forward with the introduction of its "Model T" in October, 1908. This was a four-cylinder car, Ford's first model with a left-hand drive, priced at $850 and built on the principle of standardized parts. An attractive buy, effected by manufacturing economies, it sold fast (to the extent of a half-million replicas within

* Mar. 24, 1908.

five years). The census showed a total United States production of 123,500 pleasure cars in 1909, and 3,500 trucks; but despite the increasing consumption of rubber, Brazil's supply did not keep pace.

From 26,750 long tons in 1900, Brazil had advanced to only 42,000 tons in 1909, but the price had jumped from a $1.10 high to $2.15 a pound. This could not yet be offset by plantation rubber from the Far East, for the acreage there was still too recently planted to yield significant quantities. Moreover, another factor increased the demand for rubber: the call for tires in larger sizes. Treads of four inches and five and a half inches were becoming the order of the day.

The wider tread meant a greater area of contact with the road. In the case of smooth-faced tires, the result was weaker traction. The element of speed spelled more trouble, namely, skidding. To overcome this tendency, tire manufacturers devised anti-skid treads such as metal rivets, leather protuberances, or rubber buttons molded on the surface. These were copies of bicycle treads. Firestone had already introduced the dual tread, with its circumferential dividing line, and had corrugated the ridges. Now Harvey Firestone thought up a new idea.

He wrote the words FIRESTONE NON-SKID on a sheet of paper and gave instructions that the letters be drawn to form a tread design. In block lettering, approximately an inch and a quarter long, they were placed obliquely across the arc of the tread, FIRESTONE on one line, NON-SKID below it, repeated again and again along the circumference. Engraved inside the vulcanizing mold, the design was forced into the tire tread by hydraulic pressure on the hot rubber. Here was a pattern that presented an effective wearing and tractive surface, and a self-description: a revolutionary improvement born in September, 1908, the first angular non-skid tread.

Thus the name prevents the slip. . . . The letters of the words form more angles and points of contact than any other non-skid tread. The spaces in and between the letters cause just the right amount of suction to grip the slippery road and prevent the side slipping.*

The innovation proved more than sales talk. It gave service. Gripping the road and averting accidents, it lengthened the life not only of the tires but of the car itself. Public acceptance was reflected in the sales. Forty percent of the 105,000 tires sold in 1909 were non-skid, sixty percent (of 168,000 units) the next year.

Incidentally, profits in 1910 exceeded a million dollars for the first time. They had totaled $355,801 on $2,128,-354 sales in 1908 and $538,177 on $3,017,958 sales in 1909. Now they were $1,394,835 on a volume of $5,271,-040, rims of course included.

. From the engineering standpoint, the character of the tread had to be considered in relation to the casing, for there was always a danger that toughness of wearing surface might intensify strain on the sidewalls. A non-skid design must not jeopardize resilience. The ideal was a balanced tire. As a further step in durability, Firestone increased the thickness of the tread by one-fourth on smooth tires and one-third on non-skids. In time the design was simplified, retaining only the words NON and SKID, one under the other, molded on the tread at an elevation of approximately two-tenths of an inch.

Progress, in a swiftly growing organization, had to be made on many fronts simultaneously. About a year after engaging Thomas, Harvey Firestone decided to give him a broader background in the rubber business by putting him into the production end. Thomas took off his white collar and pitched in as night foreman of the washers, mills, and calenders. First he hired another chemist,

* Advertisement in *Motor Age*, Oct. 8, 1908.

selecting one with knowledge of organic chemistry, for it was now realized that coal-tar derivatives made better accelerators than mineral substances; and only small amounts were necessary to hasten vulcanization. There was a saving in time, labor, equipment, and floor space. Other organic chemicals served as improved reinforcing agents in the compound.

Thomas started with the rubber washing machines. This apparatus tore apart slabs of rubber under a stream of water; it removed impurities thus exposed and delivered the clean rubber in the form of long thin sheets. The sheets were placed on racks or trays to dry. Formerly, drying had taken many days, but the factory had recently installed a vacuum drier and thereby cut the time to several hours. Rubber must be perfectly free of moisture particles, otherwise these would appear as blisters after vulcanizing.

The next step: the sheets were masticated and blended into a uniform mass, rendering them sufficiently plastic to receive other ingredients, the powders carefully weighed. The compound was then thoroughly milled into an even mixture, and again the mass was rolled out into sheets. Dusted with soapstone to prevent sticking, they were "aged" a few days. Rubber needed a rest after that considerable mauling.

Other mills warmed up the aged compounded stock, which was next quickly transferred hot and plastic to feed the calenders. These machines received rolls of dry cotton fabric at the same time, the fabric being impregnated with the rubber between hot rollers. Now the calendered fabric went through the machine once more, to be skimmed with a coating of rubber, and was rolled up with a lining of duck in between. This was the birth of a ply. Later it would be bias-cut, spliced, and conveyed to a tire-building machine, to be applied under tension, layer after layer, on a building core. Thomas was to superintend those operations before receiving his next promotion.

Thus, he worked, six nights a week, in twelve-hour stretches, a budding executive in overalls. For his chief really was training him for top-level work by giving him experience in actual production. It was Firestone's way of developing and molding an organization.

Processes of production, details of operation, opportunities for economy were watched from day to day. Costs must be lowered to attract greater volume. Volume must be won in order to lower costs. Efficiency was an endless chain. The waste of used rubber was avoided by putting up a reclaiming plant in which rubber was restored to its original state of plasticity. Every step toward conservation of energy and material was a step in the direction of greater value in the product— better tires for the money—more miles per dollar.

The company was not big enough to accomplish all Firestone envisioned. The factory was not big enough. He had seen the low tile building reach a timid story higher, the two other buildings on the plot come into the fold, a three-story unit rise to four floors and soon join another of equal height; and now a massive plant of nearly 140,000 square feet occupied the corner at Miller and Sweitzer Avenues. It was a dream come true, but only part of a dream. There was no room in which to make further additions.

After scouring Akron for a larger factory, Firestone called in "the boys" early in 1909 and asked them to look for the best place within the city limits to serve as their future site. He wanted ten acres; ten at least, twenty if possible.

At the extreme southern end of town there was a corn-field in the midst of other farm land. Plenty of fresh air here! And near by, the tracks of four railroads, convenient for freight. The property belonged to the estate of the late Moses Falor, and there were nine heirs whose ideas would have to be reconciled.

Firestone went before the annual meeting of stockholders that August and received "full authority to act as in his judgment seems best" in the matter of purchasing a new site.

After resolving the difficulties presented by the heirs, he agreed to buy fifteen acres and took an option on eight more. The total area eventually acquired by the company cost on the average $1,000 an acre.

"This," he announced, "is only the first step in our plans for an expansion of our business. We have long had in mind the erection of a great modern plant, but have hitherto been handicapped by the lack of land on which to build."

The plan was to start construction in 1910 of a factory that would afford five times the tire-building capacity of the present plant and to abandon the latter. A fully equipped laboratory would be one of the modern helps. The cost was estimated at $500,000.

This was a vast expenditure to contemplate, equal to the capitalization, though far below the surplus that had been accumulated. Nevertheless, sound thinking dictated refinancing, to keep the company in a liquid condition. If the current pace of business continued, even this project would be overshadowed by enlargements. The upshot of the thinking along these lines was to propose a reorganization. An Ohio corporation would be formed, to buy out the present company. This was approved at a special meeting of the stockholders on March 5, 1910, and the management issued the following public explanation:

The company was originally organized under West Virginia, when the laws of Ohio imposed a double stockholders' liability. Since the laws have been changed it has been the intention of the company to incorporate under Ohio but the time did not seem opportune, as the company has been working along with a small capitaliza tion, allowing its earnings to accumulate to take care of its increased business, until its surplus had increased to many times its capitalization.

Even with the surplus the volume of business has increased to such an extent that when it was decided to build a new factory necessary to take care of the present volume, which would require an outlay of almost $1,000,000, it was thought best to increase the capitalization sufficiently to take in additional capital.

The policy of the company has been very conservative on financial matters and would not go into this venture without sufficient capital to insure financial solidity; and while the present stockholders are loath to give up any share of the common stock it was discussed and was the feeling of the stockholders that the capital be increased to $4,000,000 ($3,000,000 common, $1,000,000 preferred stock) and that $500,000 of the preferred stock should be offered for sale.*

The preferred stock, seven percent cumulative, was marketed through the Central Savings Bank and Trust Company and the National City Bank, both of Akron. It was quickly oversubscribed. Of the common stock, $2,400,000 was issued to present stockholders at the rate of eight shares of the new in exchange for each share they held in the old corporation; in this way they participated in the division of the surplus.†

The officers of the new corporation were the same as before: Harvey S. Firestone, president; Will Christy, vice president; Stacy G. Carkhuff, secretary, and James G. Robertson, treasurer.

Toward the end of May, the construction contract was let, and by the time of the September sales convention the branch managers and salesmen were able to pose for

* *Akron Beacon Journal*, Mar. 7, 1910.
† Later that year the directors voted to issue the remaining $500,000 of the authorized preferred stock and gave the stockholders the privilege of subscribing for it at $100 par. In 1912, common stock still in the treasury was offered to them at $250 a share ($100 par value) to the extent of ten percent of their holdings.

their picture in front of the steel framework of the structure that would produce the Firestone Tires of tomorrow. The buoyant mood was heightened a fortnight later when Harvey Firestone concluded a deal with the Ford Motor Company, for 10,000 sets of tires, and soon he was able to announce that he had booked $2,000,000 worth of business from car manufacturers for the coming year.

"You can't stop the tire business," he observed. "There will be a steady, healthy development."

Automobile registration in the United States had reached 350,000 in 1910, and he paid no attention to self-appointed sages who predicted a saturation point. This was America, a country that did not stand still, a country of free men aspiring to the benefits of a free society and working hard for them. He had the same optimism that emboldened the car manufacturers and other industrialists.

Patiently, with a scale model of the new plant, Firestone concentrated for many months on ways of arranging the most efficient layout. By passing a string—representing work material—from one department to another, from floor to floor, he studied the movement of the material through the miniature factory. Now he was a bit worried that construction might not be completed in time to handle orders for delivery early in 1911.

The building would have a frontage of 265 feet and a depth greater than this—360 feet. These were the dimensions of the first floor and basement. Three additional stories would be built in the form of wings spreading across the full width, four wings on each side of a central passage; each wing sixty feet deep, forty feet apart, thus affording abundant light and ventilation from the courts between. The fourth floor would accommodate the offices. Capacity would be 5,000 tires a day, and if more space should be needed, the design permitted extension of the wings without interruption of work.

Set back from the street a considerable distance, with an intervening lawn, the new plant proclaimed adherence to the first principles of modern industrial hygiene: a departure from the agglomerate huddling of dingy factories that had defaced the passing era. In fact, the whole plant was modern, built of steel, concrete, and brick facing, with glass comprising three-fourths of the surface. New economical equipment was installed; curing presses, for example, in place of pot heaters; larger mixing mills; variable-speed, motor-driven calenders. Auxiliary buildings were erected, such as a power house, a water-softening plant, a cement house, and a pumping station. The latter was part of the company's independent water supply system; while other rubber concerns obtained their water by leasing rights to the old canal that meandered through the city, Firestone was going to pipe it from Summit Lake, nearly a mile away.

Months passed, and the overworked factory at Miller and Sweitzer hummed through the night. The opening of the new plant was postponed from January to March, and there was further delay. The company intended, when the day should come, to transfer all activities and abandon the old site; but now it looked as if the new building would afford no room for rim manufacturing.

All Akron was heartily enjoying a boom, and thousands of men migrated to the city, mainly from West Virginia and Kentucky, to take jobs that the undisputed capital of the rubber industry offered them. The population had grown sixty-one percent in the ten years since the 1900 census—from 42,723 to 69,067—and every other person employed was a rubber worker.

At the height of operations at the old plant, the company employed a thousand people. Four hundred had been added in the past year. Five hundred more were immediately taken on when the first whistle shrilled at the new plant. Production began on June 8, 1911.

Here, in the spaciousness of South Akron, with novel techniques and new machines, the transformation of the rubber into tires for a mobile America was achieved at a considerable reduction in cost. With 81,000 pounds of rubber consumed each day (13,000 for solids, 2,000 for hoof pads!), the saving in the milling room alone was $100 a day. Four eighty-four-inch mills each mixed more than 300 pounds at one time, which was twice the capacity of the old-type mill. The new calenders gave a twenty-five percent increase in production at the same cost. The curing presses saved fifty percent in labor, or $120 a day. This is what the mechanical engineer reported on power saving in response to Firestone's inquiry:

Our new power house has 3,000 horsepower in the two turbine units. When operating at rated capacity it will require 24 tons of coal to generate the necessary power. To develop the same amount of power at the old plant with the old type of equipment it would require 49 tons of coal.

The new plant equipment is designed to use slack coal, which costs us $1.60 a ton in storage. At the old plant it is not practical to attempt to burn this cheap grade of coal, consequently we must use coal that costs us $2.10 a ton in the house; this gives us a comparative cost of $38.40 at new plant to $102.80 at old plant on the same horsepower output.

The labor cost is also quite an item; in a 24-hour run it required 22 men in two shifts at a cost of $66 to operate the old plant boiler room, while in our new boiler room a 24-hour run in two shifts requires 6 men at a cost of $18—a little less than one-third the operating cost at the old plant.

This gives a total saving in fuel and labor of $122 for each 24 hours, or 68% of cost at old plant.*

* Memorandum, Sept. 7, 1911.

The sales organization of a hundred men, gathered for the convention in September, were guided through the plant and treated to a view of the economies and the thoroughness of the new system of production. It heartened them to see what a progressive company they had, backing up their efforts. At the annual dinner, served in the building by the girls of the office force, Harvey Firestone fanned the spark of their manifest enthusiasm and whipped it into a speech glowing with zeal to forge ahead.

So much achieved in so few years! From scratch to front rank, The Firestone Tire & Rubber Company had advanced, earning a reputation for quality and holding it. The head of the firm had always refused to let quality bow to any exigency. He was conscious of prestige. Firestone tires were giving twice as much mileage as formerly.

Along what paths chemistry and engineering would lead the company further to benefit the public, no one could foretell. But striving persisted . . . and better compounds, cords, gum dipping, and balloon tires were destined to bring longer life.

5

Human Relations

THE days when one could call all the employees by
their first names were over. Harvey Firestone re-
gretted this as he looked at the size of the big new plant.
But there was no turning back. Industry was on the
march, and the multiplication of goods for wide consumption meant large-scale employment.

Firestone recalled the times when he used to pull a
single sheet out of his desk drawer—a list of workers and
their rates—to see the size of the payroll he would have
to meet that week. Every morning at seven o'clock he
would make the rounds when he arrived and greet each
one of them. In those days there was no place for employees to relax at lunch time, so he rented (and later
bought) a small house on the opposite corner to use as
a restaurant.

He recalled also the supper dance, given Christmas
week, 1908, celebrating the completion of the four-story
factory addition; he had sent a car to collect some of
the girl office workers at their homes. A thousand persons
filled the tube room on the top floor for the merry get-
together.

Summers afforded a natural opportunity for social life
and recreation. The company held outings at a nearby
lake resort, and Harvey Firestone enjoyed the fun as
well as the next fellow. Picnics became a standby, gen-

erating friendliness that carried over into workaday relations. A special success were the annual sales meetings, begun in 1906, at which the salesmen mixed the business of learning the Firestone viewpoint with the pleasures of mutual exchange and had a rollicking good time at the banquet. These conventions were lively with the pep of a typical booster affair. Only twenty-three salesmen composed the first gathering—he took them on a junket to Cleveland to witness the start of the Glidden tour—but in 1909 the number of branch managers and field men attending was seventy, and in 1911 it was a hundred.

The refinancing of the corporation, marking its great financial growth, gave the company the occasion to offer stock to the employees on a monthly payment plan. One share, preferred or common, was allotted for each year's service.

The shift to South Akron posed a lunch problem. Isolated "out in the country," before there was time to set up a restaurant in the building, the workers were a half-mile from their old haunt and there were no other eating places in the neighborhood. A company truck was released to convoy those who did not want to miss a hot meal.

Harvey Firestone was deeply concerned over the dangerous grade crossing at the foot of South Main Street, the chief artery to this side of town. He knew it was only a matter of a few years before a new community evolved south of the plant, and traffic would be heavy, but even now the employees' hazard of running the gantlet of five sets of tracks sweeping down at a sharp angle aroused him. Thus began his agitation for a viaduct. He took the chairmanship of the Akron Chamber of Commerce grade separation committee and stirred up not only the railroad officials but the voters as well. It was a long fight.*

A unique chance to render a public service came soon after the company had settled in its new quarters. That summer, the city's water works had to be shut down because a pipe burst. Firestone at once placed the firm's private pipe line at the disposal of Akron, supplying drinking water and water for fire protection at the company's own expense. This simple act unconsciously demonstrated that a business enterprise was part and parcel of civic existence.

As the business grew, its social responsibility increased, and so did its "sense" of responsibility; but here again nobody put the thought into so many words. People were too busy to philosophize. The factory was clean, the prevailing wages for ten hours' work stood higher than in most industries through the nation ($3.50 a day for tire building), and forced up the general level of the city. The men had steady work, were well dressed, and many owned the homes they lived in.

More and more workers were attracted to Akron. Firestone opened an employment office in the downtown district. The influx created a housing shortage—a perennial problem in this fast-growing city—and Harvey Firestone attended a national housing conference held in Cincinnati to seek remedies.

The company's tire production in 1911 exceeded 200,000 units and almost doubled this figure in 1912, virtually all the pneumatics being of non-skid design. Rim manufacturing operations had taken over the entire three and a half acres of space at Miller and Sweitzer and yet, with 80,000 rims produced in 1911 and 120,000

* The chief protagonist did not live to see the viaduct in operation. The Harvey Samuel Firestone Memorial Bridge was dedicated Dec. 20, 1938.

the next year, did not meet the demand. The latest machines for rolling, shaping, electric welding, and galvanizing rim steel had been acquired. Bases for solid-rubber tires were also made in large quantity. The new demountable rim had a quick-detachable feature and was of one piece, no longer a split rim. A friendly rivalry grew up between the two plants, fought out in baseball battles at company picnics.

Sales to Ford alone amounted to $931,510 in 1911 and $1,366,623 in 1912. Although the capacity of the tire factory was 2,500 pneumatics daily, this did not suffice; two of the wings were extended. Total sales of $11,688,188 in 1912 yielded a net profit of close to $1,200,000, but no more than $7 in annual dividends on the common stock was declared, a surplus of approximately a million being set aside to establish new branches and otherwise to expand. Harvey Firestone did not believe in fancy dividends but in using the money in the business.

He squelched a rumor of impending consolidation with Goodyear.

I do not want to bury my identity in a merger. I have worked hard to place my company on a substantial basis. Now that it has been accomplished I don't feel like stepping into the background. There is something more than money in life. I have five sons who will grow up and take a hand in the company's affairs in time. I want to have those places prepared for them.

These rumors are a great injustice to the stockholders and to the public who are misled by rumors of high financing, inflating rubber stock values to a point that must eventually be detrimental to the rubber interests and the citizens and city of Akron, who are directly and indirectly interested.

The Firestone Tire & Rubber Company will not sell out, consolidate or absorb with any other rubber company. It is built upon a substantial foundation to manufacture tires and sell them to the public, and it is going to continue along that line. There is no stock or cash consideration which will change that policy.*

By the end of July, an improvement in the manufacturing process, long overdue, was achieved by Firestone engineers. The company's first tire-building machine had been constructed. Other companies were paying Goodyear a royalty on each tire made by machine, and were producing much more economically than by the strenuous manual method. Firestone, preferring freedom, had been delayed in his mechanization program by having had to concentrate on refinancing and the tremendous undertaking of the new factory. On September 1, the first machine-built Firestone tires were made.

No longer would human muscle need to stretch plies over the iron forming core and smooth them down with tense fingers, layer after layer. The machine fed each strip of fabric to the rotating core with proper tension and fitted it around, a little wheel on each side "stitching" the ply with precision impossible by hand. It saved time. It saved strain.

By the end of November, Firestone had ten such machines, with ten others being built in its shop; and when the new year came the twenty machines were in operation, ten more nearing completion. This important technological advance, like any apparatus replacing hand labor and multiplying an operator's daily output, necessitated a wage readjustment.

Formerly a man constructing a tire performed all the stages himself. Now the work was divided into building (by machine) and finishing (by hand). A new classification of employee was established, the finisher, and he was put on a piecework basis, given a rough allowance of one-third the rate previously paid for making a whole

* Statement in *The Akron Press*, July 13, 1912.

tire by hand. The scale was provisional, intended to be corrected by experience; intended also to enable the finisher to do a good job and maintain his $3.50 wage. Under the new machine system, the direct labor charge in the cost of building up a tire casing was cut in half.

The builder's work ended after two taut plies were laid on the core, the beads applied, and successive plies stretched secure. Still on the core, the casing was then sent down to the other end of the room for finishing. The old hand operations obtained. A chafer strip of rubber-impregnated fabric was smoothed on, to reinforce the bead. Sidewalls of specially compounded rubber were next applied to protect the foundation. Now a cushion of rubber was laid down longitudinally for the eventual function of uniting tread and body. At this stage came the initial curing in a pot heater.

The Firestone plant used a "two cure" method of vulcanization. If the tread with its breaker strip were cemented on before this, the heat would not penetrate thoroughly because of the varying thicknesses of the assembled parts. The result would be uneven curing. By means of the preliminary vulcanizing, proper treatment of the wall construction was assured. After the first cure the tire was sent to the tread applying department for the breaker strip and the cementing of the tread. It was next cross-wrapped with duck tape and then placed in a horizontal heater for a final cure which made it a firm unit, better prepared to withstand wear, shocks, strain, heat, and weather.

The number of employees now averaged around 1,800. Thomas was factory superintendent. Firestone, engrossed in the buying of rubber, in the financing, the advertising and selling, and other duties, commented: "I don't even know the names of my foremen. It used to be different."

On a Monday in February, 1913, after a tryout of the rate for finishers, with time studies made for an objective appraisal, a new scale was posted. The company thought it was a fair one—calculated to enable an experienced finisher who was an average worker to earn the same pay he had got originally, though the work was lighter. Scientific management had been introduced in many factories in America, usually suspected by labor but hailed by outstanding friends of labor as a lever for increasing productivity and raising the worker's status.

The posting of the notice was a routine matter in a routine day. Some of the men were critical. They complained that under such a schedule they could not keep up the pace day after day. It was revised, and the finishers' foreman said that if it wasn't right it would be made right, as they knew the company was always fair.

At five o'clock the next afternoon, February 11, as the day shift was leaving, the entrance was blocked to workers arriving for the night shift. Some men standing there in close rows were chanting: "Everybody on strike at the Firestone!" Most of the workers got inside.

What had happened was that 150 men in the tire finishing department walked out in protest against the new schedule. The ready-made demonstration at the gate was staged by the I.W.W. (Industrial Workers of the World).

A city-wide rubber strike to organize the industry was the manifest intention. The next morning 600 employees failed to report for work. Pickets appeared, here and at the Goodyear and the Goodrich-Diamond plants. Smaller rubber factories, taken by storm, were completely shut down. A general cry was raised against "speed up," "the man with the stop-watch and notebook," and "unsanitary conditions."

Not since an abortive attempt in 1902 of the American Federation of Labor to form a union had there been more than a half-hearted move to organize. Now the A.F. of L. stepped in and contended with the I.W.W. for the allegiance of the men.

The industry blamed outside agitators led by "Big Bill" Haywood for the disruption and disturbance; they had boasted that a victory in Akron would be the prelude to tying up the whole automotive industry. Firestone maintained that the points at issue would have been settled but for a misunderstanding and could easily be resolved now but for these instigators.

There has been nothing in the present situation that we could not or would not have adjusted to the satisfaction of the company and its employees. *

On February 20, although many of the finishers had come back, fifty percent of the Firestone workers were out—"mostly on account of fear, some in the hope that they would be able to form a rubber workers' union."

The other factories fared worse. The number of strikers kept increasing until a peak of 15,000 of Akron's 22,500 rubber workers towered over the turmoil. Even fewer were able to cause a crippling effect, for the work of the various departments in a tire plant was interdependent; a stoppage at one stage meant an overflow or a drought at others. On February 24, the Firestone plant turned out only 200 tires and 200 tubes.

"Many of the good men who were employed in Akron have left," Firestone wrote his son, Harvey jr., who was at school. He kept him posted on events.

On March 1, a state senate committee headed by William Green, of Coshocton, who had introduced a resolution for an investigation of the Akron situation, opened hearings at the Portage Hotel. Ten days later, a riot broke out. The mayor swore in several hundred

* H.S.F. quoted in *Cleveland Plain Dealer*, Feb. 16, 1913.

deputies to scout the town in autos and break up groups of intimidators and demonstrators.

As the month wore on, men returned. Firestone had more than a thousand working, and the power was on for twenty-four hours a day. On March 31, after most of the industry's men had already been reinstated, a handful attended an official union meeting to vote the strike at an end.

The investigating committee's report opposed speed-up wherever it might exist but found tire industry wages high. Firestone had testified that the rate schedule was not intended to speed up the work, for hurried performance might impair quality.

The material that goes to make up a tire is expensive by comparison with the labor on that tire. To have the man do his best work— not to be rushed too hard or try to do more on a speeding-up system to make more money and thereby neglect things that he wouldn't neglect otherwise—we set the time that we think he ought to use in making a tire and making it right and to the best efficiency.*

One of the state senators asked, "Your plan, then, is the very opposite of the speeding-up system?"

Firestone answered, "Yes, sir."

The committee had visited several factories and found them fireproof, well lighted, well ventilated. Firestone had testified that he was very proud of his plant, "trying to make it the most sanitary in the United States," and a corps of sixty porters kept it clean.

I am a crank about good water, good light, and good air. You can keep men happier, healthier that way. . . .

Dust is deadly to adhesion. So we must be careful to keep dust away from our goods. We employ suction fans in some of our mills, and where there is a good deal of soapstone and dust, or any fumes, we have a suction fan over a hood to take it off.†

* H.S.F. testimony, Proceedings before Special Committee of the Ohio Senate: In the matter of the Investigation of Conditions Relative to the Strike in the Rubber Industries at Akron, March, 1913.
† *Ibid.*

According to the committee report, the most salient feature of the evidence was that employees refrained from submitting grievances for adjustment, in fear of discharge, but there was no evidence of a blacklist. The companies were advised to post notices informing the workers that they might submit any complaint with the assurance of no discrimination.

Queried on his company's policy regarding complaints, Firestone answered:

> We want the men to come. Our office is open. Up until last October, I was acting as superintendent. I was through the factory almost every day, and any complaints could be brought to me. . . . It is perfectly free for any man to come to me—doesn't make any difference what position he occupies. I am accessible at any time.
>
> We were always looking to the human side and trying to make our men feel a part of the organization. We are handling expensive material. We want them interested, and we used every effort.
>
> I believe that we have as loyal and as fair a body of men as you can find in any factory. Now, that loyalty and that fairness can only exist by our fostering and helping and doing our part of that proposition, and the Firestone company, I believe, occupy that position. *

On the day the strike ended, the Firestone plant produced 2,000 pneumatic tires, 1,700 tubes, and 20,000 feet of carriage rubber. Beginning the first week in April, output was greater than at any previous time in the company's history. Soon it averaged 3,000 pneumatics daily (for a calendar year's total of 609,477). It caught up on the losses of the unlucky seven weeks, on a Ford order for 200,000 tires, and the regular spring demand.

There were at least twenty classifications of workers besides builders and finishers,† not to mention the large

---

* *Ibid.*

† Among the specialized factory occupations: assembler, bead maker, bias-cutter operator, tube buffer, calender man, compounder, curers (bead, tire, tube), drier, tire duster, tube finisher, laborer, millman, tube skiver, tube splicer, strippers (core, tube), soapstoner, tear-down man, tread cutter, trucker, tube-machine feeder and operator, tube roller and wrapper, and valve inserter.

staff that handled the endless stream of paper work.

The superintendents and foremen numbered 101. On a Saturday in June, 1913, Firestone took them in an auto cavalcade to the Homestead Farm in Columbiana. The party started with lunch in the plant restaurant on the fourth floor, drawing lots for places in the procession, except of course that H. S. was to be in the first car as "pathfinder," and fifteen-year-old Harvey jr. took the wheel of the second, entrusted with the duty of scattering confetti at the turns in the road so that stragglers would not lose their way.

Bedecked with banners, thirty cars rolled along the countryside and came to the yard of the farmhouse, where Firestone's mother and his wife greeted each man. A hungry pack, they needed no special urging to sit down at the long tables under the trees and fall to.

"I think they are a fine-looking lot of men," Firestone wrote to José Alvarez, his customer and friend in Havana. He decided to make this an annual outing of superintendents and foremen, with an early-morning start in order to get in a full day "down on the farm" (for fishing, quoits, baseball, and cat naps). In his diary, the night after enjoying the following summer's event, he entered: "One of the happiest days of my life."

This longing of a man who had created an organization which in a sense was an expression of himself, to recapture intimate contact with his creation, found an outlet in new welfare measures.

In planning the factory, he had taken thought of ideal working conditions, for safety, comfort, and health. Artesian wells had been sunk on the property to provide drinking water; safety devices were attached to the machines; an emergency hospital was staffed by two nurses and a physician. In July, 1913, the company's Industrial Service Department began functioning. It was

charged with maintaining these provisions and further-
ing them. Recreation facilities came within its purview,
and a baseball diamond was laid out adjacent to the
factory. A new restaurant was built across the street from
the main entrance to encourage the people to go out into
the open during their lunch period. Meals were served
at cost.

A step toward fusing the interlocking interests of management and labor was the adoption of the suggestion-
box idea with generous awards for meritorious proposals,
and the publication of a house organ. The airing of
grievances was encouraged. The company did not wait
for the newly enacted mandatory Ohio Workmen's
Compensation Law to go into effect; it had been one
of the first participants under a voluntary compensation
law of 1911. Firestone paid its premium to the State
Industrial Commission several months ahead of the
required time to make it possible for benefits to com-
mence at once.*

The problem of keeping a balance between production
and sales naturally had its counterpart in labor relations.
In April, 1914, for example, Firestone recorded: "Business is exceptionally good—the factory is running full
capacity and we are not able to make enough tires. I
just O.K.'d plans for two more extensions." On May 8:
"We are now turning out over 5,000 tires a day and it
makes a lot of work to get them out through the country
and to the customers." But on May 14 business was
"fairly good" and "our sales are not quite as large as I
would like to have them." On May 18, after an Akron
competitor had let 400 men go: "We are keeping all our
men but have as many as we can use." In the middle of
June, Firestone was "quite busy just now trying to sell

---

* The first beneficiary was a rim worker, who suffered a broken finger, had
to stay away from work for three weeks, and was paid for his lost time and
medical expense. He returned to his position, which had been held open for him.

some of the tires we are manufacturing. . . . We are doing a great deal of advertising and pushing hard for sales." *

He put the Service Department on the job of studying the causes of labor turnover, which, with absenteeism, often exceeded twenty percent a month. It cost at least $25 to break in a new man. His own conviction was that the high rate of turnover was due to unskillful handling of the personnel; dissatisfaction must be erased, the power to discharge must be examined.

While awaiting the results of this study, Firestone encouraged the sale of stock to the employees as a means of giving them a greater stake in the company's prosperity. Some of them had already bought stock (to the extent of $85,726 as of August 1, 1913), but a plan must be formulated to facilitate purchases and make such stockholding widespread.

Harvey Firestone's mind, piercing one phase of the business after another, dwelt constantly on human relations. His thinking soon bore fruit in the emergence of a four-story Club House, free life insurance, a savings bank, and the thousand-acre community development—Firestone Park.

* Excerpts from letters, H.S.F. to his sons Harvey jr. and Russell.

6

"We Are All One"

STEEL skeletons of new extensions being added to the wings of the factory would meet the eye of a visitor virtually every time one crossed the tracks at South Main Street and approached the Firestone factory. Construction tried hard to keep pace with demand. No sooner had the company achieved a productive capacity of 5,000 pneumatic tires a day than plans were drawn for an output of 7,500. The automobile had captured America.

Passenger-car production had been jogging along in annual gains of 10,000 until Henry Ford's imaginative leap into the mass market and Henry Ford's defiance of restrictive licensing freed the automobile industry of its narrow bounds. The first spurt into six figures came in 1909, bringing auto registration to 350,000 in 1910. The next surge occurred in 1912, with production of 356,000, and registration the following year at 1,250,000. It was no coincidence that this expansion came directly after Ford had beaten the broad claims of the Selden patent holders. More than half a million cars were assembled in 1914.

With America on wheels—self-propelled, rubber-tired wheels—Firestone's name for good performance commanded increasing business. Sales had advanced thirty-four percent in 1913 (half the cars equipped with Firestone rims) and sixty-five percent by 1914.

"Extraordinary year," Harvey Firestone noted in his diary. The sales total of $19,250,109 was all the more impressive because tire prices had been reduced, meaning a proportionately greater number of tires marketed (more than 900,000). This company's financial showing was the best of them all. Profits were $3,227,719. Common dividends, raised from $7 to $10 in 1913, were supplemented with a $2 extra payment, and the stock was put on a $12 per share basis.

"Nothing but mileage . . . at the lowest cost . . . would have done this," declared an advertisement in announcing that the 1914 demand had brought the company fifty percent more dealers and "made us grow into the largest organization of tire specialists in America." A 37x5 Non-Skid tire, "seven plies instead of six," was priced $39.80, "twenty percent below the average of four widely advertised makes." Back in 1908, the company had sold 36x5½ tires for $74.

Harvey Firestone predicted an even brighter picture for 1915. Two additional elements hove into view: the growing use of motor trucks and, because of the rising cost of horses, wider adoption of autos by farmers. He proved right. Car production jumped close to the 900,000 mark; truck production, only 25,000 in 1914, presaged greater possibilities by taking a sharp upturn to 74,000. Registrations now totaled almost 2,500,000.

For the Firestone company the harvest was 1,342,225 tires (besides rims, tubes, and solid bases), a sales volume of $25,319,475, profit of $4,517,272, and an extra dividend of $4. In the course of the year, quotations on the common stock ranged from 365 to 804½.

Persistently there was a shortage of labor. The nation's industrial growth, the spread of population, the advance in purchasing power, the art of advertising—all these had broadened markets, and the demand for commodities resulted in a scarcity of skilled workers. Agents dispatched from Akron to other cities in Ohio, where many unemployed men were said to be available, found mostly inexperienced people. Labor recruitment had to be energetic and thorough.

Five thousand employees now thronged the company's gates. These, and the vision of many more arrivals when still further factory extensions would be ready, fixed Harvey Firestone's attention. Wage increases were not the only answer, although machinists received a flat fifteen percent raise and piecework employees also were given more money (tire builders and finishers earning $4 to $4.25 a day). Other equations were involved. The machine age posed the crucial problem of man's impersonal attitude toward his job. How to hold the workers' interest in the organization?

Through the Industrial Service Department measures were devised toward this objective. The shifts, instead of rotating, became permanent, with older men getting preference for daywork and newcomers having this to strive for. An innovation in factory management removed the power of discharge from foremen and transferred it to superintendents and departmental managers. The rate of turnover consequently declined. After the power was lodged with department heads alone, turnover went still lower. Finally, when the authority was vested in the superintendent of labor, the rate dwindled to less than three percent a month. Promotions were made now through the same office.

The new system did not rob foremen of dignity. On the contrary, their responsibilities were heightened, for Firestone assigned to them the role of tactful industrial psychologists studying subordinates for ability and proclivity—also trying to see situations through the men's eyes—to the end that the men should be happy at their work. Where foremen gave confidence, they reaped trust. If a man failed to make good in one department or slipped behind in strenuous work, the operative principle was to save him for some other task. A Firestone employee was worth keeping as a Firestone employee.

Harvey Firestone ranked personnel with finance among the factors governing success in a business enterprise. Was not the welfare of its workers part of a company's success? The prosperous condition in 1915 ushered in an ambitious program.

First came the Club House. Plans for an addition to the outgrown restaurant across the street were canceled in favor of putting up a $350,000 building. More than an eating place, it would be a meeting place with lounge rooms, clubrooms, library, classrooms, gymnasium, swimming pool, bowling alleys, barber shop, and a large auditorium. Medical and dental service was set up.

Next, a land company was formed to buy up farm property southeast of the plant and pave the way (literally) to employee housing. Meals at cost, homes at cost; individual houses set apart amid trees and lawns.

Firestone harbored still more ideas for bettering the basic conditions of living. Looking ahead to an opportunity to translate them into action, he analyzed various benefit plans.

He felt that the welding of family unity had progressed far. At the third annual outing of superintendents and foremen to the homestead in Columbiana, he sensed their spirit. Speaking to them at the long tables under a huge tent, he said: "While I am glad to be host today, I dislike the idea of you thinking of me as host. I want each of you to feel that you are all in a sense hosts—that this is *your* homecoming—that we are all *one*."

The deathtrap at the grade crossing, closing in on more victims each year, alarmed him. He had a count taken of the number of pedestrians, autos, horse-drawn vehicles, and bicycles entering South Akron, to demonstrate the urgency of a viaduct at South Main Street. He had photographs taken, and motion pictures, vividly portraying the menace on a winter day. Flagmen and gate tenders failed to synchronize. Often gates were lowered after vehicles had started across the wide expanse of track. Autos followed so close behind each other that drivers absorbed in avoiding collisions had little chance to look out for onrushing trains.

"My company is doing everything it can to protect the lives of its employees in the factories," Firestone told a Chamber of Commerce meeting. "The only three employees who died during the past year were killed at the South Main Street railroad crossing. A girl employed by us was seriously injured at the same point."

If the city was unable to pay its share of the project in concert with the railroads, he was willing to cooperate on a plan to take care, for several years, of the sinking fund and interest charges on bonds that would have to be issued. But before city officials and railroad engineers could arrange an agreement and the work of surveying and preparing specifications could be done, the United States was at war.*

The year 1916 opened with contracts on hand for nearly a million demountable rims. This harbinger of continued prosperity did not belie its promise. Passenger-car production almost doubled, truck production kept climbing, and Firestone made a few short of 3,500,000 tires, with sales reaching $44,135,325. This unfaltering ascent would have been monotonous were it not thrilling.

* Construction had to be postponed until the end of the war; then was further postponed. H.S.F. continued to serve as chairman of the Akron Chamber of Commerce grade separation committee and to press for progress. In October, 1919, the signatures of railroad officials were obtained on an agreement to build a temporary bridge. Time, like traffic, dragged.

Despite the increasing cost of labor, Firestone profits were $5,926,568. Dividends were placed on a $5 quarterly basis.

Thousands of additional employees were enrolled. While a fifth story was superimposed upon the plant and new five-story wings sprouted from both sides of the structure, and a separate mechanical building was going up, and ground was broken for Plant 2 (to be devoted wholly to Ford-size 30x3½ tires), the immensity of the physical equipment did not dwarf Harvey Firestone's perception of the human element.

The institution of an eight-hour day in Akron rubber factories was one of the year's achievements. Firestone introduced three-shift schedules first in the bead press-ers' room as early as March, and from there they spread to other departments. It meant revisions of rates, so that the men earned at least as much money in eight hours as in ten or twelve. As a matter of fact, production increased and so did wages. The men began their day feeling more fit. Quality of the larger output was assured by rigid inspection.

Rubber City won national publicity as "Ohio's eight-hour town." Harvey Firestone explained:

There is nothing sentimental, paternalistic, or philanthropic in our adoption of the eight-hour system. But you can't make men do their best unless you get them fully interested, proud of what they are doing, happier in mind, better in body and spirit, and producing something for themselves while they produce something for the business organization of which they are a part.*

The Industrial Service Department reported to him statistically: increases of thirty to forty percent in piece-work rates, but a reduction in number of man-hours per tire, so that labor costs actually advanced only twelve to sixteen percent.

* Quoted in *India Rubber World*, Dec. 1, 1916.

To encourage thrift, Harvey Firestone brought other South Akron manufacturers and merchants together and organized the Rubber City Savings Bank in September, 1916, taking temporary quarters in a nearby store. The company opened an account for each person on the payroll by depositing a dollar to each one's credit. The passbook was a passport to prudence. Sixteen thousand active savings accounts were on the books by the beginning of 1919 when the renamed Firestone Park Trust & Savings Bank moved into a building of its own at the corner of Miller Avenue and South Main Street and boasted deposits totaling $1,917,000. Guardian at the gateway to Firestone Park, the bank stood as a constructive force in the life of this new community.

A half-mile from the factory, the Park was opened in October, 1916, landscaped to preserve the natural beauties of the countryside. At the start there were only 600 acres, with a sixteen-acre area in the center of the allotment reserved for public recreation. Home sites were offered for sale to employees, and 177 were bought the first day. Within a year, about 600 houses were built and occupied, sold at cost price on a five percent down payment, the balance defrayed by $20 to $30 a month including taxes, insurance, and interest. Another hundred acres had been added, and in a few years there would be a thousand, dotted with a thousand homes. Locations were set aside for schools, churches, and a shopping section.*

It was a healthful community on high, dry ground, with eye appeal—a fine place to live. The architecture, the boulevards, trees, and ornamental lighting of the streets (wires in underground conduits) created an environment worthy of an American with a pay check. By

* The general selling plan was ten percent down, one percent monthly on the unpaid balance, paying out in thirteen and a half years. The lot owner could elect to furnish his own building contractor and materials, in which case the initial payment was $500 against the loan.

October, 1917, the company had invested $2,981,000 in
employee happiness through this project, half the sum
going for improvements such as miles of paving, side-
walks, water mains, sanitation sewers, storm sewers, and
street lighting. To handle this operation a separate unit
had been organized, the Coventry Land & Improvement
Company.*

A week after the opening of Firestone Park, the Club
House was dedicated. Employees, their wives and children and friends, came to the auditorium to shake hands
with Harvey Firestone and enjoy with him this realization of his dream.

> I can see clearly that I am not the only one happy today. I have
> an idea that the reason for this is that we have so many women and
> children with us this afternoon, and after all they are the ones in
> our families that are almost always happy and inspire happiness in
> others.
> Today my thoughts have taken me back to South Akron as it
> was when we started. . . . I had a picture of this Club in my mind
> back in 1903.
> When we moved into our new factory we needed more employees
> and so we saw the need of their being able to have pleasant, healthful
> homes near by the plant. We saw that our employees needed certain
> definite things to be happy, contented, and efficient, and in order
> to get the most out of life.†

Happy homes, a reliable savings bank, safe railroad
crossings. Besides these, Firestone continued, one other
facility:

> A congenial social gathering place where Firestone folks and their
> friends may mingle together and enjoy social affairs and entertain-
> ments under best possible conditions. . . .
> You may imagine that after dreaming of this Club and holding
> the picture in my mind for so many years, it gives me supreme

* The name Coventry came from the original designation of this district.
Here in 1823 George Adam Falor bought his first farm. In dramatic contrast
with the pioneer village, an Akron streetcar line sped into the modern development in the fall of 1918, with H.S.F. handling the controls of the head car.
† H.S.F., quoted in *The Firestone*, November, 1916.

pleasure today to turn it over to the Firestone organization, because they, after all, by their loyalty and cooperation, have made it possible.*

But the list was not complete. He had other things to tell; he must hold them back until the stockholders' meeting three weeks later. One was the setting aside of a million dollars as an employees' welfare fund, with a provision for free life insurance. This was authorized by the meeting on November 2, 1916.†

On the same occasion, the capitalization was brought up to $15,000,000. The company retired its preferred issue of $1,000,000 seven percent stock. It was authorized to issue $10,000,000 of new six percent preferred with a view to obtaining more working capital as needed; half of this was immediately offered and was several times oversubscribed. Also, in place of 30,000 shares of common stock ($100 par), the company was authorized to issue 500,000 at $10, the shareholders receiving ten for one in the exchange. Of this, 350,000 shares were issued, making 50,000 available to the employees.

"Every employee a stockholder, is the object of the stock distribution plan of the Firestone Company."

Harvey Firestone described its attractive terms at a dinner for 500 superintendents, foremen, and departments heads, and their wives, held at the Club House. He himself owned 163,913 shares of common.

"We want to hold the interest of our employees," he explained. "The only way to do that properly is to give them a real interest in the company. It is better for the company and better for the men. If you have a real interest in the work you do, there is nothing in the world

* *Ibid.*

† The board of directors adopted a plan in August, 1918, to carry out the insurance phase: automatic coverage of $500 after thirty days in the company's employ, $600 after one year, the benefits being graduated to $1,000 after five years' service.

that gives you more pleasure than your work, and at the same time you become more efficient."

Subscriptions were open to all grades of workers at $100 a share, the allotments being based on length of service. The current market quotation was $140.

Purchasers could take five years to pay, in weekly installments of fifty cents for one share and ten cents for each additional share; but even if the stock were paid up before this it must remain with the company that length of time in fairness to stockholders who bought at the market price. Employee-subscribers would have all the privileges of full-fledged stockholders; dividends would be credited to them in the interim. Where failure to pay an installment was justified, an extension of time would be granted.

In case of resignation or dismissal before the five years expired, the subscription would be canceled (an exception where women workers left to be married). Payments would be fully refunded with six percent interest and an additional sum representing part of the difference between the purchase price and a higher market price. All stock acquired by the company through cancellations would be turned over to the Employees' Stock Department (situated at the bank) and sold to employees at average cost, on the same plan.*

In the nine weeks within which employees could take up this offer—January 2 to March 8, 1917—eighty-nine percent of the 10,500 factory workers, virtually all the home-office force of 1,500, and eighty-four percent of the 1,000 employed at forty-nine branch houses sub-

---

* Distribution of stock on the basis of length of continuous service was made as follows: less than six months, one share; up to one year, two shares; up to two years, three shares; up to three years, four shares; up to four years, six shares; up to five years, eight shares; five years and more, ten shares.

In computing length of service, no deduction was made for layoffs, or for less than a year's absence through illness, or for time between voluntary leave and reemployment if not more than ninety days.

scribed. The foremen and managers had done a fine job of presenting the plan to the people. Firestone was delighted.

Payments were to begin on the first payday after March 1. A number of intended subscribers dropped out, leaving 9,484 contracts signed for a total of 28,012 shares—almost one-tenth of the outstanding common stock thus going into employees' hands.

> I have worked a long time [Harvey Firestone wrote] to get a plan that I thought would mean something to the men and which would make a stronger and better organization, and I know that they cannot fully appreciate what I believe it means to them.
>
> It is just human nature to wonder what the reason is when we can buy anything below the market price, and then we are all apt to despise small things. This is especially true at the present time on account of everything being inflated and the country, as a whole, going at such a terrific rate, and that is just the reason why you had to make such an effort to get the men to only receive one share, but that one share may help start many of our men to a small savings and to a greater interest in their work and the company, making better and happier men of them.*

As the year advanced, quotations on the stock touched 150 but also dipped to 97. The country was engaged in war. The money market was quite tight. Government needs for large sums caused declines in all industrial and railroad stocks as well as high-grade bonds. Harvey Firestone assured the employee-stockholders that their stock was "worth more to you today than when you purchased it, as the profits for the past year have added to the value of your stock."

Sales had skyrocketed to $61,587,219. The volume would have been even greater but for retrenchment in midsummer.

> We found that we had more business and were attempting to

* Letter, Apr. 3, 1917.

make more tires than we were equipped to make well and hold our
past high standard and reputation for making the best tire, and,
consequently, as you know, we reduced our operations to two shifts.
We want to urge upon every employee that he give the most careful
attention to his work, and that every tire he makes or any work he
does will be a credit to him and to the company.*

Common stock paid a $4 dividend. The company
made good the difference between this and the six percent interest charge on the deferred payments. In 1918,
the dividend was $6. Everyone was urged to buy Liberty
Bonds.

When a bonus was awarded to salaried employees
toward the end of 1918 (matching the wage increases
that the factory employees had received), Firestone encouraged them to buy more stock. The bonus was paid
in the form of ten percent cash and an equal amount
credited to them, which was applicable either to indebtedness for company shares or Liberty Bonds or to a
further purchase of stock to be offered in a new general
allotment. If the employee chose, he could take the credit
in cash.

For most of us it is not easy to acquire the habit of saving. We
need a special inducement and this is an opportunity for you not
only to acquire the habit of saving but to use the Stock Department
as a depositary for your savings. . . .

It is a matter of record and pride that so large a number of our
men and women have become directly interested in the Firestone
Company. We believe it is good for both of us and as time goes on
we shall both realize the many advantages to be gained by a partnership of this kind. We are glad to be able to do this in recognition
of your splendid and faithful employment.†

Changes in personnel during the two war years had
brought back into the treasury a considerable amount
of stock, and this was what was offered to them now,

---

* H.S.F. to employee-stockholders, Oct. 25, 1917.
† H.S.F. letter, Nov. 9, 1918.

again at $100. As the offering was oversubscribed, the maximum allotable to any person was four shares. Even so, the 8,030 contracts for 20,672 shares, when added to previous contracts still in force, exceeded the 50,000 shares that had been authorized for this purpose. The company purchased 3,680 shares in the open market and sold them to the employees, absorbing the loss upon itself. Quotations were in the 140s.

In the middle of 1919, when Harvey Firestone was contemplating another stock distribution to personnel, there were 10,428 subscriptions of the two allotments in force, totaling 65,257 shares.

"The employees," he said, "have a real and substantial interest in the Firestone business."

7

A War and Its Aftermath

WHILE strengthening the human fiber of the organization, Harvey Firestone ran the business in its manifold aspects. He coped with day-to-day questions of finance, raw material, manufacture, and sales, integrating them in his mind. As the company grew, things were not simply on a grander scale, they were more complex. Striving for improvement of product in the whirl of expansion hardly simplified matters. And the outbreak of war in Europe the summer of 1914 had precipitated a new chain of reactions.

Ocean shipping was suspended. The company had a three months' stock of rubber, but the break in continuity of supply, however temporary, panicked the stoutest heart. Cablegrams flew into the chaos and returned small comfort. In a fortnight the price of fine Para leaped from 72 cents to $1.15 a pound.

This country consumed half the world production of rubber. Our merchant marine was miserably inadequate, slightly more than ten percent of imports of all kinds coming in American bottoms. Not only were connections with Brazil interrupted, but the plantations in the Far East, now yielding almost double the volume of jungle rubber, were mainly British-owned, British-controlled. In November, Great Britain declared an embargo on rubber to prevent any raw stock or finished goods from reaching the enemy.

Protests to the British Embassy in Washington did not beat down those doors—not until the following January, when the embargo was lifted on condition that the American rubber industry police the destination of the material. It fell to Harvey Firestone, after his election as president of the Rubber Club of America, to assume responsibility for these assurances. Vigilance was maintained, well-nigh perfectly.

Rubber prices had been declining steadily each year since the peak of 1910—tire prices regularly reduced in harmony—but the vagaries of the market in the course of a year imparted the character of gambling to forward orders. "Rubber prices are always treacherous," Firestone said. "The lower you get rubber, the greater the risk you have of its going up." At one point he remarked, "It goes up and down so fast that it makes you dizzy." In November, 1915, he recorded in his diary: "Crude rubber market has gone crazy."

He had sent a man to Singapore, the trading center for Malaya, Burma, British Borneo, Siam, and the Netherlands East Indies. In Singapore, a Firestone buying office was set up to make direct connections with planters and avoid paying tribute to London speculators. From the Akron viewpoint, it seemed logical to ship across the Pacific to the West Coast or through the Panama Canal; the prewar route for rubber was the Red Sea and the Mediterranean.

These shackles of dependence upon intermediaries, and upon a foreign power, moved Firestone to decide, that same November, that he should invest in a plantation estate in the Far East. Areas were explored for him, reports rendered, consultations with bankers held, but none of the proposed arrangements was suitable. Rubber averaged fifty cents a pound in 1915 and climbed to fifty-nine cents in 1916.

Interested in the Augusan River Valley in Mindanao, Philippine Islands, Harvey Firestone wanted to cultivate 50,000 square miles. He inquired of the War Department Bureau of Insular Affairs in April, 1916, and learned that the legal limit was only 2,500 acres. Ex-President William Howard Taft, former civilian governor of the Philippines, was scheduled to be guest-speaker at the next annual meeting of the Rubber Club. Firestone suggested a topic: The possibilities and advantages of the Philippines. "It is very important that we grow rubber under the American flag if we can." *

There was no microphone at that meeting, in the Waldorf-Astoria in New York, but Firestone made himself heard: "Rubber is the most important commodity in the world."

Taft's judicial enthusiasm did not carry him so far, but he pointed to Germany's dire need as proof that rubber was a military necessity.

As for extensive planting in the Philippines, Taft was sympathetic but doubtful. He told the audience that adverse Congressional legislation was keeping capital out of the Islands.

The limitation contained in the fundamental act of the Philippincs, forbidding the acquisition of land by corporations of more than 2,500 acres, is an absurdity in a tropical country where sugar, rubber, and other tropical products should be encouraged. . . .

The amount of land which ought to be cultivated in the Philippines is so great that the acquisition of parts of it by great corporations could work no evil at all. †

Harvey Firestone pursued the subject. Two months later, in an interview, he said: "The American people, especially those dependent upon rubber production, should invest in rubber plantations in the Malay States

* H.S.F. to G. H. Hodgman, Dec. 9, 1916.
† W. H. Taft, Jan. 8, 1917; quoted in *India Rubber World*, February, 1917.

and Sumatra . . . for the reason that they can better control their product, both as to price and output."* The United States was now consuming two-thirds of the world's rubber. Another rankling situation was the British embargo on Egyptian cotton, the long-staple cotton used for tire fabric. Firestone advocated the cultivation of this type of crop in our country. He also emphasized the need of an American merchant marine to keep the lanes of crude-rubber transportation open. "The rubber industry's weak point—its dependence on foreign sources for its raw material."†

Never a man to tolerate a hindrance, neither was he inclined to limit his attitude to words. It was a safe guess that Firestone would keep thinking of an avenue of action.

When the final crisis in our relations with Germany seemed near and war was imminent, he offered to President Wilson "the use of the factory organization and all facilities in any way that can be of service to the government in war."‡ The offer was accepted at once. Re-elected president of the Rubber Association of America (new name of the Rubber Club), Firestone announced that the industry was capable of handling any call that might be made upon it.

This was a generous promise, but by the end of the year the Firestone factories were swamped with work and were managing to get it done. Yet he noted that "the government is calling on us for more than we are able to make and deliver."

It was only a momentary twinge of conscientiousness, for schedules were always met. Despite delays in obtaining steel from the mills, which were shooting flames into the sky on high priority orders, the company supplied seventy-five percent of all the steel bases required for the tire equipment of the motorized artillery and one-third of the steel tires used on artillery wheels. (The mud in France was a severe challenge in those days before the evolution of pneumatic traction tires.) The rim plant had to be enlarged and additional machinery bought. Motorized wheel shops were designed by the company and equipment was provided for them, enabling tire repairs to be made close to the front lines. Soldiers were taught repairing in the factory.

Rubber tires ordered by the army were of the same constructions as civilian tires. They could not be produced any faster than usual, for the time was ultimately governed by vulcanization, which could not be speeded up at that stage of technical knowledge. About 500 women were employed, chiefly in bead making and finishing. This innovation of women workers proved very satisfactory and was destined to set the postwar pattern in factory life. The company's over-all production was 3,749,668 tires in 1917 and 3,036,199 in 1918.

Plant 2 was converted at a cost of $225,000 to manufacture army observation balloons and gas-mask parts. The armistice stopped an ambitious production program. Other wartime deliveries for the armed services included tubes, tires, rubber solution, cement for balloons, grooving machines, leakproof airplane tanks, steel equipment, and miscellaneous accessories. The company had been operating a footwear department in a small way; it had to expand in order to deliver hip boots, short boots, and gaiters.

The supply of rubber did not fall short during 1917, though the tonnage of American vessels had barely begun to increase. The United States received two-thirds of a record crop, and the manufacturers accumulated stocks in anticipation of Federal controls for conserving the nation's industrial resources. As foreign trade went under governmental regulation, rubber was included in the list of licensed commodities, and the industry's association executed the directives of the War Trade Board. Midway in 1918, to release shipping space, the Board curtailed imports, fixed prices for standard grades (fine Para at sixty-eight cents) and earmarked thirty-five percent for the government's needs. The remainder was to be allocated to manufacturers on the basis of seven-sixteenths of each one's 1917 consumption.

As a member of the Rubber Association's executive board, Harvey Firestone conferred in Washington with the War Trade Board on establishing regulations to further the war effort. On the War Service Committee of the Rubber Industry, he worked also with the War Industries Board, created by the Council of National Defense to promote the flow of materials and supplies and expedite production. When the W.I.B. took over the mobilization of the industry from the W.T.B., Firestone was asked to head the rubber section. Instead, he helped set it up; he was already serving as chairman of the industry's solid-tire subcommittee.*

Operations ran smoothly, even to the extent of labor harmony. Akron did not lack rubber. This center customarily took more than sixty percent of the crude rubber imports and had at least sixty-five percent of the war orders for rubber products. Moreover, to conserve man power, the War Industries Board cut down the production both of automobiles and of tires. The tire makers were limited in the last half of 1918 to fifty percent of the pneumatics produced in the corresponding 1917 period and to eight sizes. In Firestone's case, there was an over-all decrease (3,036,199 tire units in 1918 as against 3,749,668 in 1917), the first year that the com-

---

* H.S.F. was in addition a member of the Ohio Branch, Council of National Defense, by appointment of Gov. James M. Cox, and he served on its labor and industrial relations committee.

pany's production curve failed to keep on its upward
course. Dollar volume for all its goods, however, rose
substantially.

Akron did not lack labor. Many thousands of men,
drawn to "eight-hour town" by high wages, and drift-
ing in from other industries or from the mountains of
West Virginia and Kentucky, crowded the city and
created a new housing problem. Besides spurring construction in Firestone Park, the acute situation prompted
the company to erect a temporary village, barracks
style, outside the factory to accommodate 1,500 workers.
But the strangers in town were not the only ones to feel
the pinch.

Wondering at the large turnover, Firestone said to
Thomas, his right-hand man, "Why don't you put a
force of men to gather history from every man that
leaves our employ and find out why he left."

The investigators found families living in attics, sheds,
and "every conceivable nook and corner," with excessive rentals demanded. Some beds were occupied in
eight-hour shifts. Some workers lived in tents. Thomas
reported:

> The rental of a room to single employees has reached a point
> where $2.50 to $3.50 per week per individual is quite the ordinary
> thing. This means that each bed is capable of producing $6 per
> week to the landlord.
>
> Quite a number of our employees who have been renting homes
> have been forced to vacate due to the fact that the owner wished
> to turn it into a rooming house from which he can obtain a larger
> revenue.
>
> In fact, Mr. Graunke, head of our investigating department, was
> this week forced to move from the home he has been occupying, for
> the above reason. He was unable to find a suitable location on a
> rental basis and was forced to send his family to Cleveland to the
> home of his people until he can locate a suitable place here.*

* J.W.T. to H.S.F., Mar. 3, 1917.

Absenteeism was also investigated. It was caused largely by illness, a result of overcrowding. The Industrial Service Department, already on the job of ferreting out lodgings, engaged visiting nurses to attend ill employees.

With a worsening of the problem, newspapers in other Ohio cities refused to accept employment advertisements from Akron firms. Addressing the local real-estate organization, Firestone pointed out that housing must be recognized as a key to Akron's continued prosperity. "We will have to take a broader view of things and build more and more for the future. Labor is growing more and more to be Akron's largest factor."

Enlistments in the armed forces and the draft had taken 721 men from the roster by the end of the first war year, but when the armistice was signed 2,086 service stars spangled the huge flag that covered the height of the company's main building. The war over, Harvey Firestone wrote each man that his old job, or a better one, was waiting for him. While away they had been relieved of meeting installments on their stock purchases and their Firestone Park houses without losing equity.

On the home front, employees participating in Liberty Loan drives were helped by the company in buying bonds; the deferred payment plan had many uses. Together, they and the company purchased $3,791,500 worth of bonds and contributed $222,688 to the county War Chest, in both cases oversubscribing their quotas. Workers canvassed the city in teams to sell bonds. The company gave $15,000 for the government's thrift propaganda campaign. Space was provided in the Club House for the local draft board (the company sought only nine exemptions) and for Red Cross work done by Firestone girls.

Harvey Firestone derived great gratification from war gardens tended by employees on the factory grounds. The gardens got under way the spring of 1917, before

Congress recognized the necessity of food conservation by passing the Food Control Act. The company plowed the land and made 265 plots of 50 by 100 feet ready for as many workers. By the end of the harvesting, they had raised vegetables with a total retail value of $14,205.59 on a capital investment of two dollars' worth of seed per gardener. The average time each one had put in per week was checked off as two hours and twenty-nine minutes. They earned 94 cents an hour.

With pride, Firestone distributed illustrated pamphlets to manufacturers throughout the country, depicting this application of the war garden idea. Federal Food Administrator Herbert Hoover sent his compliments; its success, he said, could be used as a good example by other industrial establishments.

The next summer there were more Firestone gardeners; the plots were smaller. Harvey Firestone bought a brand-new farm tractor (the wheels had steel lugs) and drove it over the ground. The tractor was also used to till other vacant lots in the city. So worth while, from the standpoints of patriotism, healthful outdoor work, and joy in accomplishment, was employee gardening that in subsequent years Firestone fostered it on unoccupied land outside the Park and regarded the annual presentation of prizes as an important ceremony.

Besides food, another wartime concern was transportation. As the railroads were handicapped by a terrific volume of traffic, little funds for maintenance, and the priority demands of the government, the lines got snarled. Federal coordination followed. Meanwhile, many shippers had taken recourse to motor trucks for short hauls. This measure of self-help was endorsed by the United States Railroad Administration, which in operating the roads appreciated the fact that trucks could relieve congestion.

A rush of business came to truck manufacturers. Overtaking the 92,000 units they had produced in 1916, they turned out 128,000 in 1917 and, the following year, when passenger-car production was cut almost in half, 227,000. More tires and rims for trucks!

The veteran champion of commercial motor transportation found his vision vindicated by necessity. Firestone, who had striven to make the operation of trucks with greater carrying capacity feasible, had already introduced giant solid-rubber tires to replace duals and twins on the rear wheels. These solids measured eight to fourteen inches wide and they stood up, thanks to patient experimenting on special vulcanizing processes. At the end of 1916, the company was making 1,600 solids a day, having chalked up a record in its rim plant of almost a quarter of a million bases for pressed-on solids. In 1918, the sale of bases came close to a full million, whereas rims for pneumatics declined sharply.

It was in 1918 that the multiplicity of solid-tire sizes on the market encountered the stern insistence of standardization. The War Service Committee that Firestone headed reduced the number to fifteen (ranging from 32x3½ to 40x14), discontinuing some of the nonessential ones and providing for a tapering off of others.

Trucking was hampered on two counts. The paucity of hard-surfaced roads limited the radius of travel to Old Dobbin's ambit. The vibration of the vehicles, unendurable at a rapid pace, curtailed speed to about fifteen miles an hour. Trucks on solid tires had to have reinforced construction to counteract the shaking up and breaking up of parts that occurred when drivers tried to hasten deliveries. And when trucks adopted a heavy chassis and body, they curdled the indignation of taxpayers, for the solids cut up their highways.

The obvious solution was pneumatics for trucks. At first, dual tires in passenger sizes were used. They did afford more speed and (with lighter chassis) heavier loads. Also, they were kind to roads. But for greater efficiency Firestone built truck tires with eight- and nine-inch sections, some of them strengthened by as many as sixteen plies. Introduced in the summer of 1918, when the war effort was at its tensest, this was indeed a case of putting the shoulder to the wheel. Speed was trebled. Trucks ventured on longer hauls.

To make these new tires practicable, Firestone had developed a giant rim constructed with the inside flange as an integral part of the base and carrying one continuous side ring and one split locking ring. Strong drive plates prevented circumferential creeping, that old bugbear.

Inauguration of an Akron-Cleveland motor express line was evidence on the home grounds that the day of two-way trucking had really arrived. At railroad stops and terminals, trucks took on payloads and eased the pressure that less-than-carload shipments put on boxcars. The Railroad Administration posted signs in freight houses urging the employment of trucks in interurban traffic, especially to prevent the loss of perishables. The Council of National Defense helped to establish bureaus arranging for return loads, thereby making trucking cheaper for the shipper and more profitable for the trucker. The War Industries Board did not limit the production of large-size pneumatics for trucks.

On the signing of the armistice, 600,000 trucks were in use. Truck factories had stepped up their output. Now the demand receded. The builders, with whom Harvey Firestone had always cooperated for the advancement of their branch of the industry, faced an embarrassment of overproduction. Here was a challenge. Could he mark time and let their progress be braked? These vehicles had proved their mettle in army transport. They had

saved much money in commerce. The problem was not
so much to convince the country of the desirability of
trucks as to facilitate the engagement of them. In other
words, good roads and scheduled trips. These objectives
Firestone determined to attain by national educational
campaigns.

Thus he conceived the "Ship-by-Truck" movement
and furthered the good-roads movement—forces shaping a golden motor era. Highways uniting a nation,
products of field and factory flowing in swift exchange,
our ability to produce would be matched by our ability
to distribute. Those who shared this insight were close
to the secret of American abundance.

Following the war, Harvey Firestone wrote, "I am
still working on the housing problem." Using the dedication of the new bank building in February, 1919, as a
springboard, he told his dinner guests (400 bankers from
northern Ohio) that the Firestone Park Trust & Savings
Bank had more than $2,300,000 in deposits.

> We need this money here in Akron for two purposes. One, to
> build homes. The other, to increase our balance with the Cleveland
> banks....
> Every house that we have built is sold, but there is a limit to how
> much we can finance.... Now it is up to the Akron bankers.*

Through the Coventry Land & Improvement Company, approximately $4,000,000 had been invested in
Firestone Park at this time, with mortgages taken by the
Cleveland Trust Company and the Metropolitan Life
Insurance Company. More houses were wanted, not only
in the Park but elsewhere in Akron, and yet few building
permits were being issued in the city for lack of financing.
Firestone called a conference. With other Akron business
leaders, a project was fashioned to help people build at
a reasonable cost.

* Quoted in *Finance and Industry* (Cleveland), Feb. 8, 1919.

The result was the Akron Home Owners Investment Company. The Goodrich, Goodyear, and Firestone companies each subscribed for $500,000 of its stock; other firms and individuals took shares to make a grand total of $2,000,000. Harvey Firestone was president of the enterprise. They did not know they were heading into a national depression, but in two years they made it possible for 469 citizens to build their own homes.

As matters stood at the beginning of 1919, the outlook was rosy. The United States had come out of a victorious war, industrially stronger than ever, psychologically healthier in awareness of our world significance; a creditor nation. The country contained five and a half million motorists and would have a million more before the year was up. The tire industry was booming as never before. The company had a large and steady working force, and Firestone said: "Our savings and welfare programs have been of immense value both to the company and to our workers."

8

Problems of Production

CORD tires became popular during the war—the result of development activity pressed forward despite the distractions of the times. The inner compulsions of the Firestone company to improve its products, to lengthen tire life, were a constant driving force. Progress paid off in two ways. It promoted the use of motor vehicles. It brought the monetary returns accruing to leadership.

The first experiments in cords, begun in 1915, had disappointed the men who worked and the men who watched. The enemy to be routed was fabric deterioration, a cause of ply separation and blowouts. As a tire in action flexed, the crisscrossing strands in square-woven fabric sawed each other; the heat of the friction disintegrated the tough unit that a casing was supposed to be. To eliminate friction, this type of ply was replaced by a sturdy warp of parallel cotton cords having only light filler threads to hold it in sheet form.

Cords were not new. The principle had been used in bicycle racing tires in the 1890s, but the heavy strains of auto tires rendered it inapplicable, the experts had thought, for want of an effective way to insulate the cords. Current efforts aimed at forcing rubber into them. A rival company tried to rubberize the strands singly, immersing them in cement and rewinding them on spools. It didn't work. Firestone designed a machine for guiding the material into a vat and carrying it over a long table, where steam coils banished the solvent.

Test runs proved that cord tires were superior to square-woven fabric tires in efficiency. They saved in fuel consumption. But because Harvey Firestone was not yet satisfied with the construction, he rejected it at a product meeting, telling the department heads: "There isn't a cord tire on the market that is an economical tire from a standpoint of cost per mile. We are not going to make that tire as it is made today."

It was decided to try multi-ply construction, formerly regarded with suspicion as a technique for cords. At the same time, a new curing process was employed. Instead of being vulcanized on the core, these tires were stripped off before going into the molds and expansible airbags were inserted. Cord tires were built a bit smaller than the wanted size; the pressure that expanded them not only forced them against the inner wall of the mold to receive the tread design, but stretched the cords evenly in all directions. This even tension was of paramount importance.

Merely twenty-five a day in February, 1917, cord-tire production was about to be increased with the arrival of additional equipment. On test cars they did "exceedingly well," according to report. They looked good for many more miles than fabric tires. Each cord was sheathed by rubber and embedded in rubber. This material, cut on a bias by a new Firestone machine, produced plies with the cords running at a forty-five-degree angle. In building a tire, these plies were placed longitudinally around the circumference, with alternate layers reversed; thus the cords ran in opposite directions to give greater strength and flexibility. New skidless designs were adopted: a "Double F" tread with angles, recommended for rear wheels, and a triple-grooved tread for front wheels.

Before another year ended the company was producing a full line of cord tires in sizes ranging from 30x3½ to 44x10, about 1,000 a day—a sure sign of public favor. And finer, stronger strands were used.

A further improvement that lengthened tire life came in the composition of the tread. Zinc oxide, for long a filling ingredient in rubber compounds, afforded increased resistance to abrasion. In large quantities, it resulted in white treads, which had a certain vogue. Mixed with lampblack, it further toughened the tread and lessened stretch. Besides these elements there was carbon black, derived from burned natural gas and sparingly used for color effect. When the war created a shortage of zinc, larger amounts of carbon black were substituted for it. Discovered: that this coloring agent was a marvelous reinforcing agent. Treads now had acquired vastly more stamina, longer wearing quality.

And the board authorized the sales department to make adjustments on a basis of 6,000 miles for fabric tires, 8,000 for cords, 10,000 for solids.

Incidentally, a trend away from the two-cure method of vulcanization had begun. The single cure, with simultaneous imprint of the tread, saved additional time. This coincided with a need for faster tire-building machines—apparatus that would stitch the ply on the core as rapidly as it was laid down, in a continuous operation. Such a machine, designed by Firestone engineers, was built in 1916 and used for three-and-a-half-inch tires. Developed with it were mechanical means for applying the beads, so that one man could produce 100 tires in eight hours. Molded tires were gradually displacing wrapped tread tires in other sizes as well.

The company's highly profitable rim division, which

did close to $3,000,000 business in 1916—the year it was threatened by a patent owner who had won his claim to the demountable rim—grew to more than $5,000,000 in 1918, the year that saw the birth of the Firestone Steel Products Company.

Consuming 3,000 tons of steel a month, the rim division delivered only forty-five percent of its output to Firestone, the rest to automobile manufacturers and the trade. Its size and proportion made Akron, the rubber capital, a steel center as well. Stalwart enough to make the most of its prospects as a separate entity, Steel Products was incorporated on May 1, 1918, with a capitalization of $100,000, all the shares being held by the parent company, whose directors and officers served in like capacities with the subsidiary.*

"Firestone started the demountable rim in America and has led ever since," said a trade-paper advertisement. "The rim business of The Firestone Tire & Rubber Company alone gives the new concern dominance in that field."

Small wonder that Harvey Firestone had fought the interloper. Louis H. Perlman, of New York, having obtained a demountable rim patent in 1913, won an infringement suit against Standard Welding Company, of Cleveland, and upon affirmation of the decree by the Circuit Court of Appeals in 1916, he sold the patent to William C. Durant, head of United Motors Corporation. The Perlman Rim Corporation, organized by Durant, forced Standard to close down until $1,010,000 was paid over.

Firestone wired his patent lawyer: "Refuse all negotiations with Perlman's attorneys. From what I know of

---

* The original capital advances made by The Firestone Tire & Rubber Company to Steel Products amounted to $1,977,202. Two years later Steel Products had a surplus account of $1,327,823, representing the accumulated profits earned during this period. Sales in 1920 totaled $7,749,672.

Perlman patent it is ridiculous for automobile industry to pay tribute. I will not stop voluntarily and want you to lay plans to fight to last court if proceedings started against us."*

In a follow-up letter he wrote: "If we lose, we can drop out of the rim business, pay the damages, and quit."†

But he did not expect to close up shop. He considered those harassed auto manufacturers who feared they might have to revert to clincher rims. "I do not think they should be forced to do this," Firestone said. "I think we should furnish them demountable rims, at least all that we are able to furnish. I believe that if we stand with the automobile industry we will win in the end." And he gave orders to put on a full force in the rim plant and make extra inducements for greater production.

He had watched the litigation from the start. He had engaged investigators. When the Perlman company sued Firestone in the United States District Court in New York, in 1917, an injunction was denied on a showing that new evidence had been gathered on the character of the testimony given by Perlman in the Standard case. The suit came to trial before Judge Learned Hand in June.

It was Firestone's intention to expose as fraudulent the Perlman claim of inventing the demountable rim in 1903 and first using it on a car in 1904. But the trial stopped abruptly. After a startling cross-examination of Perlman, plaintiff asked leave to discontinue the action. Under existing rules the motion was granted, but his exhibits (wheels and rims) were impounded, and he was indicted for perjury.

The court stated, when Perlman sought to deny the grand jury the use of the exhibits, "A man who can

* H.S.F. to C. C. Linthicum, Mar. 13, 1916.
† *Ibid.*, Mar. 18, 1916.

remember so minutely the incidents in connection with his invention fourteen years ago should undoubtedly remember whether or not he was in jail for two months twenty-two years ago, or whether he was in London and escaped therefrom as a fugitive from justice."*

The sudden ending of the patent trial prevented Firestone counsel from presenting their evidence: that a partially obliterated mark on the rim Perlman allegedly converted into a demountable in 1903 was the inspection stamp of a rim association made some years later. This information was privately disclosed to Judge Hand afterward, and as a result of the case the judges of the circuit adopted a new equity rule whereby the court could refuse to permit plaintiffs to discontinue.

Despite the absence of a judicial determination of the patent, the case was a victory for Firestone and for everyone else concerned in breaking a rim monopoly. The threat of permanent injunction, accounting of profits, and payment of treble damages was removed—not to mention a royalty of about fifty cents a rim.

"This means," Firestone announced, "an annual savings to American motorists of $1,500,000 to $2,000,000 in royalty tax."

For the past three years he had been keeping tabs on the progress of another patent suit against the company, one brought by Frank A. Seiberling, president of Goodyear Tire & Rubber Company, who claimed a monopoly on tire-building machinery. Other tire manufacturers were paying Seiberling from seven and a half cents to twenty-five cents a tire, according to size. Firestone refused, still denying validity and infringement after losing in the District Court in Cleveland in 1916. Argu-

---

* *Perlman Rim Corp.* v. *Firestone Tire & Rubber Co.*, 244 Federal Reporter 304 (1917), affirmed in *Perlman* v. *United States*, 247 U.S. 7 (1918). The patent had been upheld in *Perlman* v. *Standard Welding Co.*, 231 Federal Reporter 453 (1915) and 231 Federal Reporter 734 (1916).

ment on appeal was heard in the Circuit Court of
Appeals in Cincinnati early in 1917, and now he waited
word.

The principal feature of the Seiberling patents was
spinning rollers (stitchers) that advanced against the
sides of a building core and smoothed down the ply,
shaping it as the core rotated swiftly. There was nothing
new about the spinning process or rapid core rotation,
Firestone contended. But here were new combinations,
the lower court judge had decided.*

The best defense—prior use—did not come to hand
till the fall of 1917, after one of the Firestone lawyers
had discovered the existence of a Belgian patent predat-
ing Seiberling's. Here was strong proof of anticipation,
and the appellate court was persuaded to reopen the
case and permit reargument. The Belgian machine was
assembled and set up in the basement of the Cincinnati
courthouse. "Perfectly successful performance in court"
—to quote the opinion delivered in December, 1918.

The last line of the opinion was the sweetest: "The
decree must be reversed, and the record remanded with
instructions to dismiss the bill." Most of the Seiberling
claims were held invalid, the others not infringed.

There is no true combination . . . mere aggregation . . . nothing
broadly new either in his method or in his selected tools . . . so far
as some details may be new, they are not used by defendant. . . .

It is conceded that the Belgian patent is a complete anticipation
of State [one of the Seiberling patents] as to the matter of employing
a radially-moving spinning roll in this type of tire-making machine
for shaping the side of the tire . . . the Belgian tool in its radial
progress was bound to stretch and reshape the fabric in substantially
the same way that is done by State. Putting all these things together,
State cannot be considered as the inventor of the method. . . .

Defendant uses a different tension device. . . .

Defendant gets its stretch from the slip or wipe that is impelled
by the fact that the spinning disc cannot roll unobstructedly in its

* *Seiberling* v. *Firestone Tire & Rubber Co.*, 234 Federal Reporter 370 (1916).

own plane, which fact results from its inclination toward the plane
of the core axis. This very inclination puts part of the disc out beyond
the supposed line of "hinging and folding," and prevents a fold at
the point of contact. *

Speaking of victories, here was one farther-reaching
in savings to the automobile industry and the public
than that in the Perlman case. Seiberling would have
collected on every machine-made tire in the country
(23,000,000 produced in 1918 alone). "One of the most
important commercial battles that has confronted us for
a number of years," Firestone characterized it, but also
"more than a commercial victory." Car and truck manufacturers congratulated him, and themselves.

In turn, he paid public acknowledgment to a company
engineer. The occasion, coming a few days after the
court decision, was the second annual employee-stockholders' meeting in the Club House. Harvey Firestone
rendered his report "with the feeling," he said, "that I
am talking with my partners, each of whom is working
in his own way for the same end as I am working." After
noting that Plant 2 was being reconverted to peacetime
work (Ford-size tires) and that new machines were being
installed there with a sense of security owing to the
breakup of the monopoly, he singled out W. Clyde
Stevens in the audience.

. . . a source of great satisfaction that the high court has upheld the
Firestone machine, patented and developed by an employee-stock-
holder of this company. I want to congratulate Mr. Stevens, the
inventor of our machine, for his victory, and I congratulate the
company and you as stockholders that our employees are studying
the needs of the company and working for its improvement and
development.

Convinced that the spirit of mutual interest for which
he had striven was accomplished, Firestone thanked the

* *Firestone Tire & Rubber Co.* v. *Seiberling,* 257 Federal Reporter 74 (1918).

employees as a whole for their attitude toward efficiency.

You have at all times shown yourselves anxious to install whatever methods or machines that seem to be conducive to the saving of time, labor, or materials. This . . . is highly important and during the past year has brought about the saving of hundreds of thousands of dollars.

Rubber manufacturing had always been a speculative business, profits being contingent to an unusually high degree on the fluctuating prices of the materials used. With a sixth sense, the vagaries of the crude rubber market had to be anticipated. The stress of competition necessitated operations on a larger scale in order to realize a profit. Strategic buying and superior manufacturing management became increasingly essential as an overproduction of tires in the country loomed for 1919. In a contest for survival of the fittest, Firestone planned "so to manufacture and sell as to be the survivor."

On the management side, the pattern of integration and concentration, manifested in forming Steel Products and in specialized use of Plant 2, prevailed in the overall picture. Work was departmentalized. Departments were harmonized with each other.

An executive committee had been formed to bring together the various department heads for discussion, at least once a week, of significant matters as they arose, such as unusual sales problems, special purchases, factory organization, engineering problems, reports on amounts invested in raw stock and finished goods, and contemplated real-estate purchases or construction of branch facilities.

The watchword was efficiency, in industrial engineering, factory, merchandise, sales, and advertising. The development department was so organized that a definite responsibility rested with each individual division: cord tires, fabric tires, solid tires, rims. A fabric department was established to study not only finished goods but raw cotton, cotton raising and marketing, to learn far in advance the conditions that would prevail at the time of use, for cotton costs had increased in their bearing upon the price and quality of tires.

Making tires in Akron, the company took more than an entomological interest in the boll weevil; the pest had inflicted enough damage in the Sea Island cotton belt (along the coast from South Carolina to Florida) to cut the crop materially. The war had reduced Egyptian cotton acreage; laxity of supervision had resulted in deterioration of quality. On the other hand, experiments with long-staple cotton were being conducted in Arizona and California's Imperial Valley. Yes, important industrial consumers must know what was going on far back along the line.

The rubber buying department was divided into two branches: one in Singapore, which supplied thirty percent (5,200 tons) of the company's requirements in 1918; the other in Akron, which purchased the balance from brokers and operated facilities for receiving, preparing, and washing. In time, Firestone hoped, seventy-five percent would be obtained from Singapore, both for the economy (the cost came to three cents less per pound) and for the assurance of a higher grade on the average.

British owners of Far Eastern plantations did not sell direct to manufacturers but through brokers in London and New York. Representatives of the Firestone Singapore station covered ports and inland points to deal directly with native producers and Chinese traders.

During the war, the growers' association had adopted standard practices in gathering and coagulating latex to provide a better and more nearly uniform product. Shortage of ocean transportation nurtured ingenuity: smoked sheets, instead of being packed in boxes, were compressed into bales at a large saving in shipping cost.

The company expanded its laboratory. In spacious new quarters more than forty men were now engaged in making compounds, performing chemical analyses and physical tests, and doing research—each man assigned to a specific task. Firestone also provided a fellowship in chemistry at the University of Akron. The intimate connection between modern industry and modern science was nowhere closer than in a rubber factory, and these years brought forth new accelerators and antioxidants that enabled tires to meet greater tasks.

On the mechanical side, the power house was modernized and a 12,000-horsepower steam turbine engine was installed; it would save its $100,000 cost within two years. Efficiency, lower overhead, skill. These were the hallmarks of production.

"Much of the success of the Firestone organization is due," said its chief in a magazine article, "to the fact that I have employed good men—many good men." Without their "exceptional abilities, character, and energy I could not have built up a business of such magnitude." The board of directors, already increased from five to seven, was further enlarged in 1919 when three more were added—men engaged in the company's executive work.

A year of spectacular activity, 1919. It opened with a daily production of 5,500 two-cure fabric casings, 4,500 full-mold fabric casings, 1,250 cord casings, 1,200 solid truck tires, and 15,000 inner tubes. As the season came closer, the output was 22,000 tires and 25,000 tubes a day. Ground was broken for construction of a new plant for Steel Products, to double the size of the old. A new mechanical building was started, to release space in the factory. Firestone refining and preparation mills in Singapore began converting rubber slabs into amber crepe, with a large warehouse on the waterfront to facilitate storage and shipment. Investment in a fabric mill was another move made to obtain source-of-supply prices.

The board authorized the incorporation of The Firestone Tire & Rubber Company of Canada, Ltd., with a factory on 135 acres near Hamilton, Ontario, to hurdle the tariff wall and supply markets having preferential trade agreements with the Dominion.*

In Los Angeles, speaking at a dinner tendered to him by the Chamber of Commerce, Firestone pointed out that as most of the rubber imports arrived at Pacific coast ports, and since Imperial Valley cotton was excellent, cotton mills should be erected near by and "there is no reason why we should not make tires here." The thought was in chrysalis stage merely. But with Harvey Firestone, thought was ever the beginning of action.

Meanwhile two more decisions were made: to enlarge the capacity of Plant 2 from 10,000 pneumatics a day to 16,000 at a cost of $1,500,000 and—so swift was progress—to devote Plant 1 entirely to cord tires.

A great year—$91,078,513 in sales, the company unable to fill all its orders, and the automobile industry embarked on a gigantic program of two million cars, a third of a million trucks. There were already 7,500,000 motor vehicle registrations in 1919. The company's production tally was more than 4,250,000 tires, 1,461,000 rims, 418,000 steel bases. Its payroll, including 3,138 exservice men, numbered 11,581. Its profits came to $9,306,978. A special common dividend of $2 was declared, making $8 for the year.

For the projects that were planned to surpass this record—for the greater capacity, larger investment in material, and continuous improvements—more capital

* The Canadian company was capitalized at $5,000,000. For the first unit, a daily capacity of 3,500 tires and tubes was planned. Half of the ground was to be devoted to a housing development similar to Firestone Park in Akron.

was necessary. To obtain it without adding to current indebtedness, an issue of second preferred seven percent stock was decided upon. And to anticipate financial requirements for some time to come, with flexibility, the amount of this stock was set at $40,000,000. This was in addition to the $10,000,000 outstanding six percent preferred. As the law imposed a two-to-one ratio between preferred and common, the latter was increased to $25,000,000, thereby making the capitalization $75,000,000.

There was no present intention of issuing all the authorized common or even of going beyond the $3,500,000 common already issued, except for employee offerings a little later. All that was needed now was $10,000,000, to be acquired through new preferred stock. It sold readily and widely. The National City Company in one day sold $8,000,000 worth to clients throughout the country, averaging twenty-four shares apiece. The Cleveland Trust Company distributed $1,500,000 worth, all that remained after Firestone employees, on their own initiative, had taken $500,000 of this stock. The grand average was less than twenty shares per purchaser.

"This is the kind of distribution I think is most valuable to us in the tire business," Firestone observed.

With assets of $370 for every $100 preferred share issued, the company was eminently sound.

With the approach of 1920, Firestone had supreme confidence in the company's future. He foresaw "most unusual growth and prosperity."

9

Extending the Market

HARVEY FIRESTONE'S concept of the motor truck as a vital part of American transportation, and of transportation as a creative element in American prosperity, meant more than foresight. It was a responsibility, assumed spontaneously and affirmed by perseverance.

Recalling the early days of automobile fervor, when he did not forsake the makers of trucks although greater rewards came from serving the pleasure-car trade, he revealed to the 1919 convention of the National Association of Motor Truck Sales Managers:

> So far as profit is concerned, we would have been out of existence a long time ago had we not gone into the manufacture of pneumatic tires. The profit on these enabled us to carry the load on solid tires.
>
> This may sound strange to you and perhaps foolish for us to have allowed our competitors to unload the solid tire business on us while they were making money on pneumatic tires. But when I believe a thing is right and should be put over, I haven't sense enough to let go. Each year I was hopeful that the automobile truck would find its right place in industry and become a large business, but I am beginning to think the automobile manufacturers were like the tire manufacturers—they made pleasure cars and unloaded the truck business on you fellows.
>
> But the table has turned, and today we are going to have our inning if we build the right kind of trucks and the right kind of tires and do not allow them to be abused or do work for which the truck or tires were not intended.

Having initiated the Ship-by-Truck movement, Firestone was in demand as a speaker before trade groups that had caught a glimpse of his vision. They were enthusiastic, for trucks were selling fast again; but the idea transcended the fact of immediate returns. Business thinking must be done in broader terms.

> I haven't any doubt but that every one of you can sell more trucks this year than your factories will be able to manufacture. However, I want to urge you not to overlook the farming industry—not entirely for the amount of sales but for the helpful production of foodstuff and the development of agriculture throughout the country.*

In other words, Firestone perceived the social and economic benefits of motor transport. With this as the keynote, trucks and busses could be promoted to the public universally and put upon the permanent basis of everyday utility.

He had launched the campaign of education at the year's start when, the war over, he placed a series of full-page advertisements in national weekly magazines to inculcate the industrial lesson taught by military exigencies.

> When the French line stood at the Marne, the truck began to receive the recognition it deserved. . . . People realized, all at once, that the motor truck was essential and vital in our transportation, and therefore a basic part of our living.
>
> Like good roads, motor trucking should interest every man, woman, or child. Both are basic elements in lowering the cost of distribution, saving products now wasted, opening up resources heretofore untapped.
>
> The truck is ready and able to shoulder burdens the railroads cannot carry and to leave them free for responsibilities too long deferred and delayed. . . .
>
> Our future industrial growth depends largely upon the assistance rendered the railroads by trucks in speeding up freight movement. Communities which are not served by the railroads find in the truck the means for their rapid development.

* H.S.F. address to National Association of Motor Truck Sales Managers, Nov. 4, 1919.

Ship by Truck. Let us make this the slogan of a new business era. *

Writing to distributing agents, Firestone pointed out that "the hundred-mile radius belongs to the truck." Railroad Administration studies had shown that short hauls rarely paid the railroads; new construction of feeder lines was improbable, and even electric interurban lines had become outmoded. Wartime experience proved the cheapness of truck transportation, the reduction in delay, damage, and labor expense, as compared with railroad freight shipments and their complications of transfer, distribution of belt-road collections, their freight houses, and junction points.

The hundred-mile radius, surely. "But the truck has not stopped there," he said. "Its future is restricted only by the extent of good roads and systematic schedules."

Firestone envisioned highway transport vehicles linking every producing center with an ultimate outlet, "developing the country on a broader scale." The generalized propaganda of truck manufacturers, truck operators, tire manufacturers, and highway associations too, he found inadequate; for each group concerned itself with its own objective. The Ship-by-Truck idea must be applied definitely, practically. The individual locality was the place to do it.

As Firestone tires were already carrying more than half the country's truck tonnage, the company was a natural leader for the movement. It had contact with the truck operators through its many branches.† What remained to be done was to organize a relationship with shippers at these points and advertise locally a service as the clearinghouse for free information on rates, routes, capacity, and schedules of all trucks operating in the area.

* Firestone advertisement in *Collier's*, Jan. 25, 1919.
† The branches were in effect a national network of service stations, some of them complete wheel-building shops to serve users of solid tires. About 500 dealers had hydraulic presses for applying solids to trucks and boxcar-like trailers.

Return-loads bureaus, serving many cities during the war under the aegis of the Highway Transport Committee of the Council of National Defense, had closed down. Their work of keeping local merchants and manufacturers posted on the availability of trucks and seeing that the trucks did not return empty to their points of origin was "a national asset," Firestone said. It should not be abandoned.

With a central office in Akron, to integrate information, conduct research, and issue bulletins, the company set up bureaus in sixty-seven branches. Each bureau kept in touch with the others for swift exchange of data. They had further duties: to promote the construction and maintenance of roads adequate for trucking and to encourage uniform state legislation on the use of trucks, trailers, and highways.

To demonstrate the efficacy of long-distance hauling, the company sent a fleet of loaded trucks out of Akron on a tour through the South. Each arrival in town made news and provided an opportunity for an open-air lecture on the operating cost of a three-and-a-half-ton truck (equipped with Firestone giant pneumatics and rims). Men in cars accompanying the fleet interviewed mayors and fire chiefs en route and gathered facts for the researchers back home.

Through the spring and summer, communities stimulated by Firestone newspaper and magazine advertising sponsored truck parades on their main streets. Cavalcades of peace! Hauling livestock, coal, milk, fruits and vegetables, farm machinery, furniture, dry goods. Ship by Truck. In every state the slogan was taken up, with all its implications of local and national progress.

Much of the publicity stressed the motor truck as an agency for reducing the cost of living, which had risen to an ominous level. The use of trucks effected savings in the logging industry, the oil industry, and the coal-mining industry. Trucks provided cheap, rapid, more efficient transportation of manufactured articles. They cut the cost of marketing produce; took it to farther places. They released land for food that had been growing feed (a single horse required the yield of five acres). The horse as a means of highway transport had become, Firestone pointed out, "an expensive luxury which the American people can no longer afford."

For the enlargement of rural life, trucks not only enabled farmers to dispose of more of their perishable foods and obtain more readily the products of mill and factory, but as busses they made possible the establishment of consolidated schools and so helped their children to receive a better education.

In the summer of 1919, the Army Transport Corps embarked on a spectacular journey—to see whether it was feasible to take a complete military unit with equipment from Washington, D.C., to the Pacific Coast. Leaving July 7, the First Army Transcontinental Motor Convoy, comprising 300 enlisted men and officers, sixty-five trucks and other vehicles, with means of constructing or reconstructing roads and bridges, followed the route vigorously espoused by the Lincoln Highway Association.

The convoy rested at Columbiana. Here Harvey Firestone greeted the commandant, Colonel Charles W. McClure, and a slim young lieutenant colonel named Dwight D. Eisenhower, and entertained "the army" for a farm dinner. Speaking to them on the front lawn of the old homestead, Firestone related some local history.

The fine improved brick road upon which I am looking, and over which you have just traveled, lay here practically without improvements for more than a hundred years until a comparatively short time ago.

I can well remember how I worked out many days of what was called the poll tax to maintain this road and other roads through our township, under a supervisor selected by the township trustee. The improvement of the road then consisted of plowing up a ditch on each side to carry off the surface water and scraping the loose dirt to the center to form a crown.

Some of the loaded trucks in this convoy weighed fourteen tons, and Colonel McClure was bent upon keeping a schedule of eighteen miles an hour. One wondered what would happen when soft roads were encountered or even roads apparently hard-surfaced but actually weak because of shallow bases.

A number of alleged highways were in fact broken through by the heavier vehicles and shattered. When crossing the Salt Lake Desert road, the convoy took two days and a night to travel seventy-five miles. Elsewhere mud, all-too-yielding sand, and defective bridges caused other delays. Army trucks carried freight and rode on solid tires—but sometimes they bogged down. Two commercial trucks in this motor train, flying the Firestone flag, with cargoes of tires for the company's San Francisco branch, managed to maintain their usual rate of speed. They had pneumatics.

On September 1, as the convoy was about to enter upon the splendid highways of California, Harvey Firestone was watching a monster Ship-by-Truck parade in Minneapolis. The same day he attended the state fair and declared that the army's transcontinental run was doing the best job of calling attention to the value and economy of good roads. "The problem of food supply," he emphasized, "and the conditions of unrest throughout the country are so interwoven with this question of transportation that a discussion of the one includes the other."

The coast-to-coast convoy arrived in San Francisco.

The feat was accomplished. It had proved the practicability of trucks for long-distance freight transport and indicated the military value of a system of national trunk highways. It rallied public opinion around the principle of Federal and state expenditure for good roads.

Firestone favored centralized authority over road building, the state to take over from counties and townships and cooperate with the Federal government. Apart from the unpleasant play of politics in highway development, much waste had resulted from complications of different jurisdictions. Inadequate funds often were spread thin over an excessive length, so that a superficially good road became in a year or two worse than the old dirt road it had replaced—"and actually wears out more tires and automobiles than a good new road would cost." A single administered fund would avoid piecemeal construction and unrelated parts. Each state should have a chief highway engineer to prescribe standard specifications.

As the cure for the current high cost of living lay, said Firestone, in increased production and lowered costs, this must be accompanied by greater transportation facilities. "The Ship-by-Truck movement has come in to fill the gaps of our transportation system."

Typical of the response was a telegram from the mayor of New Orleans when the Firestone fleet reached that city:

We are confident that your efforts will materially aid in the development of a bigger and better New Orleans. Your Ship-by-Truck bureau will hasten the day when a better system of highways will traverse the whole South.*

The year 1919 marked the beginning of the applica-

* Mayor Martin Behrman to H.S.F., Nov. 19, 1919.

tion of state gasoline taxes and auto license fees to road building and upkeep. Four states adopted this device, which was soon to become universal. Congress had passed the Federal Aid Road Act in 1916, appropriating a sum in the interest of interstate travel and rural post roads. And now agitation for increased allotments to the states, reinforced by the imaginative appeal of the Lincoln Highway project, centered on integrated routes for through traffic.

A railroad strike in the spring of 1920, following the return of the lines to private operation, brought trucking into the national limelight again. Railway terminals were choked with accumulated freight. State officials and chambers of commerce appealed to Firestone bureaus to direct arrangements for moving fuel and food. The call to public service was met. This emergency and the handy alternative underscored the commercial value of good roads.

With even-handed justice, trucks came to the rescue of some of Firestone's own customers. The Yellow Cab Company, of Chicago, the city where the strike had started, could not get tire replacements by rail for its fleet of a thousand taxis. Its thanks were publicized on the delivery of several hundred tires by truck from Akron.

The railroad crisis happened on the eve of National Ship by Truck — Good Roads Week, during which Firestone released a motion-picture film to theaters in many cities. The purpose of the week, Firestone announced, was "to present to the public the necessity of a national highway system and to visualize the achievements already attained in the motor trucking industry." Notable Americans endorsed the observance, among them former Railroad Administrator William G. McAdoo, Senator Arthur Capper of Kansas, Bernard M. Baruch, Senator Charles E. Townsend of Michigan, and Thomas

C. Atkeson, spokesman for the National Grange. Even the president of the Pennsylvania Railroad lent his name: Samuel Rea, who recognized that reduction of short-haul tonnage on the railroads meant freedom to develop long-haul facilities.

Maintenance of the Firestone bureaus, the educational advertising in newspapers and periodicals, the visual demonstrations, and other means of spreading the gospel were expensive. The company spent more than $2,000,000 on the campaign up to the time of its conclusion in 1921. In that year, Congress enacted legislation greatly increasing Federal aid and concentrating disbursements upon important routes. The Federal Highway Act, designating the Bureau of Public Roads of the Department of Agriculture as liaison with the states, made it possible to create a coordinated system; in effect, made a dream concrete.

This milestone gained, Harvey Firestone still saw the necessity of imbuing future citizens with the ideal of improved highways and an understanding of the cultural benefits as well as the more obvious material ones. He had instituted in 1920 an annual college scholarship essay contest on the subject of good roads. Open to all high school students, this contest—and the six that followed—were conducted by the Highway Education Board, Firestone bearing the cost of four years' tuition and expenses.

The Board was composed of the United States Commissioner of Education, as chairman, and representatives of the Department of Agriculture, the War Department, the automotive and rubber industries. More than 200,000 entries in the first competition manifested the breadth of serious thinking on the theme. The judges selected the essay of a sixteen-year-old Idaho girl, and presentation of the award was made by the newly inaugurated Presi-

dent, Warren G. Harding, at the White House—an
event that dramatized the cause for millions of newspaper readers and for newsreel audiences.*

The miracle of America shone with new wonders. In
the free movement of people and products, barriers of
distance and isolation were broken. Our immense country became more closely a united whole, each region
making contributions to all the others. An unparalleled
level of living had been achieved for the great mass of
the population. And a central pillar of this high standard
was easy transportation.

Almost half the automobile sales were made to farmers
or to people in small towns. There was a car for every
fourteen persons in the United States (in contrast to one
for 268 in England, one for 402 in France, one for 684
in Germany). The use of automobiles was a national
habit. In an amazingly brief time, the automotive industries had shot into the front ranks of business, not only
statistically, in number of wage earners, in total payroll
and value of output, and relevance to the livelihood of
workers in other trades, but in impact upon American
life—where a business expresses its chief significance.

What had become of the dire predictions, heard in the
past again and again, that the saturation point was
imminent?

Whither the automobile went, the tire industry was
its inevitable companion. In this link of mutual welfare,
they traveled the curves of economic progress. The public was on a spending spree, and with the release of wartime restraints on production the auto makers took up
the backlog of demand, planning to assemble two million cars in 1920.

---

* Winners of the Firestone essay contests held in subsequent years were high
school students in West Virginia, the District of Columbia, Kentucky, Wisconsin, Hawaii, and Mississippi. The seven were admitted to Northwestern University, the University of West Virginia, Princeton University, Marietta College,
Ripon College, the University of Michigan, and the University of Wisconsin.

Postwar inflation was prevalent, though its self-destructive nature was not so apparent. Even tire prices, which had risen in defiance of a tradition of the tire industry's own making, had to go still higher as the cost of cotton advanced two and a half times over 1919. Rubber was more abundant than ever, but the supply of long-staple cotton fell far short of estimated needs. Cost-per-mile continued to decline, it was true, but the retail price index did not indicate this.

Inflation rode the buying wave. Manufacturers in all lines made heavy commitments for the year.

In the spring of 1920, the repercussions began. Harvey Firestone examined his figures and saw that business was "slowing down too rapidly." He told the executives and superintendents at the next summer outing that he had made plans for a European vacation but was willing to cancel them if they thought they could not handle the situation. They urged him to take his holiday.

The whole picture of the national economy was undergoing an alarming change. Farm prices cracked; industrial buying stopped; from everywhere came reports of retailers' cancellations of orders; consumers went on strike. The country was in a depression.

At the time the storm broke, Firestone was in Europe with his family. He had taken a country house in England, intending to spend the summer there with his wife, their five sons, and daughter. Cables from Akron invaded the vacation. "Sales and collections not encouraging." Their tenor became shriller. Notes to pay off rubber and cotton purchases were falling due. Material kept arriving on contracts that had been signed for record amounts. Inventories were already excessively large.

Akron cut expenses, cut production. Seven million dollars of trade acceptances were about to mature and the banks had to be propitiated. Firestone cabled back:

If you cannot handle with them or have difficulty cable me and I will come home by first boat next week. . . . Keep good courage. There are many people in the same difficulties we are without the banking interest back of them that we have and it will not take a great while until we can adjust our business.

Akron put on additional salesmen for more intensive coverage, to convert finished goods into cash. Firestone replied to the latest news:

Glad sales improving. Regret your policy of giving prize money for increased sales. It exhibits a weakness in management and impresses your branches that you do not have confidence that they are making their best effort in these strenuous times. My judgment is that all your branch organization wants is helpful suggestions, confidence and inspiration from the home office. . . . Use your energies direct for results and you will be surprised how the business will improve.

Two days later he sailed for home. Cotton and rubber prices had crashed. In the devastating consumer revolt against the high cost of living and the far-reaching paralysis of the auto industry, all industries were lumped in the slump. The season of the year that should have been the most active for the tire business proved a failure.

The company owed banks and brokers $43,942,000. Inventory and commitments were worth fifty cents, or less, on the dollar. The incoming tide of raw materials, unwanted and high-priced, must be checked. But even if Firestone succeeded in staving off financial obligations, the company needed a positive program—to boost sales.

Met in New York by anxious colleagues on his arrival toward the end of August, Firestone heard their doleful accounts. Over the week end at the old homestead in Columbiana, he reflected, and evolved a plan.

He summoned branch managers to Akron and informed them how he proposed to seize the contracted market and expand it. By an immediate price cut. Not a piddling reduction, which would have brought no objection from the sales organization—and no response from the public. But a drastic slash, to precipitate action. One-fourth off!

For the company, this automatically would mean substantial inventory losses. For the dealer, a heavy loss on his present stock. But for both it meant a revival of business. A giant advertising drive would soon blazon the news across banners, in newspapers, on billboards: "Firestone Tires 25 Per Cent Discount."

"I would like a discussion of this, men," Firestone invited the sales conference. "What is your impression? If you see any flaws in it you will not be criticized, but I will try to argue you out of it."

Here was a chance to clean house on tires bearing the "Non-Skid" design, without throwing them on the "seconds" market and having them backfire on the regular dealers.

It is a good tread, but you know there are times when the tire business seems to have fashion. That tread is out of fashion. . . .

Here is a condition. We want to help our dealers and give them a wider spread.*

The trade would be informed that no more tires of the old design were going to be built. The company's cross-and-square tread would supplant it.

Secrecy covered the preparations for "reduced price sales"—fabric tires on October 7, cords on October 15. The public was surprised. Competitors also were surprised, in a different sense. Firestone tires sold fast!

Full-page newspaper ads in branch cities carried the announcements over dealers' names. " 'Firsts' with serial numbers," were specified. "Manufacturer's guarantee 8,000 miles" on the cords. Non-Skid cords 30 x 3½ were reduced from $35.75 to $26.81, other sizes in proportion. This was what the public had been waiting for.

* H.S.F. at branch managers' conference, Akron, Sept. 4, 1920.

Henry Ford, holding the same conviction, had sprung his own sensation late in September, the first to cut prices on cars. Visiting Akron on a trip to sources of supply, Ford intimated to Firestone that the revisions (fourteen to thirty-one percent) were below his present costs. It was the only remedy for stagnation. "Prices must come down," he said.

The presence of Ford and his son Edsel as house guests at Firestone's estate, Harbel Manor, touched off a rumor that negotiations were in progress for the sale of the Firestone company to Ford. It was unfounded. The only business talk they exchanged related to the purchase and price of tires.

Probably the financial difficulties of some other tire companies suggested the story, for these concerns were in such deplorable shape that they had no recourse but to succumb to banker control. Firestone had won a full month's headway on his competitors in reaching out for the latent market, and they were constrained not only to follow him on the reduction but to acknowledge him as the pace-setter thereafter. The weight of their refinancing hobbled them.

With lower operating costs—the broom of economy sweeping every nook, the clerical force drastically curtailed, salaries and wages cut ten percent—the company came through 1920 sound and unfettered. Tire production had reached the highest figure, 5,000,000. Sales too, pushed to a new peak, touching $115,000,000, but inventory depreciation had nipped any possibility of profit. On the other hand, borrowings were reduced to $31,356,000.

It would take time to get out of the woods. Incoming materials had been slackened; personnel was reduced by as much as 73.9 percent, expenses by 78.7 percent. But new-car sales were hampered by Federal Reserve re-

strictions on auto dealers' credit. The export market for
tires and cars declined considerably, as the depression
was world-wide. Extensive unemployment persisted. Re-
sumption of demand must work its benefits by easy interlocking stages.

Meanwhile the company strained to conserve its cash
resources, itemize its assets, and turn them into money
to pay bills. Further ways of reducing expenses were
found. "Changes of policies and methods from former
days are absolutely necessary," Firestone cautioned, "as
no business could run on the policies and methods of the
tire industry in the past. We must do, and look after,
the small things and the small savings as we never have,
and that, you know, is tedious and objectionable to all
of us—we like to do big things."

But no restraint was put on projects to produce better
tires, better rims. In the old rim plant (the new factory
for Steel Products stood idle and unequipped, serving as
a warehouse for the present) bead wire was developed
to replace cables. Made into braided ribbons of nineteen
strands of 0.025 gauge piano wire, the new beads were
impregnated with gum and cured as a unit with the
plies around it. This improvement afforded greater resistance to the strains caused by the internal pressure in
tires. Another innovation was brass plating of steel bases
for solid-rubber tires. With saw-tooth ridges this electro-
plated base provided stronger adhesion of the hard rubber than a plain steel surface.

After paying $9.50 in dividends on the common
stock for 1920, and $1.50 in January, 1921, the com-
pany passed dividends on the common; but a bonus
of $1.50 was voted for each quarter to employee-stock-
holders (except officers) to maintain their morale. This
bonus applied to 33,561 shares (3,914 contracts) as a
credit to meet the interest charge on deferred payments

Wisely, almost all the employee holdings were retained. Personnel in need of funds were able to borrow on them.*

Early in 1921, Firestone went to Detroit and obtained from Henry Ford, the most active of his forty-seven manufacturer-customers, a promise of sixty-five percent of the Ford business for the ensuing year. A big order came through promptly. Besides being an important financial help, it inspired the organization. For a time Plant 2, with its simplified, straight production line turning out a single size, 30 x 3½, in a clincher fabric casing, accounted for half the company's entire output.

Sales still did not pose the only problem. Firestone met with the inflexibility of old habits. He confided to Ford:

> I find it difficult to get many men to realize that they must do things better and more efficiently than they have in the past few years. When you tell them about it, many begin to feel that they are abused. When that attitude is taken I let them go. . . . I have reached the point where there is no man around our place, no matter how big, that we cannot get along without if he does not get into line with our policy.†

The engineering department was always on the job. Now it developed a rotary bias cutter that sped up production by two to four times and automatically rolled up the ply material in liners. This saved one-quarter of a cent per tire. Fractions were matters of great moment.

In mid-1921 the tire industry's condition became worse than it ever had been. The company took cuts of twenty percent on cord tires, seventeen percent on fabric tires. In the fall, further reductions, to put life into laggard business. Sales for the year declined to nearly half the 1920 sum. But by skillful operations the company

---

* The bonuses were paid in the years 1921-1923. Dividends were restored in 1924, on a $4 annual basis, employee-stockholders receiving $2 in addition. In 1925, the rate was advanced to $6, so the bonus was discontinued. Dividends on the preferred stocks were paid throughout the stringent period.

† H.S.F. to Henry Ford, Mar. 3, 1921.

made another deep dent into bank indebtedness, down to $21,680,000. Visiting the banks with the balance sheet, Firestone induced all but one to confirm their credit lines for 1922, and he impressed one bank so favorably as to obtain a half-million increase.

The new year went well; very well. Sales and distribution methods were simplified, effecting a marked decrease in cost. The dealer organization was enlarged and strengthened. Intensive local advertising and dealer effort directed at small-town car owners brought exceptional success. Automobile and truck production leaped to 2,500,000, raising registration to 12,000,000, and offered a beneficent industrial climate. Firestone raised wages and salaries ten percent, saying that the men were entitled to share the good years as they had shared the bad.

The time was ripe to resume construction of the Canadian plant, long delayed; this was financed by the sale of $1,500,000 seven percent first-mortgage bonds. The floors of the Steel Products building were about to be finished.

Summer saw fresh price cuts—30 x 3½ gum-dipped cords, for example, retailing at $12.45. One reason was the glut of rubber, which made quotations plummet to the depths of the planters' despair. Another was Firestone's policy. He briefed the salesmen: "I realize that we have been the leaders in reducing prices to the consumer. This policy is based upon fundamentally good business, not only for ourselves but for all dealers who want a permanent and profitable business." Consequently, unit sales returned to the 5,000,000 bracket, though dollar volume slipped a little. What counted most was the final reckoning—a profit exceeding $7,000,-000 and an increase of close to $6,000,000 in the surplus.

The depression, short but incisive, was now a thing of the shadowed past. For some, it had been a crippling gash; for Firestone, a sobering setback generating new energy.

The company entered the year 1923 in excellent form: inventory valued at or below the market, commitments on a very favorable basis, expenses at their lowest point, factory efficiency at its highest. The daily average of 26,000 tires and 28,000 tubes registered a net profit of $13 a share and enabled the company to slice the bank debt from $12,775,000 to $5,770,000.

After another year of mounting sales and mounting gains, Firestone had a happy-ending inside story to tell:

> It was only the confidence of a few of my friends in the banking business that saved the company from refinancing, such as was done by other large rubber companies. I laid a program before my banks each year for the past four years as to just what we would do, and while I do not think they felt I would be able to accomplish what I told them I would, they seemed to have enough faith.
>
> I did accomplish each year what I promised and usually went over. Now we don't need to make any promises to the banks as we do not owe them anything.*

He had been obliged to retrench to advance. He had been spurred to exert herculean vigor. And yet this did not fully explain how the company managed to come out in the clear by October, 1924, with $5,692,000 more added to the surplus account. Nor did mass sales at deflationary levels complete the answer, although in soaring over $8,000,000 in profits for the first time since 1918 Firestone had had to make twice as many tires and do $10,000,000 more business than in that year. There was another story—in the merchandise itself.

One contributing factor was a secondary line of tires, the "Oldfield 999," produced under the name of the Oldfield Tire Company, in which Firestone had installed Barney Oldfield, the popular racing champion,

* H.S.F. to Harry Chandler, Dec. 27, 1924.

as president. A greater leavening force, however, was the enhancement of the quality of the regular line by gum-dipping the cords—giving 10,000 miles and more. These tires were priced to compete with the standard cord grades of the other prominent manufacturers. Gum dipping in 1921 led to balloons in 1923. Firestone had delivered the goods.

And in the unromantic rim division, which lacked interest for most of the top men in the executive entourage, but which modestly added several millions to the annual sales volume, another economic service had been performed. It was here that Harvey S. Firestone jr. undertook to get his early training in management. Here an interchangeable giant rim for pneumatics was developed as a godsend to trucking.

Where was the dirge of yesteryear? Vision, striving, resourcefulness—by these qualities the company ensured its future and its growth. They were sinews, and they squelched joyless jabberings of market saturation. Balloon tires, better truck equipment, better highways. America traveled by car and shipped by truck, and Firestone forged new opportunities for progress.

10

Happy Anniversary

ONLY a short way to go, and the Firestone company would round out its first quarter-century. The recency of one of its great contributions—the balloon tire gave proof that instead of coasting along on fame, the company was performing its social and economic function more ably with the years. History making had a prospect as well as a past; Firestone had an eager department devoted to product development.

The balloon introduced a new basic principle, but despite its complete reversal of high-pressure tire construction it was evolutionary. A logical outgrowth of the adoption of cords, it proceeded—a big step at a time.

Cords had presented a problem in rubberizing. Calendering the plies was not enough. Every fiber of every cord in every ply must be impregnated with rubber to increase flexing life. With the express purpose of minimizing friction and heat within large truck tires, Firestone engineers sought the proper technique of insulation.

At first single strands of cord, unreeled from spools, were guided through a vat of rubber cement and over a steam-heated table; several strands were twisted into a heavy cable cord. But it was found that the solvent had dried too quickly, and in the rapid evaporation the rubber particles were drawn back from the interior and came to the surface. Then by horizontal spreaders, next by vertical spreaders, sheets of cord fabric were immersed. Slow drying could be had in an atmosphere of benzol vapor, which was feasible only in an enclosed chamber and by the same token likely to cause an explosion.

In the fall of 1920, a new drier was designed; an inert gas was added to the benzol vapor. The cords remained soaked. The solvent was recovered. Gum dipping— another Firestone extra—was thus achieved.

The resultant gain in truck-tire strength and flexibility, as tested on the Indianapolis Speedway the following January, meant more mileage. Gum-dipped cords went into regular production the following month. And their success led naturally to utilizing the process in preparing passenger-car tires.

Motorists could now enjoy greater buoyancy, and to ensure firmer traction a tread was designed of cross-and-square pattern. Full public acceptance became a certainty when the Indianapolis Sweepstakes honors in 1923 fell to Firestone gum-dipped cord tires used by eight of the ten drivers who shared the prize money. The winner, Tommy Milton, maintained an average speed of 90.95 miles per hour in the 500-mile classic without a single tire failure. Soon the public pleasantly learned that these new tires were capable of rendering 12,000 miles of service.

The development department had already taken the next step. Since 1921, it had been experimenting with larger cross sections, made possible by the resilience of cords and even more practicable by the greater permissible deflection of gum-dipped cords. Since many car owners had shown partiality for oversize tires, "to smooth out the road," the increase in sectional dimension was right welcome. It was this quest for comfort rather than the expectation of further extension of tire life that inspired the developers.

They lowered the air pressure. Engineering object: to support the load on cushions of air instead of rigidly inflated casings. This was found physically feasible as the enlarged air capacity with reduced pressure equalled the high-pressure tire in volume of supporting air.

Here was a reversion to the fundamental principle of pneumatic tires—the containment of air, the casing acting simply as container. Having a low bursting stress to withstand, the casing now could be made lighter; four plies of strong, gum-dipped cord served in place of eight stiff plies. The thinner walls played their part, giving a greater degree of deflection. The larger contact area with the road gave full benefit of the lower pressure. The cushioning took away none of the durability. Tires rolled over bumps instead of riding on top of them and jouncing the car.

The Firestone company evolved the first satisfactory set of low-pressure tires in October, 1922. Compared with high-pressure tires of equal height, they had twice the air capacity, about half the pressure (twenty-five pounds), half the number of plies, and a lighter tread. They were molded to a section of seven and a half inches, to be mounted on wheels of twenty-inch diameter. Hence rims were wider and smaller. The outward aspect of so much blownup rubber inevitably begot the designation "balloons."

The important thing was that balloon tires performed splendidly. By counteracting vibration, they enabled a motorist to drive at greater speed. He did not have to slow down for rough spots ahead. The fewer plies lessened internal friction and the lower compression of air lessened the danger of tread separation and ply separation. There was less need to fear punctures; the softness of the tires yielded to sharp obstacles, whereas taut tires were pierced by them. A new tread construction made treads as yielding as the new casing, the design being a ribbed center with flexible shoulders.

Factory production of balloon tires began on April 5, 1923. Harvey Firestone planned to put them on the market "in a limited way" as they would necessitate—for all their inherent appeal—radical changes in car design or at least, for existing cars, changeovers in wheels and rims besides tires and tubes. He urged Henry Ford to adopt balloons as optional equipment on the Lincoln car, and quoted their fellow camping companion, Thomas A. Edison, as being "thoroughly sold" on them.

However, Henry Ford was not the first. While the rest of the tire manufacturing industry looked askance at balloons—some makers advising the trade to go slow with these "experimental" low-pressure tires, and at least one openly opposing the innovation—several auto manufacturers were testing them. And at a conference of rubber companies mulling over the issue in September, Firestone concisely told them he had already taken an original equipment order.

The Cole Motor Car Company had switched from 33 x 5 high-pressure tires (twenty-three-inch rim) to 34 x 7 balloons (twenty-inch rim) and announced:

Cole Is First to Introduce the New Balloon "Air Cushion" Tires.

Here are the advantages . . . superlative riding comfort, logically and practically obtained. Double the braking power due to doubling the braking surface. The best answer to date for skidding. Lower upkeep and longer car life because the big, soft tires protect the car against vibrations and road shock. Far less chance of air leaks and blowouts due to greatly reduced air pressure (only 25 lb. front and rear). Unquestionably the greatest single motor car improvement of recent years.*

It was a try. A trial balloon, so to speak. Firestone himself was uncertain how popular balloons would be, though they were giving service beyond his expectations.

* Advertisement in *Motor Age*, Sept. 27, 1923.

Dealers did not begin to sell them actively until November. They had not only tires to sell, and tubes, but complete changeover units: rims and wheels of smaller diameter (produced by Firestone Steel Products) to apply to the car. Soon, however, they had the advantage of standardization in five balloon sizes: 4.40, 5.25, and 6.20 sizes for twenty-one-inch wheels, 6.20 and 7.30 for twenty-inch wheels. With a small investment a Firestone dealer thus could reequip all makes of cars. His prestige in the community would grow. In fact, the response was electric.

In mid-December, when all the balloons that could be made were being sold, Harvey Firestone wrote Edison: "I feel sure it is the coming tire."

The company's first consumer advertisement appeared in *The Saturday Evening Post* at Christmas time, a double-spread in color:

Balloon Gum-Dipped Cords . . . unusual comfort, safety, and car conservation . . . without sacrificing mileage or increasing fuel consumption. . . .

The special Firestone gum-dipping process, by which each cord is impregnated and insulated thoroughly with rubber, adding greater strength and flexibility to the carcass, made it possible to carry out the new principle in tire design and construction so successfully. Soft and pliable, yet sturdy and tough . . . smooth out the bumps and ruts of the road . . . cling tenaciously to the pavement, due to the increased flexibility of the tread and the larger traction contact. . . .

The huge air chambers, the greatly lowered air pressure, absorb all road irregularities, preventing jars and jolts from reaching the chassis. They relieve the car of much of its vibration and preserve it from the shocks that cause squeaks and rattles, which are especially annoying in closed cars that have been in service for some time . . . a superlative degree of riding comfort, together with greater security and a longer life for your car.*

Even during the winter months, when business was ordinarily slow, Firestone dealers set new sales records.

* *The Saturday Evening Post*, Dec. 22, 1923.

The swiftness with which balloon tires caught on was truly amazing. "Going wonderfully well," Firestone recorded the following February. A large number of important new dealers swung over. In March, 1924, the factory was producing 25,000 balloons a week, and that month Ford agreed to adopt them. Sales of replacements continued strong into spring.

Today the majority of leading car manufacturers and more than 60,000 individuals endorse Firestone Balloon Gum-Dipped Cords by placing them on their cars.*

Tests by use in service on Chicago Yellow Cabs showed that the 7.30 size, compared with standard 35 x 4½ cords resulted not only in a substantial reduction in number of flats per month but in an appreciable saving in gasoline. And as for doing this "without sacrificing mileage," to quote the first cautious claim, these taxicabs averaged 16,114 miles on the balloons, many of which ran as high as 18,000 and 25,000 miles.

Ford's change was indeed revolutionary. Up to this time, the Model T had clung to 30 x 3½ clincher fabric tires, four plies, with fifty-five pounds recommended pressure. For 1925, the switch was to straightsides, to cords, to balloons. The tires were 4.40 inches wide, four-ply, with thirty-five pounds pressure. Rim diameters were reduced from twenty-three to twenty-one inches, rims being of a new, drop-center construction. The new Buicks abandoned five-ply sixty-pound pressure tires (31 x 5) for thirty-four-pound 5.25s; the new Packards, eight-ply sixty-five pounds (33 x 5) for thirty-pound 7.30s.

Balloons were applied to trucks and proved practical. Motor busses, which had come into greater use in the few years past, took to balloons with smooth sailing, Firestone introducing special bus tires to render long service.

* Company advertisement in *Journal of the Society of Automotive Engineers*, June 9, 1924.

At the races the news flashed: "Firestone Balloons Win Battle of Tires." The same brick track; virtually the same cars and drivers as in the 1924 Indianapolis Sweepstakes, whose winners had used thick-walled, high-pressure, Firestone gum-dipped cords; yet the new balloons in the 1925 contest beat the previous year's world record of 98.23 miles per hour. Peter DePaolo, in a grueling test under a blazing sun, averaged 101.13 miles per hour without tire trouble. Every one of the ten racers who finished in the money had Firestone balloons.

Quick to capitalize on the achievement, an advertisement declared:

These wonderful Gum-Dipped Balloons that stood this terrific grind will give you additional safety and comfort—and thousands of additional miles—on bad country roads, worn-out macadam and broken concrete.

See the nearest Firestone Dealer today. He will make you a substantial allowance for your present tires—will change your car over quickly—and bring it up to date so that you will enjoy all of these advantages this summer.

The shining triumph of the new tire was reflected in official statistics. High-pressure cords had taken much longer to win their place in the rivalry with fabric casings. They had accounted for only ten percent of a total national production of about 26,000,000 tires in 1917, not reaching fifty percent until 1922. But within a single year after the introduction of the balloon, this newcomer represented 11.5 percent. And in 1925, out of approximately 59,000,000 tires produced by all manufacturers, 34.1 percent were balloons. In another year they would lead the field.*

The comfort and performance of balloons established

* High-pressure cords stood at fifty-one percent in 1925, receding from their peak, while high-pressure fabrics had dwindled to 14.1 percent. As old cars went out of service, all high-pressure tire replacements diminished, the fabrics vanishing in 1929. Balloons accounted for 53.9 percent in 1927, high-pressure cords for 44.6 percent, fabrics 1.5 percent. (E. G. Holt, *Rubber Industry Letter*, No. 11, Bureau of Foreign & Domestic Commerce, Dec. 1, 1933.)

a new standard in automobiling, and car makers were stimulated to match these qualities in the structure and design of bodies. As broader tires required a modification of fenders, so smaller wheels affected brakes and brake drums. The higher speed at which autos could travel called for four-wheel brakes. Absence of vibration rattles encouraged more customers to buy closed cars, which in turn engendered year-round riding. A man's car became an expression of his taste. Besides durability, accent was on beauty.

New highs in production of passenger cars, trucks, and busses were reached in 1925. Registrations came close to 20,000,000, more than double the figure of 1920. It was an amazing market. Tires to keep all these vehicles rolling meant consumption of an enormous amount of rubber, particularly for balloons.

The world supply of rubber was far below the requirements of the industry.

Supply had been reduced by the Stevenson Rubber Restriction Scheme of 1922, adopted by the British Colonial Office at the instance of owners of British plantations in the Far East. At that time, American manufacturers had not yet recovered from their overbought condition; demand was then so feeble that the price sank to fourteen cents a pound. The scheme, born of the desperation of the depression, aimed to penalize shippers whose exports exceeded specified quotas, and it was contrived to bolster price by manipulating these releases of rubber.

When restriction was announced, Harvey Firestone insisted that the ones to be penalized were American tire purchasers—by a shortage forcing costs to exorbitant levels. As the United States imported 301,000 long tons of the 378,000 produced in the Far East, and this production was ninety-three percent of the world total, and seventy-five percent of plantation rubber was British-owned, the domination was real. Crying shortage in those days sounded like crying wolf. But Firestone was right. The advancing quotations leaped in the summer of 1925 to $1.23 a pound, as predicted.

As soon as the news broke that the colonial governments of British Malaya and Ceylon had enacted the restriction policy, late in October, 1922, Harvey Firestone summoned his associates to his office.

"I am going to fight this law with all the strength and vigor that is in me," he told them. "I do not believe that for the benefit of a few stockholders any government has the moral right to make a law restricting the output of a product of the soil so universally used as rubber."

A law that set the 1920 output of plantation rubber (335,000 long tons) as standard production, curtailed it to sixty percent, permitted a quarterly increase of five percent if the market price averaged thirty cents during the previous quarter, and required cutbacks of five percent if the average went lower—such a law was basically unsound.

Firestone believed it was uneconomic, arbitrary, inflexible. It was erroneously predicated on a continuation of subnormal consumption. It would intensify price fluctuation instead of promoting stability. The fixed procedure for releases could not act with sufficient promptness. Buyers were put in the anomalous position of bidding as high as possible.

Plantation owners—having allowed their production costs to run riot during all the years in which demand exceeded supply and the high prices paid investors dividends of 50 to 250 percent—said they faced ruin. They sought the easy road of government intervention instead of trying to trim costs, as other industries had been obliged to do in coping with depression.

Firestone dispatched a personal representative to London to look into the origins of the act—the pressure of the British Rubber Growers Association on the Colonial Office, the appointment by Winston Churchill, who was Secretary of State for the Colonies, of an advisory committee to develop a scheme, and the recommendation of this committee, headed by Sir James Stevenson and composed mainly of members of the association. British industry did not want it. Leading British economists did not favor it. The planters had imposed their private interests in disregard of the public, in disregard even of the fact that restricted production would further increase unit costs of operating an estate.

With data thus gathered, Firestone went to Washington and laid it before President Warren G. Harding, Secretary of Commerce Herbert C. Hoover, and members of Congress. He made a strong case for a protest to the British Government, pointing out that the Stevenson plan placed American highway transportation under a critical handicap; that it interfered not only with the rubber industry but with the rapidly growing automobile industry. But our government could not properly protest against foreign legislation. The demand for repeal must arise from public opinion.

Firestone would see to the agitation for repeal. What Washington could do was help America grow its own rubber and break up this dependence. He persuaded Senator Medill McCormick, of Illinois, to advocate a Congressional appropriation to investigate suitable sources of supply that were not under foreign domination. He enlisted also Senator James Couzens, of Michigan, erstwhile his customer (when secretary of the Ford Motor Company), and informed Couzens of his purpose to get American capital interested in production in the Philippine Islands.

Overnight, restriction had doubled the price of rubber.

On the Senate floor Senator James A. Reed, of Missouri, quoted Firestone:

This present advance represents an increased cost to the United States of over $100,000,000 on the estimated consumption for 1923. This must be passed on to the tire consumer. This is the time for the United States to pass such legislation as will encourage American capital to develop rubber plantations in the Philippine Islands, where the soil and climatic conditions are equal to any rubber-producing belt, and to negotiate with South American republics to develop production in their rubber regions.

Rubber is growing each year to be more important to the economics of commerce and transportation, and great opportunities are before us to make the Philippines one of our most valuable possessions and to have a secure supply of this important product.*

While Firestone was making preparations to hold a conference in Washington of the rubber manufacturing, automotive, and accessory industries as an organized protest against the Stevenson plan, and as a means of arousing the public, the Administration also acted. Secretary Hoover asked for $500,000 to study rubber production possibilities; the President made this a budget recommendation, and Hoover warned in his testimony before the House Appropriations Committee against foreign monopoly of vital raw materials. Rubber ranked fourth among our imports and was "essential to our national welfare." The War Department and the Department of Agriculture added their support.

But in his own industry Firestone faced opposition. The Rubber Association of America, although formally rejecting restriction, invited the growers' group to send a deputation here "for joint consideration of the probable effect." Firestone objected to this as a waste of time. The British delegates came, listened politely, gave assurance that only stability was intended, and went home counseling against relaxation of the controls and reporting that only one manufacturer was unfriendly. The

* H.S.F. at stockholders' meeting, Dec. 14, 1922.

Rubber Association, in turn, frowned on individual agitation. It sent telegrams to the membership urging them to abstain from Firestone's conference.

The day before the conference opened, the House of Representatives passed a deficiency appropriation bill including $500,000 for the Department of Commerce "to investigate and report on the possibilities of developing the rubber-plantation industry in the Philippines and Latin America" and the Department of Agriculture to survey the prospects in continental United States.

Hailing the appropriation, Firestone reminded the 200 businessmen attending the conference:

Rubber is a commodity vital to our modern-day commercial prosperity, but what is equally if not more important, it is one of the five raw materials most necessary in case of a national emergency.

I hope that we will go on record as supporting . . . our government in every way . . . to make us independent in our source of rubber supply and protect our industry from being threatened in the future by selfish interests.*

Firestone called for repeal of the Stevenson law.

But it is necessary that we all pull together in this matter, take an aggressive attitude, and act immediately. . . .

I realize that we have no legal redress. . . . I have faith enough in the sound common sense and business ability of the British Government to believe it will give consideration and act favorably upon a request from us in conjunction with the manufacturers and consumers of rubber products from their own country and other countries of the world to repeal this legislation.†

He heard Senator McCormick speak of the bold breadth of his thinking, which was to extend the area of planting both as an insurance against arbitrary monopoly and as a provision for future great need. The Senator, who was chairman of the Foreign Relations Committee, struck a note of warning:

* H.S.F. address, Conference of Rubber, Automotive and Accessory Manufacturers, New Willard Hotel, Washington, Feb. 27, 1922.

† *Ibid.*

Sound public policy forbids the Government of the United States to permit the continuance of a rubber monopoly which can be cut off from the United States in time of war. You may grow rubber in the Philippines, but you must do more. You must grow it in countries with which our communication will be unbroken, no matter how widespread or immense a war of the future may be.*

During the second day's session, the Senate committee in charge of the appropriation bill reported it favorably. The next day the Senate passed it. The quest began.

With conference resolutions endorsing the survey and denouncing restriction, Firestone turned to the board of directors of the Rubber Association of America. They refused to join in a protest to Great Britain. He continued his lone campaign.

In England, criticism of the Stevenson policy impelled Churchill, who was no longer Colonial Secretary, to defend his course in a statement to the *London Evening Standard:*

It was impossible for the Colonial Office to witness the financial ruin of the rubber-producing colonies owing to the continued sale of their products below the cost of production. . . .

It is too early to say what the ultimate results of this scheme will be, but if it should succeed in sustaining the vital industries of these colonies and in addition should tend to improve the rate of exchange between Great Britain and the United States, it should be the cause of general satisfaction to us. . . .

One of the principal means of paying our debt to the United States is in the provision of rubber.†

Taking the same tack, that restriction was necessary to safeguard supplies, the presidents of several tire companies publicly belittled predictions of a shortage. They said that American manufacturers did not wish to kill off the producers by buying below cost. As if this were the issue! One of Firestone's critics condemned his agitation as "exceedingly unfortunate and mischievous,"

* Sen. Medill McCormick, *ibid.*
† Quoted in *New York Times,* Mar. 13, 1922.

and the Rubber Association's board secretly voted a
publicity fund to counteract his work and "quiet any
misapprehension." This last was the last straw. Firestone
resigned his company's membership.*

On a speaking tour, he acquainted business groups
with the nature of the crisis and explained that while
rubber had temporarily fallen from the thirty-cent pivot
price (May, 1923), the principle involved was the power
of restraint and the entrenchment of restriction. His concern was for tomorrow as much as for today. At the
speakers' table at the annual meeting of the Chamber
of Commerce of the United States, a tire company
official retorted: "There is no rubber crisis."

Firestone hammered home the magnitude of the problem. This country consumed more than seventy percent
of the world rubber harvest and put eight out of every
ten pounds into automobile tires. In the past year, the
automobile industry had become the second largest in
the nation, the $2,558,000,000 wholesale value of its
products surpassing steel and yielding place only to
agriculture. "Its rapid recovery was a big factor in contributing to the speedy return of our prosperity," he
pointed out.

I have opposed this legislation from the start as I felt that as a
manufacturer I have a responsibility and duty towards the consumer, to protect his interests and give him the benefit of as low
prices as it is possible to obtain.

I need not tell you that from a purely selfish point of view the
immediate effect of the legislation might be looked upon as of benefit to the manufacturer, as you know that more money can be made
with high-priced materials than with low; and from the standpoint
of the bigger manufacturers with large capital and resources the
legislation tends to give an advantage over the smaller manufacturers whose resources are limited.†

* May 8, 1923.
† H.S.F. address. Kiwanis Club, Akron, May 17, 1923.

The campaign was not entirely oral. Firestone maintained an office in the Munsey Building in Washington, gathering statistics and communicating with officials in the Philippines and other countries. The Brazilian Embassy announced that plantations would be welcome in Para, the home of wild rubber. Inducements were offered for the investment of American capital. Governor General Leonard Wood, aiming to promote the resources of the Philippine Islands along sound lines, worked on bills to amend the land law and took a broad view:

> We must go at it not only from the standpoint of American interests but of the whole rubber situation or the rubber of the world will soon be in the hands of the British. . . .
>
> I wish Firestone would have some of his people come out here and look things over. . . . I think Firestone is entirely right in urging rubber development in those lands under our control.*

Independently of the government investigators, Firestone cabled his Singapore manager to engage a staff of experts to explore all feasible areas in the tropics and subtropics. Millions of acres were found in the Philippines and South America, in Central America and Africa. The survey men went into southern Mexico, were caught in the whirl of a revolution while inspecting a plantation that had been started during the 1910 Brazilian boom, and withdrew to other parts. In December, 1923, a Firestone man, Donald A. Ross, arrived in Liberia.

American rubber manufacturers were still dipping into their accumulated stocks of rubber. The market for recent production remained feeble, and releases under the Stevenson plan were cut first to fifty-five percent, then to fifty percent. Spurts of improvement in demand

---

* Gov. Gen. Leonard Wood to Maj. Gen. Frank McIntyre, chief, Bureau of Insular Affairs, Apr. 13, 1923.

strengthened price, but the artificially controlled supply failed to show a sensitive response. The result was a chaotic pattern of prices in 1924, a most uncomfortable state of instability, as quotations ranged from seventeen to thirty-six cents. But at the end of 1924, a definite revival of demand occurred. Yet the release stood at only fifty percent.

Balloons had stimulated tire sales. Balloons used about a third more rubber than high-pressure tires. They sent manufacturers in feverish pursuit, for world stocks of rubber were low.

A cautious increase of five percent was permitted in the release for the second quarter in 1925, although prices realized justified ten percent. The strong demand forced another lift in the quota, but it was not liberal enough. By the end of June, with a release of but sixty-five percent in effect, barely more than one month's supply remained in this country. Then it was that the price shot up to $1.23. Till the end of the year it hovered at $1, and by this time the whole industry was up in arms against the Stevenson scheme.

While keeping up his campaign with the slogan "Americans Should Produce Their Own Rubber," Harvey Firestone secured the company against an insufficiency by strengthening its outpost in Singapore. Additional purchasing offices were opened, in British territory and in Dutch. Estates in the Netherlands East Indies were not parties to restriction (except British-owned, voluntarily), for the Netherlands Government had refused in 1922 to collaborate with the Stevenson Committee. Instead, rubber growers in Java and Sumatra reduced their costs by scientific propagation. They took advantage of limitation of supply by planting more trees, and when prices rose they stepped up tapping; moreover, natives were encouraged to farm small holdings. Result: Dutch shipments threatened British supremacy.

All this time, Firestone was trying to interest outside capital in large-scale plantations. A $100,000,000 corporation was what he had in mind. The best lands for rubber cultivation were in the belt ten degrees north and ten degrees south of the equator, and this was narrowed down to two countries where Americans could best produce their own rubber—the Philippines and Liberia. He received little encouragement.

There were no new developments in the Philippine situation. But Liberia quickened the tempo of Firestone's thinking, for his investigator had hurried back with an impressive report. Conditions in Liberia were favorable as to climate, rainfall, soil, drainage. Fifteen miles inland from the capital a hevea plantation, overgrown with bush but containing 125,000 mature trees, gave tangible proof. It had been started in 1910 (fateful year) by a British company and abandoned during the depression. The government offered a lease on it. Liberia was an independent republic, historically a ward of the United States. And the latex sampled was high-grade.

In April, 1924, Firestone sent his personal representative to accompany the expert back to Liberia. The assignment was to open negotiations for a concession and explore the interior for other suitable sites. The topography of the country was of a gently rolling character, the jungle of virgin growth; the natives were strong and healthy and eager for work, as they had little opportunity but to bind themselves to contract labor in some neighboring colony of a European nation.

In June the existing 1,500-acre plantation at Mount Barclay was taken over on a ninety-nine-year lease. It would be useful for gaining experience and establishing nurseries. Agreements were tentatively reached on leasing tracts up to a total of a million acres, with Firestone to build a harbor, roads, and other public improvements.

Work began at once on rehabilitating Mount Barclay

and clearing jungle. The agreements meanwhile were submitted to Secretary of State Charles Evans Hughes to ascertain whether they accorded with American foreign policy. They were approved, except for a proposal that the United States make good an old pledge to extend a loan to Liberia—a loan needed to relieve Liberia of a customs receivership held by three European governments. Firestone felt the latter essential to the vast undertaking that was contemplated.

In August, the Liberian Secretary of State, Edwin L. Barclay, arrived in this country as a commissioner to negotiate the loan and sign the agreements.

In August—

It was the twenty-fifth anniversary of The Firestone Tire & Rubber Company. Flowers filled Harvey Firestone's office, and employees came in all day long to wish him well. His five sons gathered round. There were no ceremonies, no speeches that day, but inevitably he recalled another August 3, when the world was young. Not even the rosiest of those young dreams had pictured the immense scope of the present day.

"I have done the very best I could." Speaking at the dedication of the Firestone Stadium and Athletic Field a few days before, to thousands of members of the organization, he expressed himself as if he were alone with each one. "And the regretful thing is that I cannot come in closer personal touch with you—in your home life, your recreation and activities." In this impromptu fashion he came near summing up his creed. "All we can do is try to do our duty according to our position." Thought of the joy that the field and stadium would bring them made him joyous. "That is about all we get out of life—trying to do something for the other fellow and making somebody happy."

More formally, on the occasion of receiving an honorary degree from Mount Union College, he had stated his concept of business success:

I have spent my life in the profession of business. . . . I believe there is no other profession where so much real good can be accomplished. I do not refer simply to the accumulation of wealth but to building up this great country of ours and helping to make more happy the lives of others.

The successful businessman of today gives as much thought, or more, to the welfare of his employees as he does to the profits of the business. He builds upon a foundation of honesty, integrity, and service.*

A tire company. This was what he had started in 1900. A tire company still. But what a difference! In the modern world, witness of the marvelous march of automotive transportation and its transformation of American life, a business was ramified. If grown to large proportion in serving a large need, it must be versatile.

On the principle that a manufacturing firm of great size must exercise closer control over its basic supplies than it could do by buying in an open, speculative market, Firestone had acquired Sanford Mills in Fall River, Massachusetts, in November, 1924. The purchase was financed by an issue of $2,000,000 in mortgage bonds. By mid-1925 the renamed Firestone Cotton Mills were providing the parent company with half of its cord requirements.

At the other end of operations, the control of waste products, the small department that had begun in the old plant chemically to reclaim vulcanized rubber, and that had expanded into a six-story factory by 1916 under the name of Xylos Rubber Company, was now an independent unit with annual sales of about 5,000,000 pounds to other rubber manufacturers. With the rise in rubber prices to extravagant heights under restriction, stimulating greater use of reclaim, Xylos quadrupled

* H.S.F. at Mount Union College, Alliance, Ohio, June 18, 1923.

its capacity in 1925. Secretary Hoover publicly advocated this substitute as a conservation measure, to cut down imports from the Far East and lessen American dependence.

Now the buildings aggregating "Firestone city" extended over an area a mile long. (The company owned 235 acres in Akron exclusive of Firestone Park.) An interplant railroad conveyed materials across the expanse. In the course of the year the company consumed 100,000,000 pounds of rubber, 30,000,000 pounds of cord, 142,000,000 pounds of steel.

Economy of handling ruled the roost. In Steel Products' one-story structure, straightline operation prevailed, from steel storage to shipping platform. The machinery was mostly of the company's own design. A monitor-type roof, the full length of 850 feet, afforded plenty of light and ventilation to the men turning out rims and bases, wheel units for balloon tires, tractor wheels, and bead wire. The new drop-center rim made tire application easy by allowing the bead to be depressed into the middle well at one point of the circumference and lifted over the rim's edge at the opposite point. A soft rubber toe on the bead was beveled, formed to fit the curve of the rim, keeping out water and preventing rust.

The drop-center rim was the 1925 successor to a split rim which Firestone had developed in 1913—called "split" because of a transverse opening at one point in its circumference which permitted contraction and facilitated mounting. Other manufacturers developed their own types of split rims. It was at the instigation of Henry Ford, at the time he was considering wide rims for balloon tires, that the industry adopted the drop-center type.

Progress smiled all over the grounds. Apparatus was devised for building and finishing tires at one position;

for extracting airbags mechanically from cured casings. The newest machine, to build balloons on a drum instead of a core, was constructed in May, 1925, introducing a higher standard of perfection besides saving a great deal of time.

Fortune smiled. The silver anniversary year brought the largest sales volume to date. On $125,598,000 business the company earned a net profit of $12,800,000. Book surplus was increased to more than $39,700,000. Every one of the 10,000 employees was a stockholder, a partner in the business and in its fruits.*

The directors elected in 1925 were Harvey S. Firestone, John W. Thomas, Stacy G. Carkhuff, Carmon A. Myers, John J. Shea, Harris Creech, and Harvey S. Firestone jr. Two Firestone sons were now active in the business. Besides Harvey jr., engrossed in plantation preliminaries in addition to managing Steel Products, there was Russell, who had recently been assigned to the Miami warehouse on his first job after completing a training course in a class of thirty college graduates.

The college training program was Harvey jr.'s idea. He had broached it to his father in view of the fact that the business was growing faster than the potential of executive personnel. Let scouts be sent to colleges and universities each year, he said, and select from the graduating classes a group of men who would be brought to Akron for intensive training in the various phases of

* By an issue of 25,000 shares of the authorized common stock, a new allotment had been made to employees. In April, 1921, on the president's invitation to purchase at least two shares, the response was universal, and thereafter (until 1927) every new employee signed a stock purchase agreement for two shares. The stock was paid off at the rate of fifty cents a week per share.

Basically this was a six percent savings account, but in 1926 and 1927 the dividends were $7, in 1928 the dividend was $10, and the next year $8 plus a 400 percent stock dividend (five shares for one).

Another allotment was made in 1927, offering two shares to employees who had completed at least five years' service; all new employees bought one share of common and one of seven percent preferred.

the industry and indoctrination in Firestone methods. Let them be given jobs for which they showed special aptitude.

"By following this plan every year we'll have a continuous complement of good men on hand acquiring the experience necessary for filling important posts," Harvey jr. explained. "Their first jobs will merely be stepping-stones to their future responsibilities."

Here was foresight to his father's liking. On Firestone's approval the program went into effect in July, 1924, the trainees completing their course the next January.*

At the time of the 1925 stockholders' meeting, President Firestone observed that there were several reasons for "our wonderful growth," naming "honesty of purpose, loyalty of the organization, a determination to serve better than any other company in the rubber industry."

Balloon tires. They were distinctly serving the public. Cost per mile on the average was down to a tenth of a cent, despite onerous restriction. And crossing the threshold of its second quarter-century, the Firestone company embarked upon production of its own rubber.

---

* Addressing the class of 1949, Harvey S. Firestone jr. said: "The success of our training program is most emphatically proved by the fact that a large number of men who now hold key executive positions in our company started their business life with Firestone in the college classes. They have come up through the organization step by step. And, since they are thoroughly familiar with the duties, responsibilities, and problems of the men who are now holding their former jobs, they are especially well-qualified to supervise and direct those men."

ⅡⅡⅡⅡⅡⅡⅡⅡⅡⅡⅡⅡⅡⅡⅡⅡⅡⅡⅡⅡⅡⅡ

I I

Liberia and Restriction

TAPPING the trees on the small Mount Barclay
plantation in Liberia began early in 1925, and a
nursery of a million seedlings was started in the fall with
a view to planting large tracts as soon as the major
agreements should become effective. The Liberian Secretary of State came to Akron to discuss the details of a
loan. At the same time, Harvey Firestone continued
investigations in other countries.

His friend, Thomas A. Edison, whose eternally young
mind had seized upon the concept of American production of rubber, turned botanist and experimented with
latex-bearing plants and shrubs at his winter home in
Fort Myers, Florida. Guayule plants and seeds were
obtained in Mexico for him by Firestone. Desert milk-
weed also seemed promising. In August, when Harvey jr.
went to see him at his laboratory in Orange, New Jersey,
Edison's enthusiasm centered on a Madagascar vine,
Cryptostegia grandiflora; it could be gathered like hay by
modern machinery, two crops a year, macerated and
put into huge tanks containing a rubber solvent.

Harvey jr. reported on interviews concerning various
plantation offers: in Guatemala, Venezuela, Mexico.
The most attractive of these was the development at Las
Palmas, in Chiapas, Mexico, planted to 350 acres of
Hevea brasiliensis and two million indigenous *Castilloa* trees

on about 5,000 additional acres. The estate was only 500 miles from the Texas border, in contrast to the 11,000 miles distance from Far Eastern ports. Firestone signed the Mexican lease in August, sent out a small organization to install tapping and refining equipment in September, and soon began to receive rubber.

While the heveas at Las Palmas were large trees, their yield was meager, for the climate was not sufficiently hot and humid. The castilloas also proved disappointing; they could be tapped only two or three times a year, for a maximum of about one pound of dry rubber, whereas a good hevea gave at least four pounds. The results of the Mount Barclay operation were infinitely more satisfying: 96 tons before the end of the year, with rubber selling at a dollar a pound.*

The same September, after continuous negotiation, the preliminary draft of a loan agreement was initialed. Firestone had decided against making a further quest for investors to go into a joint venture, and he was ready to extend to Liberia a private loan of $5,000,000. He set up the Finance Corporation of America as the vehicle, arranging to furnish half the amount during the first three years. In this connection, the United States government offered to designate loan officials and arbitrate such matters as might arise.

As an officer of the newly formed Firestone Plantations Company, Harvey jr. at once went to London to assemble a group of planters and other experts and dispatch them to Liberia equipped to start clearing and planting operations on the first new unit—a soil-tested area a dozen miles up the Du River and about forty-five miles northeast of the capital city of Monrovia. His father intended to spend no more than $500,000 to $1,000,000 in 1926,

* The Las Palmas estate was abandoned by termination of the lease in June, 1926, the controlling factors being the unsettled political condition of Mexico and the difficulty of obtaining an adequate labor force.

then wait and see. The lease and loan would, of course, have to be ratified by the Liberian Legislature.

The Liberians delayed, though their current economic condition was most critical and the United States State Department repeatedly advised acceptance of Firestone's proposals. These contracts would "promote the country's welfare," Secretary of State Frank B. Kellogg pointed out. He lamented the possibility that disagreement over terms might prevent realization of this "immense advantage to Liberia."

A unique relationship existed between the two nations. From 1819 to 1847 the American Colonization Society had fostered the resettlement of former slaves on this West African coast. In the latter year, a republic was established, its constitution modeled on our own, and since that time the territorial integrity of Liberia had been preserved from encroachment, her national independence protected, by the United States. Her history hung on a tenuous, if not tortuous, thread of economic progress.

Although the commitments in Liberia were heavy, Firestone was still keenly interested in the Philippine Islands. In January, 1926, he sent Harvey jr. with a staff of engineers and experienced rubber men on a six months' trip to the Far East—to confirm the reports of previous investigators on the feasibility of the southern islands and to make further study of cultivation and production methods in Malaya, Sumatra, Java, Borneo, and Ceylon.

The same month, Firestone renewed his appeal for American freedom from foreign monopolistic control. Testifying before a Congressional committee, he proposed the simple expedient of government encouragement of long-term capital investment on a scale commensurate with the industry's needs.

I do not presume to speak with reference to our foreign policy. Surely, however, it is practicable to recommend that our government take active steps to remove those laws in the Philippine Islands which are an effective barrier against large-scale development of rubber plantations there. . . .

An awakened public sense of the dangers which threaten our sources of supply may be regarded as of the highest importance.*

Harvey Firestone jr. and his party were welcomed in Manila by Governor General Wood and by Manuel Quezon, president of the Philippine Senate. At Quezon's invitation, they chartered a revenue cutter and inspected Mindanao, Jolo, and other islands; soil and climate were ideal, labor was abundant.

Upon our return to Manila, interest in rubber was very great. . . . At the request of President Quezon, I worked up a bill for the Philippine Legislature, with the assistance of local attorneys . . . the Rubber Land Act . . . to assure up to 500,000 acres . . . on a basis which was both fair to the Filipino and to the American investor.†

Under the proposed law, no individual tract would exceed 50,000 acres, leases would run up to seventy-five years, and the wholesome fear of absentee ownership of idle lands was respected by proper safeguards. The bill was drawn with full awareness also of political agitation against American corporations; Quezon himself felt that the entrenchment of American capital might militate against a future grant of independence. However, the bill was introduced in August and the legislature assigned it to a committee for study.

Harvey Firestone jr. was home by this time and he had paid a call on President Calvin Coolidge, reporting on the Philippine situation. At the end of the month, he departed for Liberia. The agreements with that country were nearing final form.

* H.S.F., before the House Committee on Interstate and Foreign Commerce, Jan. 15, 1926.
† H.S.F. jr. talk, Firestone Club House, Feb. 28, 1927.

His ship rode anchor more than a mile offshore from Monrovia. There was no harbor. By surfboat, manned by skillful Kru tribesmen, he reached the beach and then ascended to the city on the heights.

He found the Mount Barclay plantation in fine shape, the trees of splendid size, free from disease and yielding more than 400 pounds per acre. (Output in 1926 was 190 tons.) Many of the 500 native laborers here had walked ten days from their villages in the interior, through bush and jungle, to obtain employment—of their own accord, a fact noteworthy in a country where a tradition of forced labor had not yet died. The men received a thorough medical examination and vaccination; strong and healthy, almost all were accepted.

A sanitary program was the next step, based on a medical and biological survey made by ten scientists from the Harvard School of Tropical Medicine and financed by Firestone. A permanent medical staff would be installed, a hospital built, as the recruitment of thousands of natives would mean the assumption of a social responsibility.

On November 10, 1926, the Liberian Legislature ratified the agreements. The main lease, covering a maximum of a million acres for ninety-nine years, provided that the Firestone Plantations Company develop at least 20,000 acres within five years. (As a matter of fact, this minimum area was felled, burned, and cleared, with 748 acres planted, before the prolonged negotiations were concluded.) Firestone agreed to pay an annual rental of six cents per acre taken over and an export levy on rubber shipments of one percent of the New York price.

Through the Finance Corporation of America, Liberia received the loan wherewith to liquidate internal and international debts and administer the government's affairs adequately. The bonds at seven percent (later reduced by Firestone to four and a half percent) were to be amortized over a period of forty years. Liberia agreed not to refund for twenty years nor make any other loan without the consent of the Financial Adviser, who would be nominated by the President of the United States.

Under a third agreement, Firestone would build a harbor at Monrovia at a cost not to exceed $300,000, to be repaid by the Liberian Government.*

Prospective operating plans called for the construction of houses for the administrative staff and native workers, the building of a hundred miles of road, exploration of new areas to determine the best locations for planting, the generation of hydroelectric power from several rivers, well drilling and other engineering work to ensure a safe water supply, and a retail store to supply food and goods at low cost. A radio station would be built for swift communication with Akron.

Here was a social-economic undertaking of great scope. The companions of business were scientists, architects, builders, foresters, and technicians, besides engineers and physicians. Men from the Yale University School of Forestry came to make studies. The Harvard School of Tropical Medicine sent out another group for further work.

Like health, education was an acknowledged obligation. Firestone sponsored a system of public schools in cooperation with the government, the church missions, and the American Advisory Committee on Education in Liberia. A vocational training school for natives adapted them for skilled work. The tribal language Kpelle was

---

* Firestone spent $115,000 in an attempt to construct the harbor; engineers determined the project impracticable, and Firestone absorbed the loss. Work on the harbor was resumed by the United States Navy under a 1943 Port Agreement for the building of a naval base.

put into writing for the first time, to teach it to the Americans and other foreigners, and this led to printing schoolbooks in Kpelle.

Here in the fastness of the African jungle the American eight-hour day was inaugurated, a large payroll with it, and the American standard of volunteer labor was insisted upon. Workers must not be required to obtain their jobs through the government; they must be able to bargain directly with the company and free to sever their services at will. Harvey Firestone jr. reminded President Charles D. B. King of these stipulations:

> We desire to point out to the Government again that the success of our development in Liberia is largely dependent upon the organization of a permanent and contented labor force. This can only be done through a free and unrestricted employment and upon terms and conditions which are agreeable to the laborers themselves.*

It was important also to avoid doing violence to the customs of natives emerging from primitive and semi-primitive conditions to work and live in an industrial environment; to their mode of communal living, around a palaver house, and their recreations. Harvey Firestone jr. made it a cardinal rule of the administrative staff to try to understand the native and help him in his development both as a workman and as a human being. Later, an expedition of the Harvard School of Anthropology arrived to learn the elements of the tribal cultures so that these might be fostered and blended with the mores of civilization.

In 1927, more than 12,000 natives were employed under the direction of a staff of 100 (mostly American college graduates). They planted 3,000,000 trees on 15,000 acres. In a few years, the trees would be thinned about half by careful selection, leaving about 110 to the acre because of their large, dense crowns. At five years,

* Dec. 2, 1926.

they would be mature enough for tapping. As matters stood, the company was confident of producing rubber more economically in Liberia than it could be produced in any other country.

Henry Ford ventured into Brazil in 1927. Edison experimented in Florida and invited Ford and Firestone to join him.

Ford had obtained a huge concession in the Tapajós River plateau region deep into the Amazon Valley, an area recommended by Department of Commerce investigators. He built a model town and planted a thousand acres, intending to follow up with a thousand more each year. A leaf disease blighted the trees; they died. Ford ultimately transferred (in 1934) his planting operations to another section of the state of Para.

When Edison proposed the formation of a company to conduct exhaustive plant research for domestic commercial production, he asked Firestone to communicate his plan to Ford. This was the origin of the Edison Botanic Research Corporation in 1927, the three men as stockholders, the two manufacturers each paying in $25,000. After having tested 2,300 different plants, Edison reported the following year that he now had 1,700 growing in his Florida garden. Eventually he decided on goldenrod, and by crossbreeding he produced a strain with higher rubber content. There it was, Edison said, available in unlimited quantities in case war cut off plantation supply, but he admitted its inferior quality and its cost of close to $2 a pound.

Meanwhile Firestone had cleared 40,000 acres in Liberia, partly on a new plantation near the southern coast, along the Cavalla River. "I am hopeful," he wrote his son Harvey jr., "it will be one of the greatest successes of the Firestone organization." * The proposed

* H.S.F. to H.S.F. jr., Mar. 7, 1928.

Philippine Rubber Land Act had never come out of its legislative pigeonhole.

When the next rainy season began, in the torrid "spring" of 1928, a stand of seedlings ranged on 7,000 acres of the Cavalla plantation, making a total of 27,000 under Firestone cultivation. Fortunately, operations had not proceeded at a more rapid rate; the company remained flexible enough to adopt the latest scientific advances in intensifying the value of rubber trees. In Sumatra, the art of bud grafting had been perfected, and a Dutch scientist skilled in this work was brought to Liberia. Clones of proven high-yielding trees were imported from Sumatra and native workers were trained in grafting the buds from these clones to seedling stumps in the nursery beds. If the buds stayed green after three weeks, the stumps could be transplanted in the field. The method promised to double the flow of milky-white latex. A basis would be laid for the richest expanse of heveas on the face of the earth.

But, shortly thereafter, expansion was slowed down. The Stevenson Act reacted, also a world-wide depression came on.

The chaotic pattern of events went back to the dollar-rubber days of 1925, when frightened rubber manufacturers—all the more panicky because they had not thought through this danger before—turned to Secretary of Commerce Hoover for help. He advocated conservation of supplies and echoed Firestone's theme: provision of independent American sources. There was talk in January, 1926, among rubber and auto manufacturers, of joining in a grand plantation project; talk, but no sequel.

Announcement of a 100 percent release from the Stevenson-restricted countries on February 1, in combination with sales resistance to high prices and with wider use of reclaim, sent rubber costs tumbling from a dollar to thirty-six cents. The new level cut clear across the value of four months' supply, for this was the amount a large tire maker usually owned at any given time; it included purchases in the Far East, shipments afloat, and stock at home. One reliable estimate put total losses at $115,000,000.

Restriction officials realized that their policy was not elastic enough to stabilize price. They changed it. They raised the pivot from thirty cents to forty-two; if the next quarter failed to average this, the release would be lowered to eighty percent. Despite wide fluctuations and a further break during the summer, the release remained at 100 percent for the greater part of 1926. Reduction to eighty percent in November failed to block the decline. So the plan was further revised: slashes would be made only ten percent at a time and none would be restored unless forty-two cents was averaged for three consecutive quarters. However, an average below thirty cents would send the release down to sixty percent.

Before the year was up, rubber and car manufacturers decided on cooperative action. Reserves must be built up in New York to offset the unpredictable irregularities in price; to offset also the power of London speculators who maintained reserve stocks to suit their own purpose. Thus Firestone combined with members of the Rubber Association of America (without rejoining their organization) in forming a buying pool, the Crude Rubber Agency. London kept 40,000 tons on hand; they would go out and buy 60,000 tons. Rubber was selling at around thirty-seven cents.

The pool was effective in 1927 in holding the price down, although another considerable influence was the expanding exports of the Dutch colonies, not to mention the reclaiming of rubber from old tires for use in compounds for cheaper lines. The Stevenson reflex responded. First, the release was cut to seventy percent, next to sixty percent, and there it stayed. But the manufacturers had all the raw rubber they wanted.

The Dutch had developed new tapping methods and were tapping to capacity. On government experiment farms, they strove for high-yielding trees by seed selection, soil fertilization, control of leaf blight, and lately bud grafting. Latex was already flowing more abundantly, an acre was averaging 650 pounds of dry rubber; production costs were lowered. From twenty-five percent of the world's supply in 1922, Dutch territories had come to contribute more than fifty percent. What would happen when the heavy planting of 1922-1923 came into bearing in 1928?

Growers in Malaya and Ceylon had been rolling in dividends for two years, and the events of 1927 had shorn the Stevenson plan of any pretense as a stabilizer. And it wasn't working any more. In November, despite a sudden jump from 33½ to 41½ cents, the British Colonial Secretary recommended to the Prime Minister that the scheme be reviewed.

The day in February, 1928, that Prime Minister Stanley Baldwin let it be known he had appointed a review committee, the market sagged. Rubber fell from thirty-eight cents to twenty-eight. Firestone read the handwriting to mean that restriction would be abandoned and America would win a great moral victory. Others in Akron scoffed. They had bought heavily. They held much at a thirty-two-cent average "which looked good when it had been selling at forty-two cents," Firestone remarked.

The day in April that Baldwin announced restriction would end in November was not a golden one but a black one. The price soon dipped to seventeen cents. The large accumulations in this country suffered an inexorable blow. Firestone inventories and rubber stocks were near their peak of the year, and so too the company's interest in the Crude Rubber Agency. Its net cash loss in the pool alone was $3,250,000. Its inventories were depreciated more than $12,000,000 by repeal.

Prices hung low in 1929, a year of enormous automobile production (more than 4,500,000 passenger cars, more than 700,000 trucks and busses), with total registrations passing 26,500,000. Rubber consumption had never been greater, rubber supplies never more abundant. With rubber selling at sixteen cents in the December after the stock market crash—and at nine cents a year later—there was no point in headlong development of the plantations in Liberia.

Only small quantities were shipped out of Mount Barclay at this time. The seedling trees that had been planted in 1926 would soon be ready for regular tapping but, except for a curiosity as to how well they would produce, they were untouched. The depression was on. Planters and engineers were returning home. But the time was used by scientists to develop a long-range research program that would one day realize the full potential of Liberia.

12

Planning for Strength

BEFORE the depression of the 1930s smote the country with bewildering swiftness and loosened a flood
of economic panaceas, the Firestone company had built
a solid edifice. Years of boom prevailed, and they were
used as a time for expansion and greater efficiency.

Besides being true in a literal sense—with the construction of a seven-story addition to Plant 2 in Akron,
an extension to the Canadian plant, a factory in Los
Angeles, and another in England—this meant inner
strengthening as well. The basic task was to manufacture
tires giving the public "most miles per dollar." And to
attain further economy in production, new machinery
designed by the company's engineers was installed on
a sweeping scale. Prosperity was taken as a signal to
reduce costs. Each year, huge sums went into efficiency,
reaching a climax of $4,000,000 spent in Akron plants
in 1929 for modern equipment.

Chief among the improvements were tire-building
machinery, conveyor systems, and facilities for producing
the company's own power. The flat-band method of
building balloon tires saved considerable time and space.
Cord fabric was applied to a drum in endless bands
(spliced two plies per band), laid without strain or distortion, by axial tension. Next came the power-driven
collapsible drum. Beads, tread, and sidewalls were as-

sembled on it, and automatic stitching locked the parts together.

Removed from the drum, the tire at this stage was a broad, flat hoop. In a hydraulic press it would be squeezed from bead to bead and expanded, with inflated airbag inside, into doughnut shape, responding to the bag's intensive pressure because the cords were resilient. A conveyor carried the green tire to the curing mold.

In the vulcanizing procedure, machinery replaced arduous hand labor. Conveyors had already been put to use in lifting off the top halves of molds after the molds were pulled by hook from the pot heaters; but men worked a punch bar to break the mold open and they dug out the cured tire manually. Now an electrical pulling device supplanted the hook, the mold was broken by another machine, the tire was removed by a mechanical remover which delivered it to a roller conveyor whereby it traveled to a debagging machine. These technical advances were made during the nation's lush years 1926-1928. They did not wait for adversity.

Sales in 1926 totaled $144,397,000, an increase of fifteen percent over the year before, which had gained forty-seven percent on its own immediate predecessor. Net profits, however, did not quite reach $8,000,000, thanks to the irregularity of rubber prices.

With rubber costs lower in 1927, and tire price reductions correlated to them, dollar-volume declined to $127,696,000. But unit sales were greater; that is, sales to dealers. It was a year when car and truck production eased, hence original equipment business declined. Replacement tires more than offset this drop, and profitably so. The net was $13,780,000, making one of the most satisfying records in Firestone history. A modest extra dividend was declared, and close to $9,000,000 was carried to the surplus account.

In 1928, the year that restriction was repealed and prices collapsed, units continued to swell and volume held at $125,664,000. The company took its losses on rubber gracefully, earned $7,072,000, and added close to $3,000,000 to surplus. As expanding production required corresponding provision for it, resources were husbanded.

Large quantities of raw cotton were purchased for future needs. A plethora of it had sent price exceedingly low, and the government advocated buying as a patriotic act to relieve the distress of the cotton states. Following through, Firestone acquired a mill in New Bedford, Massachusetts, in 1927, the largest and best equipped in the world for the fabrication of cords. With the 115,200 spindles there and 62,000 spindles in Fall River, the company was able to supply itself at a very favorable cost. The Firestone Cotton Mills financed these undertakings by issuing and selling $12,000,000 worth of five percent gold bonds.

In the midst of astute moves for efficiency, Harvey Firestone always kept in sight the primary goal, a better tire. He sent a memorandum to John W. Thomas, the vice president: "We must continually improve the quality of the tread to equal the wearing quality of the carcass."

Manufacturing matters having been mastered, he analyzed the over-all picture and put his finger on the remaining problem: How to merchandise and distribute at a lower cost.

For several years, Firestone had considered erecting a factory on the Pacific Coast, and in 1927 he sent his son Russell to Los Angeles to close a deal on a forty-acre site. Southern California had an exceptionally large registration of cars and trucks; tires could be distributed by truck to branches in this region, and quicker deliveries and better service could be rendered to all Western states. It would be a cheaper way to handle exports to the Hawaiian Islands, the Philippines, and the Far East in general.

Firestone Tire & Rubber Company of California was organized and sold $10,000,000 of five percent sinking fund gold bonds to build a plant, reimburse the parent company for advances, and provide working capital. Next year, construction and the installation of the latest machinery were completed, giving a daily capacity of 7,500 tires. The Xylos Rubber Company also built a reclaiming plant in Los Angeles and used a new high-pressure steam process to reduce operating costs.

In 1928, the prospering Firestone Tire & Rubber Company of Canada, Ltd., financed from its own resources an extension to increase its output. With expansion in Akron too, the total capacity for all plants came to 65,000 tires a day.

The same year, the need to keep pace with rapidly growing foreign trade prompted the building of a British factory. There was urgency. To ship into England and fill orders after paying a duty of 33⅓ percent cost near $15,000 a week. An excellent location was chosen in a London suburb, Brentford, on the Great West Road, with a railroad connection and access by canal to the London docks.

Ready in October, the plant of The Firestone Tyre & Rubber Company, Ltd., was something new on the British industrial landscape—architecturally decorative, on twenty-seven acres, and set back from the road (in the Firestone tradition) to provide the greenery of a surrounding lawn and the fresh air and light of spaciousness. As the Home Secretary, Sir William Joynson-Hicks, observed at the dedication exercises, working conditions here were excellent; he wished that British manufacturers had a similar regard for the health and comfort of labor.

Brentford was officially declared in operation when

Harvey S. Firestone jr. took the first tire built and placed it into a mold, the assembled guests watching the mold descend into the vulcanizer. At luncheon a voice was heard from Akron. By radiotelephone the guiding genius of the Firestone enterprises greeted his colleagues in England and urged them on to success.

Brentford kept busy. The venture proved decidedly worth while and in 1929 the factory had to be enlarged. Nor were bicycle "tyres" neglected!

In that busy year, Los Angeles erected a duplicate factory, doubling capacity; Akron expanded further; cotton manufacturing increased with the acquisition of a 24,700-spindle mill in Newburyport, Massachusetts, and an addition was built to the Firestone Footwear Company plant in Hudson, Massachusetts.* Still another subsidiary was established, the Firestone Battery Company, and a building went up in Akron to manufacture not only batteries but brake lining and other accessories.

The battery business was directly connected with Harvey Firestone's deep concern over a more efficient method of distributing tires. For even as he reported an advance of thirty percent in unit sales for 1929, a volume of $144,586,000, and net profit of $7,727,000, he pointed out that the weak link was retailing. If the dealers' stores could be modernized and the public drawn to them not merely at seasonal peaks but through the year for the purchase of Firestone products and services, the dealers would be fortified financially. They would be able to compete with the new chains of up-to-date stores opened by mail-order houses in year-round contact with the motorist.

These chains were vigorously promoting special-brand

---

* The rubber boot and shoe department had been moved in 1920 from Akron to Hudson, Mass., where the company had bought the Apsley Rubber Company. The name was changed to Firestone-Apsley Rubber Company and the new firm was capitalized at $2,000,000. This became Firestone Footwear Company in 1926. The business continued until 1935, when it was sold to a subsidiary of the United States Rubber Company.

tires. They had choice locations at busy traffic intersections. They knew how to merchandise. This competition in distribution, which was menacing Firestone outlets, must be met. By forming partnerships with dealers in setting up One-Stop Master Service Stations, Harvey Firestone envisioned the instrument for combating it.

Partly to raise funds for broadening this retail program, partly to expand production to 80,000 tires a day, the corporation was recapitalized at $135,000,000 and a new stock offering was made in October, 1929. The proceeds would also retire a portion of the funded debt and all the outstanding preferred stock (six percent and seven percent issues). Included in the revision of the financial structure was a stock dividend of 400 percent (five shares of new common to be exchanged for one of the old). The latter had been quoted in the high 200s most of the year.

Of the newly authorized $100,000,000 preferred at $100 par, $60,000,000 of six percent cumulative stock was offered and sold. Purchasers received warrants entitling them to buy one share of new common at $55 with each share of preferred.

Of the newly authorized $35,000,000 common at $10 par, only 2,250,000 shares were issued. There had been 450,000 shares outstanding of the old common (from 2,500,000 authorized), and these were turned in for 2,250,000 shares. Before the stock dividend, 50,000 shares were sold at $260. And this new money entered the treasury before the crash on the New York Stock Exchange near the end of October.

The sudden deflation of values, of activity and hopes, across the nation and around the world. The cessation of demand, production, employment. Worse than a vicious circle, all this spelled a downward spiral. When would bottom be reached? No one knew, just as no one knew why the thing had happened, though universal hindsight expressed the sour opinion, "It was bound to." Highly inflated prices could not be sustained forever, people agreed. Hence the recession. (Tire prices were singularly blameless.) But it deepened and it lasted. The recession became acknowledged as a depression—not a replica of the setback of 1920—a depression in big black capital letters.

Even as the Stock Exchange break was both a disaster and a symbol, the figures on automobile manufactures told a twofold tale. The crimp in the leading industry was a hardship in itself; the fact of a forty percent decline in passenger car output for 1930, developing into seventy-five percent from 1929 to 1932, bespoke a condition of national demoralization. Car registration receded at once. It continued to fall back for several years. Truck production suffered almost as severely, although registration sturdily held the road. Busses rolled blissfully along for small but steady gains. But the number of cars in service failed to catch up with the 1929 mark for seven long years. Among innumerable victims of the depression, many thousands of dealers were wiped out.

Some of the tire manufacturers had been discriminating against their own independent dealers by giving exceptionally favorable contracts to chain distributors, who sold the standard brands under special names—and undersold. The assured volume apparently contented these manufacturers in this time of stress.

But to Harvey Firestone this was distinctly not good business. Even original-equipment orders, with their narrow margin, were worth while only in so far as they contributed to dealer selling; they lowered the overhead in mass production and led to repeat sales to satisfied car owners. Many years before, he had rejected opportunities to furnish special-brand casings to mail-order houses. He was unwilling to make a destructive sacrifice for expediency. Selling widely advertised Firestone tires through tire dealers—this was the only sound kind of business.

However, a gigantic manufacturing firm could not very well depend upon channels of distribution that lagged behind the standards of progressive retailing. Many, in fact, were underfinanced and indifferently managed. Some creative effort must be applied, not only for such dealers' salvation but for the manufacturer's sake too.

During his vacation at Miami Beach in 1925, Firestone's visits to a Miami dealer's store were marked by suggestions for changes. His thoughts were turned in the direction of helping dealers to increase their income.

The company had more than 30,000 dealers served by 140 branches and warehouses in strategic centers. In addition, more than two hundred foreign branches and distributors spread out over the continents. It was a close-knit system, and it sold plenty of tires, but a selling job was never one to relax in. Competition saw to that.

Menace reared its head in 1926 after Sears, Roebuck and Company, having contracted with Goodyear on a cost-plus basis for special-brand tires, made these the feature of its newly opened chain of stores. Prices were lower than the cost of the same quality to Goodyear dealers. Complaints arose, not only from them but from other dealers to their respective manufacturers. Sears increased its tire volume from 700,000 (by mail) to 1,090,000 (by mail and stores) that year and was fast catching up with its chief competitor, Montgomery Ward & Company.

Firestone dealers in towns where the mail-order companies operated stores were losing business. Going out into the field, Firestone saw it for himself. His advice to dealers was to become aggressive on "Oldfield" tires, the secondary line, and advertise low prices; otherwise their volume would become so small that their expenses would ruin them. From his own point of view, large dealer-volume would aggregate a large manufacturing volume and thereby reduce production costs—"which would further put us both in a position to meet this competition."

Thus 1926 marked the beginning of a price war and of another outgrowth: the Firestone store program. The company invested with three dealers who had asked for financial help, in San Francisco, Fitchburg, and Memphis. The next year six other cities were added, including Chicago, the lair of the mail-order houses. Firestone's idea grew: that dealers must attract motorists with an all-inclusive, one-stop service if they wished to remain factors in the tire business in their communities.

Firestone opened a service station development department, with Russell Firestone in charge, to help dealers in the selection of real estate, in plans for layouts and alteration work, in construction and equipment. Branch managers were supplied with portfolios of architectural drawings and engineering suggestions. They were instructed to discuss building and leasing projects with qualified dealers.

"Will the Firestone organization step up to the picture that Mr. Firestone has in mind?" Thomas put the question to the branch managers.

There are thousands of towns where there is a good man or company that, with a little help, would put up a new service station. In most cases it should be a corner location and service gas, oil, grease, batteries, and have a complete tire repair service, all or most of it under a canopy, and in the North it would be necessary to have a part of it under enclosure. He would thereby dominate the tire business in his town.

Now you will ask what help we will give him and in return we ask what help he must have, for it will differ in many cases.*

* J.W.T. to branch managers, Dec. 30, 1927.

The size of the town, the amount of business available, the character and capability of the dealer would determine the justifiable investment. Up-to-date drive-in stations in all the principal centers. They would set the mark and raise the level for all dealers.

Lee R. Jackson, who had risen from the sales ranks to general sales manager, spurred the branch managers into action.

As Mr. Thomas explained to you, in many cases you can have the property owner develop a service station and lease it to your dealer on a ten-year lease with the option to buy. There will be some cases where we perhaps will have to take the lease ourselves and then re-lease it to our dealer; other cases where you can interest a real estate company or a building and loan association to handle, or perhaps by assisting your dealer he may secure the necessary finances through his bank . . . some rare cases where we might have to purchase the property and put up the building ourselves.

With this last arrangement, I have in mind a combination branch and service station.*

In a few branch cities, the company bought property, erected a new branch building of impressive stature, and along with it an attractive drive-in station on the corner. "We arranged for a strong, aggressive dealer to take over the new service station, and it is working out very successfully," Jackson noted.

This ushered in the M&M program—separate local corporations in which the company owned a majority interest, the dealer a minority interest, on a 51-49 basis. While the investment made by the company would give it technical or legal control, the actual power to control the enterprise rested with the individual himself, for its success was dependent upon his own vigor.

But the plan moved slowly. Some men in the sales department had been opposed to a gasoline and battery service, regarding it as a handicap; and later, when

* L.R.J. to branch managers, Feb. 11, 1928.

convinced of its merit, they became critical of branch managers who were not making headway. Then again, other tire manufacturers took the trouble to spread a rumor that Firestone meant to dispense with independent dealers, and this caused confusion.

Harvey Firestone's vision was clear, as usual; which meant that his purpose was firm.

I do not think we should defend our store program any further, as what other people think about it does not interest me at this time. But what the Firestone organization thinks about it does interest me, and I hope they will not let the attacks of our competitors on this program break down the morale of the organization to decide that we have made a mistake.

If we take hold of it, handle it in the right way, look out for the details, and put that determined spirit from Akron, we will succeed.*

Again he explained to the branches the situation that must be faced and his remedy for it.

The development of real service stations in all of our pivotal centers . . . is an absolute necessity if we are to hold our place as one of the leaders in the tire industry, for the mail-order houses and chain stores are going to take a big volume away from the small dealers, and while we will always have a business with the 30,000 dealers that we have, each one of them sending us a little, it will become less and less and our expenses will soon be too high for the volume of business that we both do, so that we cannot stay in the picture as large manufacturers. . . .

Even though you put up a good service station you will not succeed, as the tire business has changed and you must have large volume at low profits. You must make money on batteries, gasoline, oil, and grease and make a real business out of a service station.†

The dealer's volume was the important thing. Firestone admitted that he had formerly thought gasoline service might be a detriment to some dealers—

but it is not a detriment to a dealer who is after the business, for he

* H.S.F. to H.S.F. jr., Mar. 18, 1928.
† H.S.F. to branch managers, Mar. 23, 1928.

will use his gasoline to get a prominent location and get people into his place, and then he will sell them tires, batteries, and everything.*

Firestone's gift for analysis penetrated the human elements. Akron representatives would have to think harder, reason this out, in order to "get the picture" themselves, else they could not spark inspiration in the branches, whence inspiration must flow to the salesmen. When calling on a branch manager, their attitude ought to be cheerful and optimistic, and should they find a situation needing correction—"show the branch manager how to correct it and get him to feel the situation is demanding his effort if he wants to be a success."

The summer of 1928 was hectic, with the mail-order houses outshouting one another on mileage guarantees, cutting prices, and pushing second-line and third-line tires. Fire fought fire. "Sears usually led in industry price declines during the period of the contracts," the Federal Trade Commission was later to find, "and the competition thus brought into the retail market in the several states was a major factor in forcing out of business a large number of retail tire dealers by reducing their volume of sales or by curtailing profits, or both." †

Many of the surviving dealers were floundering, in a mood to make changes in their tie-ups with manufacturers. The trade press carried Firestone's offer of fran-

* H.S.F. to J.W.T., Mar. 24, 1928.

† Federal Trade Commission, Docket No. 2116 (1936); résumé in *Hearings before the Temporary National Economic Committee*, Part 5-A. The findings continue in part:

"This competition became destructive and Sears was enabled, through its discriminatory price advantages, to engross for itself abnormal profits while at the same time curtailing the profits of all its competitors.

"This competition was a major factor in curtailing the number of competitors who were independent tire dealers and a major factor in substituting for them mass distributors other than large-volume dealers.

"All this, in turn, drove out of business numerous small tire manufacturers and thus reduced the manufacture and sale of rubber tires to a smaller and smaller number of independent manufacturers and dealers."

chises affording close cooperation, fresh supplies quickly available from factory branches, and "every aid to the most modern and successful tire merchandising and sound business growth." In describing the service station development policy, the company referred to "ways and means of financing." Four grades of tires comprised the line: "Firestone Gum-Dipped," which was de luxe quality; "Oldfield," standard quality; "Courier," in the medium-price class, and "Airway," denoted as "meeting all competition in the low-price field."

In June, forty-two tire and rubber goods manufacturers formed the Rubber Institute to "overcome uneconomic merchandising trade practices and unfair discriminations between customers." In the contemporary fashion of industries, a "director general" was engaged to eradicate trade evils (Lincoln C. Andrews, former chief of prohibition enforcement). A few days later Firestone, one of the directors, protested against misleading advertising on mileage guarantees. There was no peace in the single futile year of life that the Institute existed.

On a trip to the Pacific Coast with his sons Harvey jr., Russell, and Leonard that June, Firestone spent a day in each branch city to deliver personally the message that service stations were the only salvation of the dealer. He had the local manager invite dealers to luncheon so he could meet them. Working back to the Middle West, he repeated this technique and also called on many of the stores. Where they could not build by themselves, the company's offer to build and lease to them still held good. Where the dealer needed financing, the company cautiously went into a partnership.

The merchandising of tires has not yet attracted enough business-men with sufficient capital and ability to set up tire stores with drive-in facilities. . . . We are therefore willing to go into the right places and provide capital to set up these places, providing we can get good locations and become associated with the right kind of businessmen who are ambitious and energetic enough to build up a large and profitable business. . . .

Investing our money with the retailer will work to the advantage of all Firestone dealers, as we will then understand the dealers' problems and how to handle them better than we do today. The competition of the regular dealer is becoming keener and keener, and he will need the best that can be procured in both service stations and finances if he is to succeed in a big way.*

With characteristic thoroughness, Firestone hammered away on the necessity for improving retailing and for the company to acquire closer acquaintance with it through experience.

A whispering campaign about the M&M program confused and disturbed some of the dealers. Jackson explained that the fundamental principle behind furnishing finances was to enable a competent dealer with little capital to develop a more profitable business—"and the only way it would be possible for us to be of such financial assistance, to so many dealers, is to have controlling interest."

Any dealer who is able to go in partnership with the Firestone Tire & Rubber Company is most fortunate and particularly . . . to have this company's name in their business. You also appreciate that it is not our policy to use the name "Firestone Tire Stores, Inc." in any town or city where it will interfere with any of our large established accounts. . . .

It is a fact that our large competitors have been establishing dealers on practically the same basis as our M&M program. . . . Firestone is the only large tire company that is giving the legitimate dealers 100% support.†

At one point, the promotion of the program moved too fast, some managers trying to interest too many dealers without considering the merits of the case or the

* H.S.F. to branch managers, July 17, 1928.
† L.R.J. to branch managers, Oct. 20, 1928.

reason for the offer. Firestone did not want the name "Firestone Tire Stores" to be used where it might mean the loss of a dealer's individuality. Nor did he want a dealer to adopt it on the premise that it was an open sesame to success; a man lulled by a sense of security in his backing from Akron would think he was a fixture in the place. "It is more important to get the right kind of men to run them."

> I don't know of any greater help that could be given to the dealer than to invest with him. . . . The good dealer who needs finance to enlarge or develop his business is very ready to have us go in with him, and we have more such dealers than we can handle.*

"Firestone Tire Stores, Inc." was first used in September by a dealer in Portland, Maine. At the end of 1928, there was a total of only forty M&M stores, but the philosophy was so well defined by now and the procedure so familiar, that the stage was set for broad-scale action.

On the first Monday evening in December, a radio program made its bow on the NBC network as a weekly, half-hour musical concert "sponsored by Firestone Tire Dealers." This friendly visit to the hearths of a vast audience was an excellent vehicle for nurturing goodwill toward the company, its products, and the stores that sold them. Harvey Firestone spoke on this initial broadcast, expressing the hope that "The Voice of Firestone" would be "a wholesome feature in your household" and would always have "a friendly echo in your memory."

By short-wave transmitters, the broadcast was carried to all corners of the world where the Firestone organization functioned. He sent greetings to the members listening, specifically those in Liberia. The magic of radio and the imagination of the audience transported them to faraway Liberia, as Firestone said:

* H.S.F. to branch managers, Nov. 3, 1928.

I hope that our American and native staff, as they are gathered around our radio station at one o'clock in the morning, surrounded by the African jungle, will hear every word that I say and enjoy the complete program.*

Girding for the biggest year of automobile production and for a more intensive fight with chain competition, the company further strengthened the retail front. During 1929, it invested close to $5,300,000 in real estate for store operations and $5,500,000 more in the separate corporations to run them. As a means of building for the future, this was far better than making special brands for other organizations to distribute.

The number of M&M stores was 211; the total number of stores in which the company had an interest, 337. Inevitably, wholly owned stores had come into view, in localities where no partnership arrangement was feasible, where there was no one who sensed the opportunity, and where business was being lost for want of aggressive merchandising. Some dealers, acting as if they had "just a job," failed to measure up as good businessmen. "But we don't keep them there very long," Firestone said, "because we want to put some fellow in there who wants to work—who is willing to work and give service." By the same token, capable dealers were given the opportunity to conduct several M&M stores in the same city.

Equality of treatment was preserved among all the retail outlets with respect to prices, terms, bonuses, and sales helps. Firestone always bore in mind that the independent dealer was the backbone of retail distribution, although the encroachments of Sears and Ward had already engulfed more than fifteen percent of the tire replacement business—and were spreading.

He had hoped for a larger number of one-stop stores by the end of 1929, and he still kept his sights high,

* H.S.F. on "The Voice of Firestone," Dec. 3, 1928.

planning to increase the list despite the onset of the depression—"in cooperation with our dealers, as fast as conditions warrant." Counting the benefits of the store program, he noted:

These service stores have been helpful in stabilizing retail prices and have given us more intimate knowledge of retail merchandising, which enables us to give our dealers better merchandising and selling policies.

Many are equipped for warehousing our products, thereby providing better and more economical distribution to our dealers.

Firestone gained new and capable dealers at a time when the total number fell away by the thousands.

The success of these service stores has convinced us that the car owner appreciates this service and we are sure our investment in them will prove profitable to our dealers and to the company.*

Approximately 25,000 independent dealers disappeared from the industry in 1929 and 1930, lost to all tire manufacturers. It was notable that 6,928 dealers swung over to the Firestone banner in 1930. That year the company's store program swelled to 238 M&M and 192 wholly owned stores.

The wisdom of Harvey Firestone's planning for strength was manifest after the first instalment of a long depression.

* H.S.F., *Annual Report,* 1928.

13

Selling in a Depression

IN the struggle to obtain a large volume of business through dealers, instead of resorting to mass distributors as three of the top four tire makers had done, Firestone faced a worsening condition. The competition forced attention and effort on low-price lines. The weakened buying power of the public aggravated each change. It was a simple matter of arithmetic: a small figure multiplied by another small figure.

"When you think of the opportunities to sell and service our products in these service stores—." Harvey Firestone was like an athletic coach whipping up enthusiasm in his men. "They are so great that we don't comprehend them. They are so big that we go around in a haze as to just how we are going to cash in on them."

All pioneering had something of this bedazzling element, he pointed out. The bigger the prospects, the more difficulties in getting started. He chided the reluctant ones, saying they were afraid they would have to work harder.

The first half of 1930, over-all operations were far from successful. But Firestone had no pessimism, either to express or to hide. He knew the break in the dark sky was bound to come, and he proceeded to infuse his abundant energy into the organization, envisaging more business at their doorsteps.

We have the opportunity of having the greatest battery sales and distribution of anyone in this country—the same is true of brake lining.

I suppose it is going to be a hard climb. It is going to be like starting the rim business. I could not get anyone to take hold of it, could not get anyone interested, no one would stick. Why?

Well, they didn't know much about it, they didn't want to know much about it. The tire business was such an important thing that they just naturally drifted back. But I thought it was a good thing, and my stick-to-it-iveness and determination would not let go. And we kept on.

Today we have ninety-eight percent of all the truck rim business and we do a big percentage of the passenger car business, and that was a hard struggle. The rim division makes more money than you fellows. We have to go to the rim division to pay expenses in the tire business. *

If they pushed batteries and brake lining, they would reduce the expense of distributing tires, and similarly the dealers would lower their overhead. By taking on additional lines and services, a tire dealer could keep occupied through the year, increase his merchandise turnover, and put his property to full use.

Men, the stores have been a wonderful thing for Firestone, a wonderful proposition. If we closed down every store we have, they have already done our organization good. They have taught us to sit down and concentrate on how to run a business.†

As the months wore on, the tire industry suffered from overproduction despite factory layoffs. Summer came; still the warehouses were piled high. Suddenly in August rubber slumped to ten cents a pound (in September to eight cents) and cotton tumbled too. The cost-plus arrangement under which Sears paid for tires took a cue from these drastic drops. Severe price cutting set the flare to another price war. Not that many more tires were sold!

* H.S.F., at sales conference, Akron, June 20, 1930.
† *Ibid.*

To bolster the dealer, Firestone increased discounts. To slacken the pace of production, factory workers were put on a shorter work week; accumulated stocks were given a chance to move. Salaries were reduced ten percent and more sharply in the case of the officers. With the approach of winter came a real problem of providing employment, so the work was spread by running the factories in two five-hour shifts five days a week.

Altogether it was a bad year. Unit sales of replacement tires declined nearly twenty percent, original equipment tires more than twenty-five percent. On $120,000,000 volume, the profit, after writing down inventory value to market price and absorbing the expense of organizing stores, was merely $1,541,000.

The stores had done a total of $37,000,000 business in 1930, but lost money. Firestone intended to set up "very few this coming year" but rather get the existing ones on a better footing through emphasis on their individual management. The encouraging truth was that they had shown a slight profit in the last quarter.

The rubber tire industry is outstanding in the progress it has made in improved and economical manufacturing. . . . The great problem today of every manufacturer is to merchandise and distribute his products more economically. *

There was no question but that the consumer was benefiting by technological advances and receiving every inducement to buy. The machinery developed at Firestone was making tires better and more uniformly and cutting down waste. One man built ten tires in the time it had taken him to build a single tire back in the days of hand operation. The motorist was getting ten times the value for his dollar. Balloons now provided fifteen miles for a cent.

Gone were thoughts of factory expansion, except that

* H.S.F., *Annual Report,* 1930.

in order to maintain the Argentine trade profitably a factory was built this year in Buenos Aires. Top-level thinking concentrated on cutting the cost of the distribution system. Nevertheless a large advertising expenditure was made in national magazines, newspapers, direct mail, farm papers, and radio. The name "Firestone" must further establish itself in public preference through confidence in quality and value, thus making Firestone products easier to sell.

Apart from meeting a new mail-order price slash at the beginning of 1931, Firestone countered the impression given out that the public could buy special brands more cheaply (by catalog, chain store, and oil company gas stations) than they could buy standard brands from dealers. The company supplied dealers with cross sections of special-brand tires and Firestone tires and then advertised "Six Ways to Compare Tire Values," urging the car owner to visit the dealer and examine the exhibits.

"There has been such a mystery and misrepresentation about tires that the people are entitled to know what they are getting for their money," Firestone said. Pressure was put on newspaper and magazine publishers and bankers to keep Firestone from continuing this type of comparative advertising. He retorted that the mail-order houses had been advertising comparisons without giving the customer an opportunity to verify their claims.

Our coming out and backing the tire dealers on a standard brand tire has given them new life and they now realize that they are not licked, and they are going to work. If we can get this story across right to the public and keep our dealers lined up and going out to fight for the business, we will change the picture and have a very large business.

Our advertising has certainly been effective or it would not have stirred up so much criticism and opposition from our competitors and the mail-order houses. In fact, the "Six Ways to Compare Tire

Values" ad that we ran in the magazines brought us more direct results . . . than all of the magazine advertising that we have ever done.*

Firestone gained 8,613 new dealers during 1931, although the national total continued to decline. The disappearance of outlets contributed to the diminution in number of tire manufacturers participating in the halved volume. There had been six large and eighty-eight smaller makers in 1926, doing $841,000,000. Now the same six and twenty-five smaller ones remained, with $437,000,000 as the aggregate for 1931.† Competitive lines were hard to finance.

Firestone's dealers were deeply conscious of the support they received. Also, they shared with the company the honors that accrued year after year as Indianapolis Sweepstakes winners broke speed records on Firestone tires, and the fame of the founder and the presentation of a medal to him (1930) by the Race Drivers Association, inscribed:

> In appreciation of his untiring cooperation and leadership in the consistent development of tires which have contributed to the establishment of automobile safety and endurance records.

The Monday evening radio program brought the dealer to the attention of millions of listeners. In September, 1931, there began a series of brief weekly talks on "The Romance and Drama of the Rubber Industry" by Harvey S. Firestone jr., vice president of the company, whose voice created closer intimacy with the public.

The number of one-stop stations showing a profit for the year was gratifying. Fifty M&M stores were discontinued, forty-two wholly owned ones added. The total was due to become smaller for several years, while

---

* H.S.F. to Bruce Barton, Apr. 11, 1931.

† Flashback to 1910: six large and forty smaller manufacturers, $75,000,000 total; to 1920: these six and 141 smaller ones, $496,000,000 total.

the survivors proved their mettle and formed a healthy nucleus for future expansion.

Financially, the company wound up its year exceptionally well. On sales of $113,797,000, it earned a net of $6,028,000, a performance which Harvey Firestone credited not altogether to careful management but also to the loyalty and sacrifice, the enthusiasm and energy, of the personnel. The factory had been operating only six hours a day because of low production requirements, with the work rotated to give employment to as many as possible. The dividend paid ($1.45 in 1930 after the stock split) was $1. As an incentive to stockholding employees, the board adjusted their stock contracts to a price of $20 a share and set up a large reserve on this account.

The debased values of the securities market prompted the company, in its good liquid position, to acquire for the treasury a substantial block of its own outstanding preferred shares at a discount of almost $2,000,000 below par. This practice was followed for several subsequent years for a saving of large sums annually in meeting retirement payments on the preferred.

In the nationally disastrous year 1932—banks had runs, banks loaded with depreciated securities and mortgages failed—crude rubber sank to two and five-eighths cents a pound, cotton to five cents. (The company bought large quantities of both before the next rise, to provide amply for the year to come.) The lowered tire prices and the constant price-cutting competition, along with overproduction and fewer automobiles in use, conspired against a large dollar volume.

Volume shrank to $84,337,000. This reflected an unchanged number of replacement units (forced, however, into cheaper lines) and decidedly less original equipment and export business. And yet, by efficiency in manufacturing and curtailment of expense, the profit was as high as $5,151,000 in contrast to a combined loss of $17,800,000 suffered by the three largest competitors.

Harvey Firestone had stepped up from the presidency to the post of chairman, at a board meeting on January 12, 1932, and on his recommendation John W. Thomas was elected president. Russell A. Firestone was now a member of the board, serving alongside his brother Harvey jr.

One by one the chairman's sons were to climb into executive positions upon gaining experience in selling. Leonard K. Firestone managed the Firestone Service Stores in West Palm Beach, Florida, for seven months and then went into general sales department work under Lee R. Jackson (vice president in charge of sales); and after a tour of the trade on the Pacific Coast and in the Northwest with his brother Raymond, he became vice president of the California company in 1933, taking over direction of the service stores department in Los Angeles. Their youngest brother, Roger, was at college.

"Our house is in good order," the head of the house wrote at the end of 1932. Rubber had already risen seventy percent and cotton also was much higher. "With $13,000,000 in cash and no bank indebtedness, we enter the new year with every confidence."

On the mechanical side, men who otherwise would have been unemployed were given tasks of improving the plants and equipment. A new tire-building machine of the compensator type delivered to the operator all the material he needed, eliminating time lost in applying it to the drum. A newly developed stitcher, set in motion by push button, effected a forty percent increase in productivity.

On the products front, research and development workers perfected a waterproof brake lining, and a new department was organized to manufacture it. Another new department made spark plugs. Further improvements were worked out in tires, batteries, antifreeze, and other auto accessories for production by Firestone and marketing through the dealers and service stations. More products, more income. And the Firestone Air Balloon led the field.

Service store efficiency was intensified by conducting a two-week brake course in Akron for station personnel and by operating one of the stores as a school for managers and their assistants.

The most spectacular evolution came with farm tractor tires. They opened an entirely new market for Firestone in a period when economy was the best talking point anyone could have. Using the balloon principle of low pressure and wide contact area, the development department had previously worked out an airplane tire to facilitate take-offs and cushion the landing shock for the new heavy transport planes. This type of tire was applied to an industrial tractor at twenty pounds air pressure in the fall of 1931, to shift railroad freight on tracks at industrial plants. They did the work better than a switching engine.

The next spring, with a low-chevron tread design, the tires were placed on farm tractors for experiment. Harvey Firestone himself tested them on the homestead farm in Columbiana that summer, taking the wheel and observing effects. As a result, the first practical pneumatic tractor tire was offered for power equipment on the farms of America.

About a million farm tractors were in use in 1932— on steel wheels. The pounding and vibration left the man in the driver's seat worn out at the end of a day's work. The mechanism was jarred out of place, the fuel consumption was high. When farmers saw a tractor shod with Firestone tires perform in a plowing contest, their enthusiasm showed frankly. There was no slipping against a furrow bank. The tires, inflated twelve to fifteen pounds, had been constructed with consideration of over-all diameter, clearance, width of furrow, ground contact, and freedom from sidesway.

A consideration of soil conditions led to spacing the chevrons of the tread wider, and as time went on the design was recut to a deep chevron for greater traction. With each stage, the usefulness of tractor tires grew. Ultimately the Ground Grip tread was created and captured the farm—a story in itself.

In further quest of markets, Firestone Steel Products began in 1933 the manufacture of stainless-steel barrels for use as beverage containers, forecasting a remarkable expansion of this division. The year saw also the enlargement of the export market and a new foreign factory—in Bilbao, Spain, where Firestone-Hispania was formed under an arrangement with five Spanish banks.

Sound beginnings, diligent adjustment to conditions, but a meager year's total of $75,402,000 withal. Labor costs were up, in tune with the spirit of the National Industrial Recovery Act; rubber and cotton were higher; but tires sold for less than ever. Manufacturers' excise taxes cost the company more than $4,000,000. They could not be added to the price because Sears and Ward dominated the trade with their large tax-free supplies. After deducting $5,625,000 for depreciation and providing for Federal taxes and all other charges, the company had a net in 1933 of $2,397,000. The dividends declined to fifty-five cents.

One source of gratification was the certified soundness of the Firestone Bank. President Franklin D. Roosevelt had ordered all banks closed immediately after taking office. This was the first institution in Akron to receive a permit to resume banking on an unrestricted basis, thus freeing more than 16,000 savings and commercial accounts.

When the Chicago world's fair planned its Hall of Science, Firestone was selected to represent the rubber industry (1933 and 1934). And in the Firestone exhibition building millions of people witnessed the making of tires by automatic machinery, including the new marvel of vulcanization, the "watchcase" mold with its hinged top and thermostat control. A Century of Progress, the fair was aptly called. Progress—but the chaotic, cutthroat condition of the tire industry was unworthy of the word.

Six years of retrogression was a better description. Harvey Firestone bluntly blamed the discriminatory buying practices of the mass distributors. Investigate them, he kept urging.

"We aren't going to let these fellows ruin the industry if I can help it," he declared on a tour of the field with his son Russell. A meeting of industry and N.R.A. representatives was scheduled to take place in New York in June, 1933, as a first step in setting up a code under the law. He would attend. He had proposals to make for stabilizing conditions of competition, as the statute provided.

President Roosevelt had obtained from Congress power to engineer recovery, far greater power than any previous President had ever wielded. Firestone hoped Roosevelt would not attempt to use it to the hilt in controlling industry—"because you can't legislate prosperity."

Firestone sat down with his former fellow-members of the Rubber Association of America (now named the Rubber Manufacturers Association) and each concurred in the N.R.A. philosophy of price control. They were in accord on predicating cost recovery upon current replacement costs, because of the errant fluctuations in rubber. They were not in accord on the idea of allocating production by quotas.

Allocation was impractical and uneconomic, Firestone asserted as spokesman for a dissident group of tire manufacturers. It would destroy initiative and incentive for good management and good service, "which together form the keystone of every business organization." Allocation would in fact prompt manufacturers to cheapen the construction of their tires and thereby endanger the motoring public. Any manufacturer who continued improvement, though bound by a quota, "would be penalized twice—the expense of developing and building a better tire and the penalty for additional sales on a better tire if he exceeds his allocation." *

It would reduce employment in the selling, distributing, and servicing of tires because, in brief, the plan would destroy competition.

Moreover, Firestone continued, no equitable basis could be found for fixing quotas, for there was no base period that was not more favorable to one manufacturer than to another; that is, a period when volume had been built up by cut prices, or when there were uneven proportions of supply to the various classes of trade, or a difference obtained in the relation of grades and sizes to total sales volume. Allocation in units would benefit one maker, and in pounds would benefit another.

"Original equipment business presents an insurmountable obstacle to allocation," Firestone wrote to the other manufacturers and to Newton D. Baker, industry counsel. "The effect would be a more destructive price battle for this business if this field is left entirely open or, if included, the manufacturers would be penalized in their renewal business." †

* H.S.F. to Newton D. Baker, July 21, 1933.
† *Ibid.*

Why was so much effort put into formulating such a plan, Firestone asked, and so little interest shown in the causes of the industry's enormous losses?

No plan or code can successfully take the tire industry out of its present difficulties until the manufacturers are willing to be more frank and willing to correct some of the evils of the industry.

The two great evils are: First, secret prices and rebates, causing discriminatory prices and price cutting. Second, misleading and unfair advertising and unsound guarantees.

These two difficulties could very easily be eliminated if every member would follow my suggestion—lay their prices and practices before a disinterested board that they might study the situation and discuss it with the industry.[*]

At a later meeting, although every manufacturer advocated a price rise to take care of increased costs, they realized that this could not be done until the larger special-brand distributors assented to raising their own prices.

Firestone favored the registration of each manufacturer's list prices for all lines—open price filing—and maximum discounts for all classes of trade and for resale.

We earnestly recommend this program as a basis on which a code can be built that will bring greater stability into the tire industry. We are sure this stability can be attained if the industry will recognize that the one great cause of our cut prices and lack of profits in the past few years is the manufacture in large volume and sale of special-brand tires.

These special-brand distributors buy their tires at a price that enables them to undersell the independent tire dealers, and the manufacturers who do not furnish special-brand tires have found it necessary to keep their dealers in a position to meet the prices of the special-brand tires or be eliminated from the business.[†]

For example, Firestone marketed a tire of first quality under the name of "Century of Progress" and priced it to compete with the mail-order-house stores.

[*] H.S.F. to Newton D. Baker, July 25, 1933.
[†] H.S.F. to Newton D. Baker, July 21, 1933.

"It would be unfortunate to have the industry divided in presenting a code to the N.R.A.," Firestone wrote Baker. "Every effort should be made along every line to avoid this, but the plan must be fundamentally sound."*

The industry submitted its proposed code at the end of July, embodying allocation and cost recovery. The N.R.A. sent it back. A second submittal provided for resale price maintenance, but the Administration was opposed to a single code for manufacturing and retailing, so this was ruled out, along with allocation. A provision to fix price differentials on the several lines and to liquidate contracts below the maximum discount levels had been deleted. Cost control was retained, in principle.

"We have been unable to accomplish anything," Firestone announced. "The industry is becoming firmly divided between two groups—one group for the protection of the special-brand distributors, and the other group for the protection of the independent dealers."†

To his son Leonard he wrote: "If we cannot get some code that controls these special-brand tires we are in for a pretty hard ride."‡

On the Administration's proposal of open price filing, for the disclosure of each maker's prices, discounts, terms, and conditions of sale to all classes of customers, two hectic meetings were held in Washington—the upshot being that the Code Authority would make recommendations to the Administrator for establishing such a system.

And so, after much travail, including a final all-day session in December during which Administrator Hugh S. Johnson stalked in frequently—"Gentlemen, have you reached an agreement? . . . We'll eat after an agreement has been reached. . . . Gentlemen, we're going to draft this code today, and we won't leave here until we do"—

* July 25, 1933.
† H.S.F. to National Recovery Administration, Nov. 27, 1933.
‡ H.S.F. to Leonard K. Firestone, Nov. 23, 1933.

the Rubber Tire Manufacturing Industry Code was completed and the President approved it. Approved, with the problem of market stabilization left virtually untouched.

In similar wrangling over a retail tire code, proposals for cost recovery, price filing, trade-in allowances, and price differentials were fought by mail-order houses and automotive chain stores. Even as the negotiations were prolonged, warfare overshadowed them. Sears, for example, offered in January, 1934, an enormous allowance on used tires, and the N.R.A. summoned an industry-wide conference for an agreement to stop this destructive practice. But the pledge covered this one point. Immediately the mail-order people advertised new price cuts. Manufacturers helped dealers to meet them. Slash following slash, tires were retailing below makers' costs.

Again the Administration took a hand. Trade leaders were called to Washington to sign a forty-day truce starting one minute after midnight, April 3. By it, floor levels were set for the several tire lines. No differentials applied as between various makes or between dealer and mail-chain distribution. The truce began to break down. The code was rushed to completion. The President approved it in May, after two weeks of open violation.

The Retail Rubber Tire and Battery Trade Code defined destructive price cutting, declared it an unfair method of competition, and forbade it. The code also empowered the Administrator to determine the existence of an emergency—and exercised it at once. On the date the code went into effect, an emergency order classified the tires by brands and set a minimum price on each grade and size without differentials for types of sellers.

An abortive attempt to prohibit time guarantees brought on even wider use of them. But worse, mail-order houses advertised sales. Retaliation was its usual swift self. The general price level sank to the pre-truce state.

In the storm of complaint and demand over lack of enforcement, a new order in August increased the floor levels of the five largest manufacturers' tires considerably over the smaller manufacturers' and left unchanged the lines sold by Sears and Ward stores. The order also decreased mail-order catalog tires to the prices these houses had adopted in violation of previous orders.

The order did not place the Century of Progress tire in the price group of Sears and Ward store tires, and since Firestone had no special brand, he felt entitled to a competitive price instead of being obliged to sell the Century at eleven percent higher. The denial of his request for a stay of the order was not made until a month after the effective date. Meanwhile, the larger competitors had fought this tire with their first-line standard brands.

The emergency provisions expired October 1 and were not renewed. The retail business was down in its seasonal valley, slumbering till another price war should rouse it. Nor had manufacturers' code compliance accomplished much. While a cost formula was being studied, the N.R.A. adopted a policy opposed to minimum price fixing (except in emergencies) and obligatory uniform cost finding. N.R.A. rejected the principle of current replacement cost, and the industry lost heart.

All this price cutting during 1934 had made it a difficult year for Firestone's tire division to be profitable, despite the use of rubber and cotton at costs far below the market. But the company had diversified its activities. On sales of $99,130,000 a profit of $4,154,000 was earned, ten percent of which came from Xylos' doubled output of reclaimed rubber for the industry.

Firestone proudly turned to the one-stop stores in his

annual report. They now numbered 101 M&M and 322 wholly owned, the latter becoming integrated with the parent sales company and adopting the trade name of Firestone Service Stores, which soon after was changed to Firestone Auto Supply & Service Stores.

"We have been able to train and build up an ambitious and efficient organization to manage these stores," Firestone said, "which this year—for the first time— showed a profit."

14

Self-helps to Recovery

LIBERIA, one of the sinews of future strength, whereby Harvey Firestone had determined to produce rubber more cheaply than anywhere else on the face of the earth, was back in action at the end of 1934.

The plantations had lain dormant during the dismal years of low automobile production, low tire-replacement sales, and a choking world supply of crude rubber. The price of rubber languished below the cash outlay needed to tap and ship. On the 38,500 planted acres, the older trees had not been thinned, a fungus growth caused root rot, and shipshape orderliness of the groves became engulfed in bush. Nature was not idle, though man lacked incentive.

Besides the blocks carved out along the Du River, the Plantations Company had selected 20,000 acres in another area of heavy rainfall. This was about 200 miles down the coast, at the southern tip of Liberia and near the Cavalla River. Only a small portion of it was planted. The maintenance budget could not take care of this either.

Was it courage or prudence? When every penny counted and only a dozen men remained, since orders had come from Akron to stop shipping. Firestone again gave science rein. Additional clonal budding material was bought in Java in 1932-33 and shipped to Liberia to produce more high-yielding trees. Another plant-breeding program thus defied the depression.

In the autumn of the following year, the price of rubber having sharply advanced, a large force of native labor was recalled to undertake the heavy work of reclaiming the heveas from the new jungle. A preparation factory and warehouses were built. On 6,000 acres the first tapping was begun. And the large nurseries provided budded stock for new planting.

Once more the sound of the morning gong signaled the tappers to start among the trees, each to his assigned number, and make a quick, deft incision in the bark in a downward half-spiral and peel off a narrow strip. The pierced latex cells between the bark and the cambium commenced to ooze. A porcelain cup attached to the trunk at the base of the cut caught the drippings. Next morning the tapper would shave another strip, from the lower edge of the initial cut, and now he must hasten to complete today's round before the strong sun checked the flow.

In three hours, he would return to the first tree, empty the cup into a stainless-steel bucket, gather up the rest of the collection, then hurry to the preparation factory. The pails of latex were poured into a tank. Diluted acid aided the natural process of coagulation and separated the rubber (approximately thirty percent) from other elements in the "milk." Slices of this coagulum were wrung through steel sheeting rolls. The sheets were hung up to dry in heated rooms. Here was rubber for industry.

The harvest in 1935 came from 10,000 acres: approximately 773 tons (198 in 1934). Trees on 45,000 additional acres were approaching maturity, more than three-fourths being budded stock. A centrifuge was installed at Mount Barclay to produce concentrated latex (more than sixty percent rubber) from the precious fluid and preserve it in liquid form for special industrial uses. A chemical research division was organized.

On the other side of the world, in the Far East, a new restriction agreement was holding down the supplies of rubber. Dutch planting interests, as alarmed over possible disaster as the British had been on the eve of the Stevenson scheme, had lent a more attentive ear this time. The upshot was the signing of the International Rubber Regulation Agreement (1934) by plenipotentiaries of the Netherlands East Indies, the Federated Malay States, the Unfederated Malay States, Ceylon, India, Burma, Straits Settlements, French Indo-China, Siam, the State of North Borneo, Brunei, and Sarawak. They controlled more than ninety-five percent of the world's production.

"This fact," said Harvey Firestone, "again confirms the wisdom of our having undertaken to establish an independent source of supply."

The parties to the agreement hoped to beget price stability. They were not daunted by the Stevenson fiasco, nor by the history of Brazil's interference with supply and demand in the period around 1910. Instead of turning on a price pivot, the regulation provided for a committee to set quarterly changes in export quotas for each rubber-producing territory, "with the object of reducing existing world stocks to a normal figure." Supply would be adjusted "in an orderly manner," thereby to maintain "a fair and equitable price . . . reasonably remunerative to efficient producers."

At the time the I.R.R.A. went into effect, there was enough rubber in the United States to answer more than eight months' needs. The year wound up with nine months' supply on hand, and the I.R.R.A. release at seventy percent. After this came a steady reduction of world stocks as the committee exercised firmer control, even though tire shipments were rising. Result, a boost in price. Rubber cost sixteen cents as 1936 closed with only four and a half months' supply in the country. Two advances in tire prices early in 1937 followed the upward trend.

One year the release went as high as ninety percent, another as low as forty-five, and in those dips and turns the price of rubber fluctuated widely. Motor-vehicle registration reached an all-time high in 1936 and 1937, and vehicle production topped the near-peak of 1928. Rubber was on its way to twenty-five cents. But supplies were dwindling to their lowest level in a decade.

In Liberia, the harvest was greater than ever: 1,030 tons shipped in 1936, and the yield of 16,000 acres of mature trees expected in 1937. At this point, there were 64,000 planted acres.

Against such a background of rubber in the raw, the business of tire making and tire selling proceeded. Great progress in design, development, and manufacture, Harvey Firestone noted, "but the industry has not made equal progress in economical methods for merchandising and distributing its products." A hazard guarantee, imposed on the industry by special-brand distributors. A reckless increase in trade-in allowance. He cited these "unsound merchandising policies."

The era of price cutting, having another fling in 1935, flung itself hard that spring and summer. It was such a spectacle of financial dissipation that sober bankers with rubber industry interests called a halt. They persuaded the leading manufacturers to stabilize their prices to dealers.

In that year, Firestone added 109 stores and further ensured a solid volume and lowered selling and distributing expense. Store profits increased with better trained personnel and a fuller line of auto supplies. The company, by selling its tires direct to dealers and stores, kept control of its product in a way impossible for manufacturers at the mercy of mass distributors. Warehouses served as wholesale channels, affording the dealer prompter deliveries, complete inventories, and greater turnover; and affording the car owner better service.

Export business was improving. South Africa had been an excellent export market; now a high tariff went up, and now Firestone built a factory in Port Elizabeth on a site selected by Harvey Firestone jr. Arrangements were made for the manufacture of Firestone products in Pratteln, Switzerland. In England and Argentina, the Firestone factories were enlarged.

Research scientists and engineers, working in large laboratories and engineering departments, contributed new products, and this diversification was credited with bringing a healthy sales increase in 1935, the year of the lowest point in units of replacement tires. More than 500 mechanical rubber goods items were added to the line. The division that developed them found new uses for rubber in auto insulation; it produced also an air spring (after two years' work), designed to replace steel springs with rubber bellows.

This was the year of the introduction of the new Ground Grip tractor tires and the realization of Harvey Firestone's farseeing, far-reaching plan to put the farm on rubber. The National Industrial Recovery Act, on which many had pinned their faith, was invalidated by the Supreme Court. This prop gone—it had, in truth, given a fillip of confidence to business and, with other legislation, had temporarily bolstered buying power— individual resourcefulness stood out as the means of recovery. The Firestone sales total of $121,670,000 yielded, after $6,500,000 for depreciation and $8,770,000 for taxes, a net profit of $5,649,000.

The company would have had to pay royalty on every

tire it had made, and many millions in back royalties, if Firestone had not chosen to resist the United States Rubber Company. The latter claimed to control the drum (flat-band) process of building casings by virtue of its Hopkinson patent of 1921.

Assembling the component parts of a casing in tire form on a core had been universally superseded by assembly on a drum into a flat endless band—a broad hoop, which was shaped into a tire by hydraulic pressure and by expansion from within. Although the Hopkinson apparatus never came into commercial use, and other inventors had employed drum-winding and pulley bands, virtually all tire manufacturers paid tribute to the validity of the U.S. Rubber patent by accepting licenses and paying from two to four cents a tire, according to size. But not Firestone. He was a close student of rubber industry patents. Drum building was ancient history. And as for the machines he used, they had been designed and constructed in his own shops.

U.S. Rubber brought suit, filing 293 claims on the basic Hopkinson process and six related patents. Firestone denied infringement and raised a defense of "anticipation by prior disclosures and practice."

Collection of evidence to prove prior use took two years of persistence, luck, travel, and painstaking on the part of investigators. Someone recalled that a man named Doughty, no longer living, had built bicycle tires by the flat-band method in the 1890s in Providence, Rhode Island. Two old-timers were found who had worked for Doughty then and there; a photograph survived of the cylindrical metal form that he used at the time to build up bands and of his expansion mechanism; also old notebooks and letters referring to the process.

Doughty, it was learned, did not succeed in business and went to England to set up a similar plant. Men were found in England who were his former associates; the story was further unfolded. Doughty again failed to make headway but at last won the interest of a bicycle company, which joined with others in forming the Dunlop Company and used the Doughty process in England and this country as the foundation for the popularity of Dunlop bicycle tires. Now Doughty returned, went to the Dunlop Company in Canada, and they too adopted his method.

With all this testimony and supporting exhibits, the Firestone attorneys entered the District Court in Cleveland. But the court held the Hopkinson patent valid and upheld many of the plaintiff's other contentions. Firestone was ordered to account to U.S. Rubber for profits and damages. Firestone appealed.

Most of the licensees suspended payment to the U.S. pending the outcome of the litigation. If Firestone won the appeal, the entire industry would benefit. He won. This was, he said, "the biggest patent fight of my life," and it cost close to $250,000.

Yes, the Circuit Court of Appeals observed in its unanimous opinion (October, 1935), the Hopkinson process seemed, at first glance, a highly significant advance in the art of tire building—"but what is the precise advance made by the inventor?"

Hopkinson was not the first to wind fabrics flatly upon a drum instead of a core in the manufacture of casings for pneumatic tires. Doughty, in the building of bicycle tires for the Dunlop Company in 1898, undoubtedly wound his casing fabric on a flat drum . . . practiced the method of drum winding and shaping which is relied upon by the defendant as an anticipation for a number of years in the United States.

But the Doughty priority, the court continued, was challenged by the plaintiff on the ground that "bicycle tires are not automobile tires." To this the three appeals judges replied that the automobile tire was the lineal descendant of the bicycle tire, even as the plaintiff company evolved from the bicycle industry. If Hopkinson did no more than apply the process practiced by Doughty, there was no invention in the method, "for the mere adoption of a known process to a clearly analogous use is not invention."

On the other hand, Hopkinson had recognized the value of cords, whereas Doughty had built with square-woven fabric.

That which clearly turned the scales in favor of validity in the court below . . . as constituting Hopkinson's inventive concept, is that cord fabric is of greater extensibility than square mesh fabric. . . . But cord fabric was not the discovery of Hopkinson, nor was he the first to recognize that the extension of such fabric when cut on the bias results in a rearrangement of the cords rather than in their stretching to the point of weakening. . . .

[Hopkinson] did not originate flat-drum winding of bias fabric . . . if he was the first to make use of cord fabric in the assembly of a pulley band this was not an inventive step but merely the substitution of one well-known material for another in an identical or clearly analogous use. *

The court held three claims of the Hopkinson patent not infringed and four claims invalid; the District Court decree was set aside and Firestone was allowed costs. The apparatus claims of another patent (for shaping by atmospheric pressure inside and a vacuum outside) were sustained and relief was granted. Firestone had used such a shaping process for a year and a half but abandoned it after the suit started for a machine of the company's own devising. The U.S. Rubber Company claim was settled for $52,000; later this company took out a license on the Firestone shaping machine.

Back to the business of selling, a more wholesome

* *Firestone Tire & Rubber Co.* v. *United States Rubber Co.*, 79 Federal Reporter (2d) 948 (1935). Rehearing denied, Dec. 9, 1935. Review denied by Supreme Court, May 25, 1936.

atmosphere than the tire industry had breathed in many a year now prevailed, and 1936 brought freedom from destructive price wars. In March, the Federal Trade Commission finally issued an order in the Goodyear-Sears case; in June, the Commission held a trade practice conference in Chicago embracing all segments of the tire industry (mail-order houses included) and resulting in the promulgation of rules to foster fair competitive conditions; a little later in June, the Robinson-Patman Act was passed by Congress, further restricting price discrimination.

The Commission ordered Goodyear to discontinue the discriminatory contract with Sears. It found that

. . . such discrimination in prices constituted a violation of section 2 of the Clayton Act, and was not given to Sears on account of differences in quantity of the commodity sold nor to make only due allowance for differences in the cost of selling or transportation. It found that the net price discrimination, after making due allowances for selling and transportation costs, ranged from 11 to 22 percent on 8 popular sizes of tires.

The Commission also found that such discriminatory prices were not made to Sears in good faith to meet competition. . . . The respondent concealed the prices and terms at which it was selling its tires to Sears from its own sales organization and from the trade generally, and never offered to its own dealers like prices on tires of equal or comparable quality.

These exclusive advantages enabled Sears, the Commission added, systematically to undersell Goodyear retail dealers and other competing dealers by twenty to twenty-five percent, and at the same time make a profit of thirty-five to forty percent.

The practice here involved of a large manufacturer giving disproportionately large discounts was held by the Commission to be unjustified, and that such a discrimination, when made merely on account of size, tended toward monopoly and the suppression of competition.

In order to maintain the principle of equality to purchasers intended by section 2 of the Clayton Act, it was necessary that the difference in price be reasonably related to a difference in cost and not a covert means of favoritism.*

At first Goodyear failed to comply with the order. Then the Robinson-Patman amendment to the Clayton Act dispelled any doubt as to the outlawing of this type of differential. Thereupon, Goodyear announced in July that the Sears contract, which would have run six years more, had been terminated by mutual release.

The stability of tire prices prevailing in 1936 was basic to the company's growth. Sales of $135,700,000, a gain of fourteen percent, brought a net profit of $9,100,000, a sixty percent increase. Current assets totaled $75,000,-000, net working capital nearly $52,000,000. Another noteworthy item on the financial side was that the company had reacquired, since 1929, about a fourth of the preferred stock originally issued.

Heavy advertising had been done during 1936. In addition to the large sum paid for the top-grade radio network program, extensive use of newspapers in eighty-two cities amounted to 1,500,000 lines, the equivalent of more than 600 full pages.

The theme song of the radio program, *Memory Lane*, was changed. A composition especially written for "The Voice of Firestone" made its debut that year—*In My Garden*, by Idabelle Firestone, the wife of Harvey Firestone. Her sons were contributing to the company's success; here was her own direct contribution.

This wistful song soon became one of the most distinguished opening signatures on the air, and it was retained until 1941. A dispute then arose between the American Society of Composers, Authors, and Publishers and the broadcasting stations, and before it could be

---

* Federal Trade Commission, Docket No. 2116 (1936); résumé in *Hearings before the Temporary National Economic Committee*, Part 5-A.

The Firestone Homestead Farm near Columbiana, Ohio. In this house, built by his forebears in 1828, Harvey S. Firestone was born on December 20, 1868.

(*Below*) 1893, Grosse Pointe Race Track in Detroit, Michigan: Harvey S. Firestone, salesman for the Columbus Buggy Company, drives a vehicle reputed to be the first in the area equipped with pneumatic rubber tires.

1902, the first factory of The Firestone Tire & Rubber Company: a former foundry at Miller and Sweitzer Avenues, Akron, Ohio. (*Below*) The entire factory force in July, 1903: twenty-seven, including the boy.

Studies in contrast. Harvey S. Firestone demonstrates progress in tire construction, comparing a 1908 high-pressure pneumatic tire with a truck tire of the 1930s. The former shows the raised letters FIRESTONE NON-SKID molded in the tread. (*Below*) Worker operates machine for springing the Firestone Sidewire Tire of solid rubber on a carriage wheel (1900).

Lieutenant Colonel Dwight D. Eisenhower (*right*), second in command of the Army's first transcontinental motor-truck convoy, stops for chicken dinner on the lawn at the Firestone Homestead Farm near Columbiana, Ohio, July 13, 1919. At his right is Harvey S. Firestone, Jr.

(*Below*) Factory management group in 1910, including some of the original employees. John W. Thomas, engaged as chemist in 1908, is fourth from left in the front row.

Half the truck tonnage
of America is carried on

Firestone
Tires

"Ship by Truck"

—the traffic motto of today and the future

By Harvey S. Firestone
President, Firestone Tire & Rubber Co.

THE necessities of war brought home to us the importance of the motor truck. When the French line stood at the Marne, the truck began to receive the recognition it deserved.

War, in that emergency, taught us over-night an industrial lesson that we would otherwise have taken years to learn. People realized, all at once, that the motor truck was essential and vital in our transportation, and therefore a basic part of our living.

Like good roads, motor trucking should interest every man, woman or child. Both are basic elements in lowering the cost of distribution, saving products now wasted, opening up resources heretofore untapped.

The truck is ready and able to shoulder burdens the railroads cannot carry and to leave them free for responsibilities too long deferred and delayed.

It is a time for principals to confer—a time for them to co-operate. The traffic situation is one of greatest significance. Our future industrial growth depends largely upon the assistance rendered the railroads by trucks in speeding up freight movement. Communities which are not served by the railroads find in the truck the means for their rapid development.

"Ship by truck."

Let us make this the slogan of a new business era.

Truck lines already stream out from city to city, from distributing centers to the surrounding towns, hamlets and rural districts. Use the truck arteries. You'll serve yourself and the public. You'll relieve the railroads of a part of the overwhelming demands now being made upon them.

The truck is the one satisfactory solution to the difficulties of short-haul freight. The hundred-mile radius belongs to the truck. But the truck has not stepped there. Its future is restricted only by the extent of good roads and systematic schedules.

"Ship by truck."

You'll save and serve. Pass the word on to your traffic department. Take it up with your business associates. Speak of it to others in your industry.

Whether it's your truck or one belonging to a truck transport company—

"Ship by truck."

Speed traffic; aid the railroads to give the country a freighting system that can cope with the rapid growth of industry. Get in line with the future trend of transportation.

"Ship by truck."

Following World War I, Harvey S. Firestone, realizing the vast possibilities of truck transportation, pioneered a "Ship by Truck" campaign. This advertisement, dated January 18, 1919, was part of the movement that ushered in the new transportation era.

Annual sales convention in Akron, 1915: some of the executives and sales representatives. *Front row, left to right*: Stacy G. Carkhuff, A. G. Partridge, Frank C. Blanchard, Robert J. Firestone, Harvey S. Firestone, John W. Thomas, Louis E. Sisler, Roy Harris, and C. C. Carlton; *lower right*: Daniel F. White.

Introducing the Balloon tire, a Firestone development, to the general public, December 22, 1923. Within a few years Balloon tires entirely replaced high-pressure tires, and the motorist rode in greater comfort and safety.

Twenty-fifth anniversary of The Firestone Tire & Rubber Company, August 3, 1925. Harvey S. Firestone is surrounded by his five sons in his office on the occasion: Russell A. Firestone, Harvey S. Firestone, Jr., Leonard K. Firestone, Roger S. Firestone, and Raymond C. Firestone.

In the Akron Centennial Parade of Progress on July 21, 1925: Mr. and Mrs. Harvey S. Firestone ride in an old-time buggy with thoroughbred horses from their stable. (*Below*) Mr. and Mrs. Firestone and members of their family at the Chagrin Valley Hunt Club, Gates Mills, Ohio, 1927. *Left to right:* Harvey, Jr., Elizabeth, Leonard, Mrs. Firestone, Raymond, Mr. Firestone, and Russell.

Camping trip, August 21, 1918: the party stops to examine an old grist mill in the West Virginia mountains. *Left to right:* Thomas A. Edison, Harvey S. Firestone, Harvey S. Firestone, Jr., John Burroughs, Henry Ford, Harvey S. Firestone; *seated below:* R. J. H. de Loach.

Ex-President William Howard Taft, on a speaking tour discussing the League of Nations, arrives in Akron on November 29, 1920, and visits with Harvey S. Firestone.

President Warren G. Harding joins America's celebrated campers at their camp near Hagerstown, Maryland, on July 23, 1921. Discussing the day's news: Henry Ford, Thomas A. Edison, President Harding, and Harvey S. Firestone.

President Calvin Coolidge welcomes the campers at his Vermont home on August 19, 1924, and presents them with a sap bucket that had been in his family for many generations. *Left to right*: Harvey S. Firestone, President Coolidge, Henry Ford, Thomas A. Edison, Mrs. Coolidge, Russell A. Firestone, and Colonel John Coolidge, the President's father.

In quest of American-produced rubber, Harvey S. Firestone and Henry Ford
encouraged Thomas A. Edison to cultivate rubber-bearing plants in the Edison
Botanical Gardens at Fort Myers, Florida. Mr. Firestone is shown on a visit
there on Mr. Edison's eighty-first birthday, February 11, 1928.

President Herbert Hoover, Henry Ford, and Harvey S. Firestone visit Thomas A. Edison at Fort Myers on Mr. Edison's eighty-second birthday.

Resting on the doorstep of Mr. Edison's laboratory at Fort Myers, March 15, 1931: Henry Ford, Thomas A. Edison, and Harvey S. Firestone.

A giant birthday cake features the party celebrating Harvey S. Firestone's sixtieth birthday on December 20, 1928, in the Club House at Akron. Twelve hundred old-time employees and the family and relatives of Mr. Firestone attended.

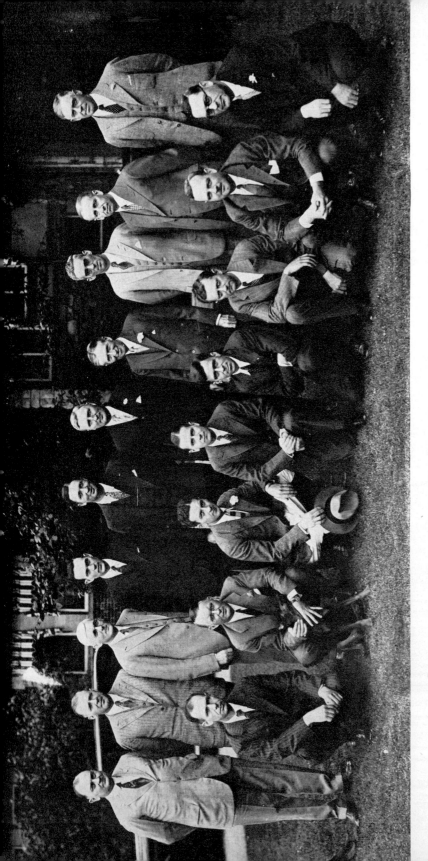

A reception is tendered to John W. Thomas on his return from Europe: September 14, 1929, at Harbel Manor, the Firestone estate in Akron. John W. Thomas was vice president of the Company. *First row:* Harvey H. Hollinger, Bernard M. Robinson, Russell A. Firestone, Harvey S. Firestone, Jr., W. T. Runals, M. E. Ake, W. A. Baker, and F. K. Starbird. *Second row:* E. A. Hoener, L. G. Fairbank, W. T. Lewis, R. R. Gross, Lee R. Jackson, Mr. Thomas, Harvey S. Firestone, John J. Shea, Stacy G. Carkhuff, and Ralph S. Leonard.

Father and sons. After an inspection trip through the Akron factory on July 9, 1930, they are photographed at the entrance to Plant 1: Leonard K. Firestone, Roger S. Firestone, Harvey S. Firestone, Jr., Harvey S. Firestone, Russell A. Firestone, and Raymond C. Firestone.

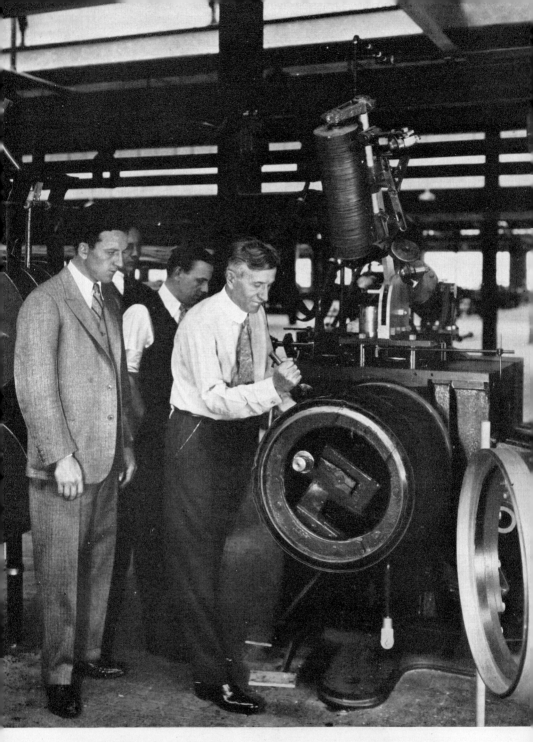

At the opening of the Company's plant in Los Angeles, California, Harvey S. Firestone builds the first tire to be produced there, June 18, 1928. Looking on, his sons Russell, Leonard, and Harvey, Jr., stand behind him.

On the links at Ormond Beach, Florida, on January 28, 1930: after Harvey S.
Firestone has made a long putt, John D. Rockefeller presents him with a dime.

A dinner in honor of the Pioneers of American Industry, held at Hotel Astor, New York City, October 24, 1928. *Left to right:* Harvey S. Firestone, pioneer in rubber; Julius Rosenwald, merchandising; Thomas A. Edison, invention; Thomas Lipton, tea; Charles M. Schwab, iron and steel; Henry Ford and Walter P. Chrysler, automobiles, and George Eastman, photography.

Harvey S. Firestone and a group of automobile manufacturers, when they appeared before the Senate Finance Committee in Washington on April 18, 1932. *Left to right:* Roy D. Chapin, George N. Graham, Mr. Firestone, Walter P. Chrysler, Alfred P. Sloan, Jr., Senator Reed Smoot, A. B. Qualey, Edsel Ford, Charles D. Hastings, and Alfred A. Swayne.

At the Indianapolis Speedway in 1932: Harvey S. Firestone, Jr., Harvey S. Firestone, Henry Ford, his son Edsel Ford, and Edsel Ford's sons Henry Ford II and Benson Ford. The winning speed that year was 104.144 miles per hour. In 1950, the all-time record of 124.002 miles per hour was made.

Liberia, West Africa: here Firestone Plantations Company produces the highest-grade rubber. These plantations became a principal source of natural rubber supply for the United States and her Allies in World War II. (*Left*) Tappers reporting for work early in the morning. (*Right*) A tapper cutting a thin strip of bark to let the latex ooze out and trickle into a cup.

Firestone Research. This structure was dedicated to "ruthless logic linked to imagination and the creative instinct," September 18, 1945. On a hilltop, it overlooks a ten-acre expanse near the Akron factories.

(*Below*) Rubber is made here. The first of the United States government synthetic-rubber plants to go into production was the Firestone-operated plant in Akron on April 25, 1942. Its rated capacity is 30,000 tons a year.

Bales of rubber are automatically split into smaller pieces by cutting machine preparatory to blending and mixing with compounds.

(*Below*) The rubber is blended and mixed with such materials as sulphur, carbon black, and other pigments in large mixing machines to make the rubber tougher and more resilient. It is then taken off the mills in strips as shown here for further processing into treads and other parts of tires.

Preparing cord fabric for plies which form body of tire: (*Left*) Rayon or cotton cords impregnated with rubber solution by Firestone Gum-Dipping process, which improves adhesion and assures greater protection against tire failure caused by internal friction. (*Right*) Cords are then passed through a calendering machine which applies a coating of rubber to each side.

When removed from the building machine, a heavy inner tube, called a "curing bag," is then put inside and inflated. As the tire is pressed between heavy plates, the curing bag expands and forces the tire into its familiar shape.

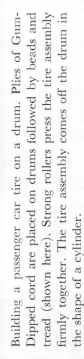

Building a passenger car tire on a drum. Plies of Gum-Dipped cord are placed on drums followed by beads and tread (shown here). Strong rollers press the tire assembly firmly together. The tire assembly comes off the drum in the shape of a cylinder.

Tire rims are made by The Firestone Steel Products Company, a leading producer of automotive rim equipment since 1910. The rims shown here are for trucks.

The tires are vulcanized in steam-heated curing presses, each of which contains two molds. They open automatically when vulcanization is completed.

Lee R. Jackson, President of the Company, compares the Super-Balloon tire, developed by Firestone in 1947, with the original Firestone Balloon tire that was made and road-tested in 1922. Wider tread, more non-skid angles, and smaller rim diameter afford more comfort and greater safety.

Harvey S. Firestone pioneered rubber tires for farm equipment. He is shown with his son Leonard testing Ground-Grip tires on a tractor and a potato digger at the Firestone Homestead Farm near Columbiana, Ohio, 1936.

(*Below*) Members of the board of directors occasionally held meetings at the Homestead. Here are Harvey H. Hollinger, Bernard M. Robinson, Russell A. Firestone, Harvey S. Firestone, Jr., Harvey S. Firestone, Frank H. Hobson, Stacy G. Carkhuff, and John J. Shea on July 30, 1935.

The largest tire mold in the world. The vulcanized tire in this tire curing press measures 9½ feet high and 38.7 inches wide and weighs 3,646 pounds.

(*Below*) Giant tires developed and produced by Firestone make possible the transportation and operation of huge earth-moving vehicles. During World War II, they served in the swift construction of landing fields and camp sites.

The farm on rubber: Harvey S. Firestone, in a realistic farmyard setting arranged for a sales conference on February 13, 1936, demonstrates tires for tractors and other farm vehicles. Having supervised the development of the first pneumatic tractor tire in 1932, he devoted much thought and energy in his later years to greater efficiency in agriculture.

On the lawn of the Firestone Homestead Farm near Columbiana, Ohio: Henry Ford pays a visit on September 17, 1936, to observe farm-tire experimental work. *Left to right:* Harvey S. Firestone, Jr., Harvey S. Firestone, Mr. Ford, Leonard K. Firestone, and Russell A. Firestone.

Harvey S. Firestone, rendering his annual report to the stockholders, addresses the meeting held December 16, 1935, in the Club House auditorium crowded with employee stockholders.

Harvey S. Firestone, Jr.

The Chairman of The Firestone Tire & Rubber Company at his desk in Akron headquarters.

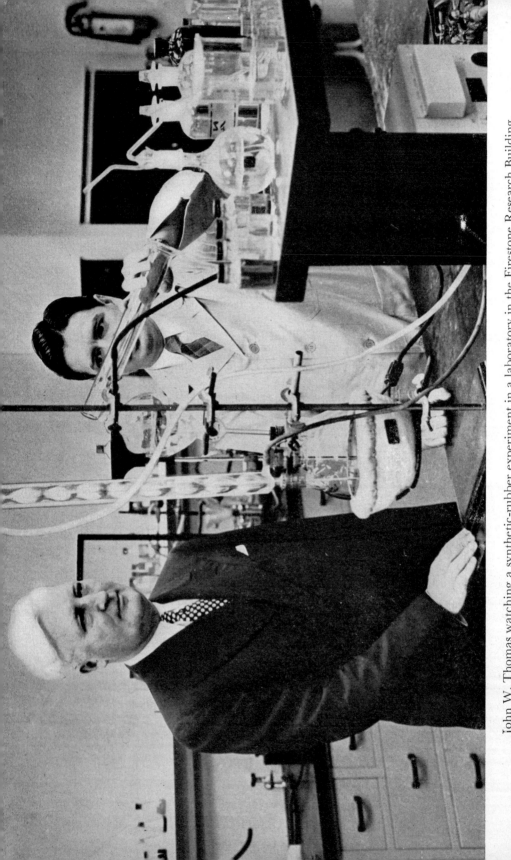

John W. Thomas watching a synthetic-rubber experiment in a laboratory in the Firestone Research Building.

Undersecretary of War Robert P. Patterson presents the Army-Navy Production Award on August 31, 1942, to The Firestone Tire & Rubber Company, the first company in the rubber industry to receive this honor. The pennant is displayed by Harvey S. Firestone, Jr. (*left*) and C. F. Richmond, president of Local 7, United Rubber Workers, CIO (*right*). More than 25,000 war workers and their families, Army and Navy officers, and guests of honor attended the ceremonies at the Firestone Stadium.

Two of Firestone's major war products: Bullet-sealing fuel cells in various sizes for Army and Navy planes; here shown, cells of 3000-gallon capacity for B-36 bombers. (*Below*) Rubber-block tank tracks and bogie rollers for Army tanks.

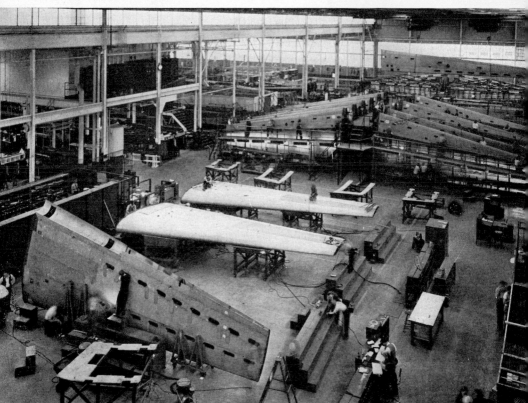

Wings for victory: An assembly line at the Firestone aircraft plant at Willow Grove, Pennsylvania, where CG-4A troop-carrying invasion gliders were produced in World War II. (*Below*) Wing panels in Plant 3 at Akron, for C-46 Commando transports.

Rubber to the rescue: Barrage balloons, produced by Firestone in Akron to protect land objectives and troops against enemy aircraft. (*Below*) Collapsible life rafts, containing supplies. Firestone was a chief source of flotation equipment for the American armed forces during World War II.

Floating bridges for United States Army assault forces: Firestone manufactured large numbers of these inflated rubber pontons that sustained marching men and heavy equipment.

The redesign and mass manufacture of Bofors 40-millimeter antiaircraft gun mounts and carriages by Firestone was an outstanding wartime production achievement. General William S. Knudsen inspects the production line on August 11, 1942; *left to right:* John Kozak, James E. Trainer, John W. Thomas, A. Bessermini, General Knudsen, Harvey S. Firestone, Jr., Harry Arnold, and E. W. Olson. (*Below*) A Bofors gun being landed on the shores of North Africa in 1942.

Equipment that made tanks amphibious, a secret "D-D" war product used in the invasion of Normandy in World War II, manufactured exclusively by Firestone in 1944. Tank transformed into boat by collapsible canvas walls enters water; (*Below*) emerging on beach, tank drops marine disguise and is ready for action.

Foamex cushioning material, produced by Firestone's industrial products division at Fall River, Massachusetts, from liquid latex received from the Firestone Plantations in Liberia. Here are automobile seat pads coming from the mold and the washer, on their way to electronic driers.

Velon Film, produced by Firestone Plastics Company at Pottstown, Pennsylvania. Giant, heated calenders operated at predetermined speeds, roll Velon to desired thicknesses. Here an operator is shown removing a completed roll of film for rainwear and household furnishings.

The board of directors of The Firestone Tire & Rubber Company, meeting at the plant in Pottstown, Pennsylvania, December 16, 1948. *Left to right:* Russell A. Firestone, Harvey H. Hollinger, John J. Shea, Lee R. Jackson, Chairman Harvey S. Firestone, Jr., John W. Thomas, James E. Trainer, Leonard K. Firestone, Raymond C. Firestone, and Roger S. Firestone.

The Harvey S. Firestone Memorial was dedicated on August 3, 1950, the Fiftieth Anniversary of the founding of The Firestone Tire & Rubber Company. The bronze portrait statue of Harvey S. Firestone, focal point of the Memorial, was unveiled at that time by Mr. Firestone's five sons during ceremonies attended by thousands of Firestone employees, Akron residents, and civic and religious leaders. The Memorial is located in the midst of twenty-five acres of lawns and trees on a hilltop overlooking a mile-long array of manufacturing plants, the nucleus of the world-wide industrial empire founded by Mr. Firestone in 1900.

adjusted, all copyright music controlled by ASCAP was withheld from the microphones, *In My Garden* fading out with the rest. Into the musical breach, Mrs. Firestone brought her warmly sincere *If I Could Tell You*, introduced by Richard Crooks. This fervent melody was so appealing that it continued to herald the program after ASCAP had returned to the networks, and her earlier refrain—better suited for a tender leave-taking—thereafter closed the famous half-hour of memorable music.

What a varied world was the world of business! Agriculture, international relations, patent suits, legislation, and music.

This was an era also of physical expansion. The company had acquired one of the largest cord fabric mills in the country in 1935 at an attractive price: 120,000 spindles in Gastonia, North Carolina. It sold its Fall River cotton mills the next year and transferred some of the equipment to Gastonia, some of it to a textile mill purchased at Woodstock, Ontario, to supply the tire factory at Hamilton. Another acquisition in 1936 was a factory at Noblesville, Indiana, for the growing demands of the industrial rubber goods division; this became the plant of the Firestone Industrial Products Company.

To come closer to the Southern market for tires, the company established a factory in Memphis, Tennessee, purchasing a General Motors plant in 1936 and re-equipping it. Streamlined for economy and benefited by the latest improvements in machinery, this factory was placed under the direction of Raymond Firestone. Raymond had entered the business via the college graduates' training class, had gained consumer-level experience in California stores as salesman, manager, and district supervisor, and subsequently he became assistant manager of the Southeastern zone; later, district manager at Richmond, Virginia. It was with such experience that two brothers went into the manufacturing branch, for Leonard was now at the Los Angeles plant.

A new subsidiary was formed in 1937, The Firestone Rubber & Latex Products Company. A plant in Fall River was purchased for the conversion of liquid latex from Liberia into Foamex cushioning material and Contro elastic thread, and for the production of plastics and adhesives (beginning in May, 1938).

Also in 1937, Firestone Steel Products constructed a plant at Wyandotte, Michigan, to produce automobile and truck rims closer to the heart of the automobile industry.

But one of the greatest joys to Harvey Firestone came from the realization of his pioneer concept of putting the farm on rubber. He lived to see its wide acceptance.

This was an outgrowth of a conviction he had formed in 1931 that tractors should run on rubber for greater economy. He met first with skepticism. How could pneumatic tires take the place of the sharp flanges on steel wheels? Impractical, people said.

His was enthusiasm that inspired coworkers, and they tackled the problem with the same blend of tingle of excitement and steadiness of purpose. The tire must have a high diameter, demanded by the clearance of a tractor in farm operations, and a wide cross section for contact with the soil and fit in furrow. This contact must be firm so that the tractor might pull without power loss, yet the grip must not cause the tire to creep on the rim. Excessive air pressure would pack the soil too hard; insufficient pressure would allow slipping on the rim.

In the original development work, flat truck rims were used. Airplane tires in sizes 6.50-16 and 11.25-24 were mounted on them.* They rim-crept. The answer

* The new designation of tire sizes was more realistic than the former method of measurement. The figure 6.50 represented the cross section and 16 the wheel's diameter. Under the old system, a tire of this size would have been a 29x6½.

was a drop-center rim with a tight bead fit. So much for creepage. As for traction, the tread must bite into earth, sand, wet clay, sod, but chevrons cut too deep would bend under the load; that is, if unsupported. And this necessity gave birth to the idea of a connected bar design—the continuation of one side of a chevron to the bar above it—and variations on that theme.

In January, 1935, the new tread design was introduced as the Ground Grip. It was an economy tire. It enabled a tractor to cover more acreage in less time than a steel-wheeled tractor took. Its larger area of contact with the ground intensified the traction. The stronger draw-bar pull saved gasoline. Stability, cushioned vibration, longer life to the mechanism, less fatigue—these were further talking points to the farmer. Harvey Firestone tried out the different designs as they came from the development department; tried them himself, driving tractors on his homestead farm.

Farm machinery manufacturers were slow to be convinced. First year's sales consisted mainly of changeovers in the field by Firestone service men, who cut down the steel-wheel spokes and welded a rim on them. With Ground Grip tires a tractor could be used as a heavy-duty road hauling machine.

At a sales conference the next year, a model farm display was set up in the old factory at Miller Avenue—a model farm on rubber—to demonstrate the potentialities. Firestone quoted statistics. There were more than 23,000,000 vehicles on American farms besides 1,500,000 tractors—"and we are laying plans to take care of this steadily increasing market." With the economy appeal still in mind, the farmer would be shown that a minimum investment, in view of demountable rims, would make it possible to interchange the tires on other wheeled machines.

The Homestead Farm was converted into an exhibit of thirty-two different agricultural implements on rubber —a mower, a combine, and a spreader, a wagon, a feed truck, and grain drill, a wheelbarrow, and others. Testing continued. Day after day the tires were used, under varying conditions. Experts from Ohio State University and the Society of Automotive Engineers descended on the farm to study performance.

After further improvement of the tread design, Ground Grip Type R was introduced in 1937. In this the traction bars had greater depth, narrowed width, and more open spacing to penetrate the soil and also permit self-cleaning. Special treads were designed for specific operating needs. Firestone's youngest son, Roger, who had become district manager in Houston, Texas, wrote home on the need for one that could work in rice fields; a new construction was created with converging ribs and open spaces to discharge mud. In general, the engineering goal was the most bars of greatest length in simultaneous contact with the soil, but not so close as to break it up and dissolve traction resistance.

The farm on rubber, no longer a dream, was soon a common sight. Growing favor for rubber-tired tractors was attested by implement manufacturers' figures. Pneumatics as original equipment increased from 17,800 out of 118,600 tractors sold in 1935 to 92,400 out of 216,000 in 1937, the percentage growing to eighty-five two years later. Changeovers on old steel wheels took place at a more rapid rate.

Tractors were seen operating over all sorts of terrain, speedily and effectively. Dual-type tractor tires were developed for lister ridge and basin farming. In 1939, the company developed a method of mounting dual-tire equipment directly on the old wheels at a saving that prompted many more changeovers.

Meantime tires for earth-movers were another boon (and source of income). An order in 1935 for size 17.25-24 amazed the beholder, but not so much as did the amended order for 18.00-24. Soon Firestone was making 2,000 of these a month. Great loads of dirt were dug up and dispatched swiftly. As bigger bulldozers were built, bigger tires were demanded. Cross sections were made twenty inches, thirty inches. Truly a wonder of the world: Firestone tires 36.00-40.

Tires—the founder's first love—were helping to build dams, highways, airports. Tires were making the world move.

For the motorist, tire quality was holding up under greater daily use and giving the average driver three years' service. Cost per mile in 1937 had declined sixty-four percent from a decade before. This was the test of a business: public benefit.

15

Labor Unrest and Peace

AFTER nearly twenty years of labor peace, the decline in production caused by the depression's lessening demand had an unsettling effect on the tire industry. All over the country, in every industry, the blight of unemployment spread, threatening the security of tire workers, who were enjoying wage rates that exceeded the average for all manufacturing industries by sixteen percent.

At Firestone, the company's interest in the welfare of the personnel—expressed by the Club House, Firestone Park housing, free life insurance and pension provisions, free medical attention, garden plots, the athletic field, free legal service at the Bank, and the day-to-day personal relationships—brought management and labor into close accord and reflected the founder's desire that the organization always be a spiritual unit.

In 1929, in the heyday of prosperity, the Firestone Country Club and golf courses for employee use were laid out and a policy of vacations with pay was begun. There were 16,945 employee stockholders, owning a total of 375,260 shares. Loans had been extended to them, aggregating $4,079,000 since the inception of stock allotments. The company had paid out more than $350,000 on insurance claims.

In 1930, the task was to soften the inexorable blows.

Tire production in the Firestone plants had declined from 12,814,000 in 1929 to 10,397,000. Akron hourly-wage personnel fell from 11,925 to 9,648. There would have been a sharper reduction in the force but for spreading the work over shorter shifts and a shorter work week.

Harvey Firestone described the situation:

> We have been operating our factory on two five-hour shifts five days a week with one supervision. Yesterday we decided to put on one or possibly two more shifts and store what excess tires we make, in order to give some employment to more people. Of course, twenty-five hours a week is not very satisfactory for many of our men but they are accepting it in order to give more men employment, for these are times when we must all find ways and means to help.*

And winter was approaching.

The surplus production continued. Output fell in 1931 to 9,098,000 tires and in the next year to 7,002,000; next, to 6,649,000. During these years, the downward trend of employment persisted, throughout the industry, but after small wage cuts in 1930 and 1931, hourly rates were left undisturbed. The difficulty lay in finding work for those who remained on the payroll. Akron factories resorted to a six-hour day, the men working three or four days a week and rotating their jobs with other employees. This situation obtained also at Firestone, where additional work was provided for members of the mechanical force by retaining them to make improvements and step up plant efficiency.

By the middle of 1933, the project of the Roosevelt administration to put a floor under prices and wages by means of the N.R.A. was under way. A revival of automobile production, presaged for 1934, stimulated tire manufacturing. The wage cuts had been restored, making hourly rates nineteen percent higher than the

* H.S.F. to Cyrus H. McCormick, Dec. 3, 1930.

national average. Firestone took on 1,500 more workers.

Wages accounted for a greater part of tire manufacturing costs than in predepression years because of the drop in cost of raw materials. Industry was receiving less for its product, in consequence of the price wars and the channeling of so much business into cheaper lines. But the economics of the situation did not comfort labor. The short work week brought low earnings. The fact that increased man-hour productivity resulting from technical improvements had been offset in the past by rising total production and rising employment, was not taken as reassurance that labor eventually would be reabsorbed.

Many workers in the tire industry clasped the hand extended by N.R.A. in the form of collective bargaining. Many joined craft unions set up by the reactivated American Federation of Labor. At Firestone, an Employees' Conference Plan was organized in 1933 to deal with management through representatives selected by the various departments; wages, hours, working conditions, safety, sanitation, and recreation were among the subject matters. The functioning of the Plan, the company noted, was "most satisfactory" to both sides.

> In spite of general industrial unrest we have had the finest co-operation and loyalty from our employees.*

About 1,500,000 more tires were produced at Firestone in 1934 than in the preceding year. There had been a twenty-eight percent increase in personnel, working thirty hours a week; a sixty-five percent larger payroll. Hourly rates were now fourteen percent higher than they had been in the peak year 1929.

Another allotment of common stock was offered to the employees in 1934, and they subscribed for 72,775

* *Annual Report*, 1934.

shares at $20 par. Three out of every four employees now held stock in the company.

The life insurance plan was enlarged the same year. Besides covering the employees for $500 to $1,000 without charge, the company had been considering a means of further protection and entered into a group insurance contract whereby the amount would be increased by $500 and sickness, accident, and hospitalization benefits would be added, the employees paying as their share thirty cents (for men) or twenty-five cents (for women) per week. "This," said the company, "together with the workmen's compensation insurance affords every employee complete protection in case of sickness or accident at a very low cost." *

Nevertheless, the A.F. of L. United Rubber Workers of America formed a local at Firestone and filed a petition with the Regional Labor Board in September, 1934, to hold an election for the determination of a collective bargaining agent for all the employees, as provided by Section 7a of the N.I.R.A. This was part of a general movement in Akron for union recognition. In December, the Board ordered elections in this city's tire factories, allowing in Firestone's case the Employees' Conference Plan to share the ballot with the union. Both the company and the Plan opposed the order, and subsequently the Board instructed the company to cease recognizing the

---

* The policy terms were liberalized from time to time. Revision in 1939 provided for $1,500-$2,000 life insurance, greater hospitalization benefits. and the extension of the group hospital plan to employees' dependents at a nominal weekly cost.

A retirement income plan was adopted in 1941, supplementing the Federal Social Security Act, whose benefits were based on a limit of $3,000 of any salary. The company now made joint contributions with the employee for the purchase of a monthly retirement income, based on the portion of salary over $3,000.

A new group insurance plan was adopted in 1946, for all employees, canceling the old one and providing greater benefits. The employee made a monthly contribution, based upon annual earnings, the company undertaking to pay the cost of the insurance in excess of the contributions.

Plan as an agency for collective bargaining until the election should decide the workers' choice.

Before the Circuit Court of Appeals came to a decision in reviewing the order, the Supreme Court ruled that Congress had delegated power unconstitutionally in establishing the N.I.R.A. Hence in June, 1935, the National Labor Relations Board was restrained from forcing an election.

Union membership fell off. Disaffection also diminished as tire production advanced; yet there was still an undercurrent. In January, 1936, Firestone in Akron was operating at ninety-one percent of capacity, with 10,368 hourly-wage employees—the largest number since 1929 and only about 1,600 short of that year. The men worked four days a week.

The same month, John L. Lewis appeared in Akron as the head of the recently organized Committee for Industrial Organization, which aimed to forge vertical unions in steel, rubber, and automobile among other mass-production industries. Here and there at the tire factories, disquietude broke out in sporadic flares; sometimes a grievance was the spark, sometimes it was personal friction.

A fist fight on a Tuesday in January between a union member and a nonmember, both workers in the Firestone truck-tire building department, resulted in the suspension of the former for the rest of the week. He was believed to have struck the first blow. In protest against the action taken against him, about 200 fellow workers in this department refused to leave their machines at the end of the day and sat down. The next shift arrived, and many of these men remained to join the sit-downers. Midnight came, and builders of passenger-car tires followed this procedure.

The effect of the sit-down was to create a bottleneck

through which no work could pass to the vulcanizing room, and into which the accumulated stock from the milling room could not enter.

For fifty-eight hours (January 28 to 30) the stoppage continued. Disturbances occurred also in other plants in Akron, the most serious being the beginning of a five-week strike in February at Goodyear, a strike which the C.I.O. supported. It won a signed agreement of settlement but did not win union recognition.

A year passed, during which tire prices advanced and Firestone increased wages, the United Rubber Workers switched their affiliation to the C.I.O. (name changed to Congress of Industrial Organizations), and a series of short strikes evidenced the ferment in Akron. Firestone production jumped to 10,029,000 tires, the largest number since 1930.

In 1937, the C.I.O. succeeded in signing strike settlements with General Motors and steel companies but did not obtain exclusive bargaining status. Rubber was another venture.

One night early in March, union men in the tire-building room in Firestone's Plant 2 interrupted their work to induce nonunion employees to join their Local 7. On the midnight shift there was an hour's stoppage of the same kind; and again on the next morning's shift. Because of these interruptions, the company announced that the plant would be closed for the remainder of the week. Work proceeded in Plant 1 on a normal basis.

Pickets massed at the gates on the morning of March 3 and balked workers arriving at Plant 1 and at the Xylos reclaiming division. The company shut down these plants and conferred with C.I.O. officials, but Steel Products continued in operation. The chief issue in dispute, the union spokesmen said, was the Employees' Conference Plan.

At a union meeting in the Armory, a vote was taken against returning to work until the Plan was abolished and the union recognized. The company told the union representatives that it was willing to grant recognition to the union as bargaining agent for union members, on condition that coercion of nonunion employees cease. The company, further, would give no assistance to any other labor organization and would take back the strikers on Monday, without discrimination. These proposals were met by the union's counterproposal that the union be the sole bargaining agent.

The company adhered to its offer. The union rejected it.

Negotiations continued. Picketing continued. This was the season when orders from automobile and farm implement manufacturers should be filled, as well as dealers' spring requirements.

A week after the start of the stoppage, Local 7 held another mass meeting in the Armory and voted to make the strike official. The motion carried by 2,668 to 93. Shacks of canvas, wood, and tin were erected as picket shelters at the gates.

Each passing week brought new hopes for the conferences between the union and the company's labor department. New hopes, new deadlocks. No attempt was made to reopen the plants by means other than negotiation of an agreement.

Harvey Firestone was at Harbel Villa, Miami Beach. Teletype messages from Akron kept him informed, but they did not alleviate his feeling of distress at this cleavage.

When the strike broke out in Akron it jarred me for a day or two. Then I concluded there must be some reason for it and that we could not help it, but the thing we should do was not to fight it but stand on what we thought was right and then let matters stand, as it was God's will we were to have a strike and there was a good reason for it, and it would be righted in the right time.

There is one thing we cannot do—we cannot bargain away the rights of our men, which is contained in their [the union's] proposals 1 and 2, and therefore all we could do was wait until the men wanted to go back badly enough that they would stand up for what is right and not be influenced by men who were trying to get control of their own liberties. Then it would be our duty to take them back—at least as many of them as we could. . . .

Whatever is right will finally prevail.*

The offer to negotiate a written agreement with Local 7 still held good—on hours, wages, seniority rights, and working conditions, but not "the personal rights of our employees." On April 12, the Supreme Court upheld the constitutionality of the National Labor Relations Act, which had been passed after the invalidation of the N.I.R.A.

Aside from this acknowledgment of the legal rights of labor, the situation remained unchanged. Negotiations went on. At one point they were broken off. Finally, on the evening of April 28, the conclusion of a written agreement was announced.

The company agrees to bargain collectively with the union through its accredited representatives and to meet such representatives to handle and adjust grievances for such of the employees as desire their services.

The company recognizes and will not interfere with the rights of its employees to become members of the union. Neither the company nor any of its agents will exercise discrimination, interference, restraint or coercion against any member of the union on account of such membership.†

The company also gave its pledge that it would not finance or otherwise aid any labor group. The union agreed that it would neither cause nor tolerate sit-downs or other stoppages; that it would refrain from intimidat-

* H.S.F. to Leonard K. Firestone, Mar. 14, 1937.
† *Akron Beacon Journal* extra, Apr. 28, 1937.

ing employees or soliciting membership on company
time or property.

In its first public statement since the start of the
fifty-six-day strike, the company thanked everyone con-.
cerned—the employees, the press, the public—for "their
patience and fairness during the long negotiations" and
added, "We believe both sides have reached an honor-
able agreement."

John L. Lewis in a telegram to the union president
urged the workers to accept it and return to work. "I
most heartily approve . . . an outstanding example of
collective bargaining in the rubber industry."

The agreement was submitted to the union employees
on April 30, and they ratified it by a show of hands
estimated at 4,300 in favor and 200 opposed.

It fixed the standard work week at six days, six hours a
day, with time-and-a-half for more than eight hours a
day, for more than forty hours a week, and for holiday
work. Before a layoff in any department, there must be a
twenty-four-hour week for eight weeks, and on rehiring,
the laid-off workers would get the preference. Wages
were unchanged; if industry conditions warranted,
they would be negotiated. Grievances that the company's labor department and the union's executive
officers could not settle among themselves would be
placed before an impartial umpire. Firestone voluntarily
agreed to continue its vacation, insurance, and other
welfare measures. The term of the agreement was one
year.

Firestone was thus the first major rubber company to
sign with the union. Later the National Labor Relations
Board ordered exclusive-bargaining elections at the
plants of the other companies, and the union won them.

The next year, on the eve of the expiration of the
Firestone contract, the Board conducted an election in

which the Firestone Employees' Protective Association had a place on the ballot with Local 7. Certified as eligible voters were 7,534 workers, but 1,176 did not vote. After 1.6 percent of the ballots was thrown out, the union won the count by 3,696 to 2,564, a margin of 1,132. Renewal of the contract was negotiated at once. It was ratified with minor alterations. Wage scales remained unchanged, but an escape clause permitted the reopening of any of the provisions on ten days' notice.*

Production at Firestone had swiftly resumed after the strike. Although total tire output in 1937 was lower than the preceding year's, the number included large tractor tires, which helped raise the sales volume, and trailer tires, a new line. In fact, this was the greatest sales year in company history—achieved despite generally poor business conditions in a relapse suffered by national recovery. On a gross of $156,800,000, the profit was $9,200,000. Common stock paid $2.50 in dividends, and $1,800,000 was carried to surplus.

Harvey Firestone was properly proud of this showing; proud also of the 561 company stores, which had increased their sales and profits.

There was no gainsaying that 1937 had been a full year—not to overlook the Indianapolis Sweepstakes, in which Wilbur Shaw broke the world's record by averaging 113.58 miles per hour for 500 miles on Firestone tires. This was the eighteenth consecutive year that cars on Firestone tires had ridden to victory in the classic.

Going South in December, Harvey Firestone stopped

---

* What the United States Department of Labor called "a major step forward for industrial stability in the industry" was the signing of a corporation-wide agreement in 1948 between Firestone and the U.R.W., covering all plants operated by the company. The company set another pattern for the industry when it granted a wage increase in that year's contract, applying to 23,000 employees in eight plants.

off at the Memphis plant and observed the building of tractor tires for cane and rice fields. With his sons Leonard and Raymond, he inspired a merchandising conference held there, outlining policies for 1938 and his ambitious plans to put the American farm completely on rubber. Memphis loomed big in his thinking. It would be an advantage to manufacture a greater part of the tractor and implement tires at this factory, "and a large part of our heavy truck tires, particularly for the South." Freight rates were cheaper on rubber and fabric to Memphis, and on finished goods from Memphis to the important centers in the South and Southwest. Power and taxes, too, were lower than in Akron or Los Angeles.

This was characteristic: the active chairman of the company still planning for growth in terms of economy. He passed through Atlanta, promising to be back in the spring for a visit. He arrived at Miami on December 20, his sixty-ninth birthday. In a press interview he said, "Our prosperity still depends on two fundamentals: work and production." At Harbel Villa hundreds of congratulatory telegrams were waiting for him.

In Memoriam

HARVEY S. FIRESTONE

1868–1938

CHRISTMAS 1937 was celebrated at Harbel Villa by a man of good will. While life had not been outward peace—for life had been action—Harvey Firestone had sources of serenity. He had revered the golden rule, a code that the modern world shyly called human relations. He enjoyed deep contentment, often merriment, in his family. And he had an abiding sense of accomplishment.

Mind and spirit were always stirring. Vacation was never wholly relaxation. Down at the gatehouse of the Miami Beach estate he had his winter office, where some time was spent each day at correspondence and in teletype communication with Akron. Friends came, executives with their wives, to share in his hospitality and lounge in the Florida sun. Of a late afternoon in a sulky, he would drive his favorite horse round the bridle path he had made for his family.

It was on a typical Sunday, February 6, 1938, attending services at the Community Church, having guests for dinner, and going for a drive at dusk, that he spent his last hours. In tranquil sleep that night he passed away.

Monday night on the "Voice of Firestone" the somber opening bars of Schubert's *Unfinished Sym-*

phony flowed into pure melody of exaltation, of yearning and tenderness; an eternal expression of immortal man.

Harvey Firestone's continuity on earth obtained in his beloved family and in the institution of social usefulness that his business genius had built. His mortal person was borne to Akron and through the silent aisles of the company's main building. The cortege proceeded to the site of his first factory and past his early home on Fir Hill and then to Harbel Manor. In the music room the casket reposed, and thousands of sorrowful men and women softly threaded by.

Services were conducted by the Reverend Doctor Walter F. Tunks of St. Paul's Episcopal Church, the church whose senior warden Harvey Firestone had been for seventeen years. Following the benediction, the pallbearers, all representing various departments of the company, bore the casket to the hearse that would take their dear friend to his birthplace, the Homestead in Columbiana. There, in the simple parlor, he lay in state and the neighbors came in. And then he was laid to rest in the cemetery near the village.

A cycle of man completed . . .

*

At a memorial service held the following Sunday, the Reverend Doctor Tunks delivered this tribute:

"We have come into the church this morning with a deep sense of personal loss. In the familiar words of Scripture, 'A prince and a great man has fallen in Israel.' Words never seem so inadequate as when we try to express our sense of loss in the passing of someone we have greatly loved. Perhaps that is why God has given us the gift of music as a means of expressing unutterable things. So this morning as we pay tribute to the memory of Harvey S. Firestone, for many years the beloved senior warden of this parish, we are conscious that nothing we can say can add anything to the luster of his achievement, or tell of the respect and admiration in which he was held by all who knew him at close range.

"What is the measure of a man? Certainly nothing external to himself, but rather the inner qualities of mind and heart and soul that are the source of true greatness. The story of the Columbiana farm boy who pioneered the early days of the rubber industry and built up a far-flung empire of business around the world is an epic of American industrial life. His farsightedness, his understanding of men and motives, his tenacity of purpose, his courage in times of crisis were all a part of his dynamic personality. Perhaps the most wonderful thing about Mr. Firestone was his capacity for growth. Although he never had the opportunity to attend college, he had a highly trained mind and the greatest respect for higher education. Few men could equal his seasoned judgment and breadth of interest. Some men, having acquired success, are content to relinquish their efforts, and settle down in easy satisfaction with what they have accomplished. But Mr. Firestone never regarded himself as a finished product. His eager mind was ever searching for new knowledge. He was always looking for ways of improvement both in the management of his business and the conduct of his personal life. With all his self-confidence, he possessed a real humility of heart and mind, which is one of the marks of true greatness, and without which growth is impossible.

"The high qualities of leadership that made Mr. Firestone one of the outstanding men of our day are familiar to all who know the story of the development of the rubber industry. His public-mindedness, his deep interest in all matters of civic and national welfare, has left a record of distinguished service of which any man could be proud. When someone went into St. Paul's Cathedral and asked to see the monument of Sir Christopher Wren, the verger said to him, 'Sir, look around you!' So much that this city looks to with pride is the monument of the public-minded citizen whose memory we honor today. Not so much in brick and mortar, as in the fine qualities of character he built into the lives of men and women, is the story of his influence written. His is a living memorial—business associates stimulated to clearer thinking, competitors challenged to more active effort, friends strengthened by the faith he had in them, and adversaries compelled to admit that here was a valiant fighter.

"But I speak of Mr. Firestone this morning in the more intimate relationships of home and family, where some of us were privileged to see a different kind of greatness than the public knew. It was here that he revealed a sweet simplicity, a tenderness of affection, a depth of devotion that made a visit to his home an unforgettable experience. Here one found that type of family life which is a survival of pioneer days—a kind of patriarchal home in which all the members of the family are bound together in strong bonds of mutual affection and loving comradeship. It was characteristic of Mr. Firestone that with him family always came first. Neither time nor distance, nor the pressure of business, ever prevented him from being with his children in the important events of their lives. Proud as he was of the business that bears his name, he considered his fine family the real achievement of his life and it was there he found his greatest joy.

"No one felt more keenly than he the responsibility of wealth and power. With quiet understanding, he turned to religion for the guiding principles of his life. There is no need for me to tell you who are worshipping in this church today that Mr. Firestone was a deeply religious man. For more than a quarter of a century he has served on the vestry of St. Paul's Parish and for the past seventeen years has been senior warden. As regularly as Sunday came, you saw him here in his pew, whenever he was in the city. On the last Sunday of his life he went to church as his custom was. In days when so many people think lightly of church obligations, it is refreshing to remember the example of this quiet God-fearing man with whom Sunday morning worship was a life-long habit. Traveling with him on many occasions, I discovered that he believed in prayers quite as much on Monday, and through the balance of the week, as he did in Sunday worship. One sensed always that his devotion to religion transcended the boundaries of church affiliation and made him a friend to all people who believe in God and His goodness. Perhaps the easiest thing a wealthy man can give to a church is his money. Mr. Firestone gave so much more than that—the greater gift of himself, his time, his ability, his personal devotion.

"Here indeed was the fundamental source of his strength—his belief in God, his faith in his fellow men. Mr. Firestone never doubted that this is a moral universe in which spiritual values are supreme. Confident that in the long run right will ultimately prevail, he faced difficulty unafraid, taking long views on life, and continuing, as Emerson has said, 'to believe what the centuries say as against the years and hours.' Here was the source of his courage, and his unbounded faith in the future. Things may go wrong for a time but in a universe where God rules, right will ultimately prevail. Believing that, even in troubled times a man can look out on the world with calm confidence, knowing that when the tumult and the shouting have died away, truth will have its day.

" 'This is the victory that overcometh the world, even our faith.' *1 John 5:4*. How inevitably we are reminded by Mr. Firestone's memory of how much our belief is belief in people. We say that we believe in this proposition or in that—we accept this creed or that theory—but always when you trace back the dominating motives that control the conduct of men, you see that we never believe in anything until we see the embodiment of it in some person.

"See how true this is. I speak to you about goodness, and instantly your mind trails off, not to some abstract ideal, but to some person you have known, a father, a mother, a friend, in whom you found the quality of goodness. So if I speak of integrity, you think of it not as a pale abstraction, but something you have seen enshrined in a person on whose inner honesty you would bank your life. So one thinks of courage, not in terms of philosophical abstractions, but in terms of some person you have seen face danger unafraid. The more you think of it, the more you will see that we do not primarily believe in abstractions but in people.

"Dr. Fosdick tells the story of how Nathaniel Hawthorne was one day dropped from his position at the Custom House. 'That position was all that Nathaniel Hawthorne had to rely on for his livelihood. And Hawthorne went home to his wife as discouraged and whipped as you would expect a man to be who must tell his wife that he had lost his position and does not know where the next month's food is coming from. But Mrs. Hawthorne fairly danced with delight. "Oh then," she said, "you can write your book!" That naturally astonished Mr. Hawthorne. He asked with some asperity where she thought they would get bread and rice to eat while he wrote his book. Then opening a drawer in her desk, she proudly exhibited a hoard of coin. She had always known, she said, that he had genius. Week by week, from their meager salary, she had saved, hoping for the leisure when he might write. Now it had come. Now he had lost his position. Now he could write his book. So that is how Nathaniel Hawthorne began *The Scarlet Letter*, perhaps the greatest American novel yet written.'

"I need not press the parable of that story. You never think of family life in terms of abstractions. But when you see it embodied in a home like that of the Hawthornes, you cannot help believing in it and admiring it. So in thinking of 'that victory which overcometh the world, even our faith,' we are not dealing with mere assent to a creed, or any formal statement of religious belief, but rather of that attitude of heart and mind which makes God seem real to us, and our fellow men more our brothers. That kind of faith some of us saw embodied in Mr. Firestone—a simple, childlike faith in the goodness of God, and in the ultimate victory of what is true and beautiful and good. No one could work with him at close range and fail to detect that here was a great believer in the fundamental truths of religion. Here was a Christian gentleman, with all the obvious limitations of this poor humanity of ours, but bearing the dignity of a great believer who wanted to do what is right, and earnestly striving to lead a Christian life.

"It is not the fashion of our day to talk much about death. We assure ourselves that it is better to take one world at a time—to live the best we can here and now and to take our chances with anything that lies beyond. Yet when death comes and touches the shoulder of someone we have greatly loved, we no longer think of this matter in terms of idle speculation where one man's guess is as good as another's, but in terms of the sure and certain confidence we have seen in someone who believed as Browning did that 'the best is yet to be.' We shall never find the assurance of immortality at the end of an argument, or in a test tube in some laboratory experiment. We shall find it where the saints of God have found it, on our knees as we remember Him who said, 'I am the resurrection and the life. He that believeth in me though he were dead, yet shall he live, and whosoever liveth and believeth in me shall not die eternally.'

"It is too bad that the Christian's faith in immortality receives only the major emphasis of Easter Day. For we need the inspiration of it every day. In the midst of life we are in death, and how we adjust ourselves to that fact is one of the determining elements of our character. One can be brave without any hope of immortality, but when we think of those we love most, then our indifference falls to pieces. It does make a difference in our way of living, whether we believe, as one modern novelist has put it, that 'we are only bundles of cellular matter on our way to the ash heap' or whether we share the lofty faith of St. John 'now are we the sons of God, but it doth not yet appear what we shall be.'

" 'This is the victory that overcometh the world —even our faith.' Faith, as someone has put it, is 'reason grown courageous.' That was the faith of Mr. Firestone, that living nobly one can die bravely, fearing nothing beyond the closed door, because the Master is there, and those whom we have loved and lost a while are there waiting to greet us. Knowing Mr. Firestone, some of us found it easier to believe in God and His goodness.

"His passing came as he would have wished it, with the tranquillity of 'one who wraps the draperies

of his couch about him and lies down to pleasant
dreams.' No better reward could any of us have
wished for so fine a friend than that the end should
have come so peacefully. Do you remember how
John Bunyan describes the passing of one of the
characters in *Pilgrim's Progress*, Mr. Valiant-for-
Truth, when he says: 'So he passed over and all
the trumpets sounded for him on the other side.'
For such a valiant spirit there must be great work
to be done in the mystery and joy of the life beyond.
May God bless him, and may light perpetual shine
upon him! and may the comfort which only God
can give, flow out in abundance to his loved ones,
turning their sorrow into joy. 'This is the victory
that overcometh the world, even our faith.' "

16

New Horizons

CONSCIOUS of its preeminence as a tire manufacturer, the company continually encouraged research and development. Applied science explored the path of progress. A fine reward of this intent effort was the achievement of the Firestone Imperial with "Rayodipt" cords in 1938, a premium tire. Rayodipt was gum-dipped rayon, a ply material of the highest known degree of strength and flexibility, giving minimum internal heat. The tread was designed with seven even ribs for firm contact with the road.

This was one of four newly engineered products placed with dealers and stores to maintain their volume and increase it. The new Firestone Champion, adopted as original equipment on 1939 cars, was not only built for long mileage but styled (six zigzag ribs, notched shoulders) in harmony with the modern trend of art in industry.

"Champion" was an apt name. A new record for endurance and safety under speed averaging 117.2 miles per hour had been made this year on Firestone tires by Floyd Roberts in the Indianapolis Sweepstakes. Now Firestone adopted racing tire construction for passenger-car tires; to integrate the tread with the carcass, tread stock was used in calendering the two outer plies.

Two new safety tubes were developed: the Champion

Leakproof heavy-duty tube, with a protective lining which sealed the inner surface to prevent air seepage, and the Life Protector, a "tire within a tire," so described because a special safety valve could offset blowout danger by supporting the car with sufficient air pressure while the driver brought it to a full stop.

A change was made in the regular line of tires. The High Speed supplanted the Standard. The Convoy and the Sentinel remained to round out a complete price range for the motoring public.

The market for farm tires grew overnight. Sixty percent of the tractors manufactured in 1938 were equipped with pneumatics (nearly eighty-five percent the next year). Firestone's triple-braced traction bars on Ground Grip tires caused this growth by reason of outstanding performance. To establish closer relationship with farmers a noon-day radio program, "Firestone Voice of the Farm," was instituted; this brought so many inquiries that the Firestone Farm Service Bureau was set up as an authoritative source of agricultural information.

Ground Grip tires had won favor also on trucks and busses, besides various wheeled farm implements. To supplement these tires, a line of Ground Grip Type S was introduced at a lower price level. There were, of course, regular truck-bus tires and heavy-duty trailer, excavator, and roadbuilding tires—one marvel a thirty-four-ply earth-mover tire, size 30.00-40. And there were bulbous low-pressure airplane tires, cured-on solids, and lug-base pneumatic industrial tires.

Such was the basic business of the company. But its activities had become multiform. The vast expansion program undertaken during the depression had been financed by bank borrowings since 1933 amounting to more than $33,000,000. These had made possible the doubling of annual volume. In order to fund this short-term indebtedness, the company decided in 1938 to issue $50,000,000 in ten-year, three-and-a-half percent debentures, designed also to retire $12,700,000 of the California and cotton mill subsidiaries' five percent bonds and provide further working capital. The issue was several times oversubscribed.

The mechanical rubber goods division, which Russell A. Firestone had taken in charge in 1932, had grown rapidly and blossomed out with a catalog of 6,000 different items, utilizing extra space in the new Fall River plant. Rubber-bonded-to-metal parts constituted the major work of this division, for automobile assembly and sundry industrial uses. Rubber served in all avenues of transportation, and in addition to bushings, bumpers fan belts, fenders, pedals, and motor mountings, this division made traffic-lane markers, third-rail insulator guards, and rubber-cushioned tie plates for railroad tracks and subway lines.

Plastics, made both at Fall River and Wyandotte in sizes and shapes hitherto impossible (but realized through a molding technique developed by Firestone engineers), appeared in radio cabinets, auto dash embellishments, instrument panels, knobs, and handles. Plastics was a new industry—and Firestone made a sweeping ascent.

But the principal activity at Fall River, with Roger S. Firestone as the head of this subsidiary in 1938, was the production of Foamex.

Foamex cushioning material gained wider acceptance as the process of foaming liquid latex was improved, avoiding the deteriorating effects of chemical agents. A mechanism forced air into the latex while giant beaters whipped it into a frothy foam; thus aerated, it was poured into the desired mold, the fluffy texture retained permanently.* The special construction of Contro elastic

* Much as this process represented an advance, it was superseded in a few years by a truly remarkable technique. By this method the latex is foamed in a high-speed aerator and flows out in a continuous stream directly into molds. The molds are borne on conveyors into a steam chest for vulcanizing.

thread—multiple laminated layers of rubber, wrapped around each other—gave Firestone entrée to sales to apparel manufacturers.

Seventy-five Firestone Auto Supply & Service Stores were opened in 1938, several more added the following year, bringing the number of wholly owned stores to 638. Trained personnel and attractive merchandise improved the profits derived from this operation. Budget departments, in keeping with modern retailing, were installed, and the stores now sold radios, electrical and sporting goods, home appliances, and other fast-moving stock. The chief thing was to have seasonable articles for sale throughout the year.

All these steps toward stability—faithful to the prescience of the founder—substantiated the correctness of their direction in a year when automobile and truck production declined fifty-two percent and even registration of cars, trucks, and busses fell. The recession of 1938, however, did no more than nick nine and a half percent off the company's over-all volume. On sales of $141,800,-000, a net profit of $5,250,000 was earned.

General conditions staged a partial comeback in 1939. The company's foreign factories continued their steady growth, export business was good, domestic sales picked up. The grand effect was a record total of $160,100,000, net profit $6,700,000. A new factory was built in Bombay, India, and another was begun in São Paulo, Brazil.

Harvey Firestone had not left a blueprint for the future, but he had given his five sons, the executives who strove with him through the years, and the whole organization a sturdy foundation to build upon, a sizable superstructure, a good name, and more—a vision of new horizons. For himself he had attained ample fulfillment. No man could live to see the final unfolding of his works. But he had initiated so many wise, practical, and anticipatory measures, that the heritage he bestowed was a rich blend of means and vistas. His rich understanding of human character had nurtured for the company such leaders as John W. Thomas, who directed the increase in production, and Lee R. Jackson, who directed the increase in sales.

It was a pity that he did not witness the completion of a civic enterprise for which he had long labored. The elimination of a grade crossing—merely that, yet it signified public duty. The traffic artery into South Akron, perilous at its worst, with cars trying to get through a thousand an hour, and trains roaring across: he had always dreamed of making it safe. As the first president of the City Planning Commission in 1920 and a man who did not dodge attendance at meetings, Harvey Firestone had created the plan whereby the railroad bed would be lowered, South Main Street turned several hundred feet east to flow into an extension of South High Street, and a bridge built as part of a straight, broad arterial highway.

He saw South High Street widened to bear traffic from downtown Akron to the northern approach to the projected bridge. In the year that elapsed, the rest of the construction was done. And on the seventieth anniversary of his birth, December 20, 1938, a city-wide celebration marked the dedication of the Harvey Samuel Firestone Memorial Bridge.

"This bridge project," said Harvey Firestone jr. at the ceremonies, "was very close to Father's heart, as was any improvement which would benefit the City of Akron and its people."

The mayor snipped a colored ribbon. The bridge was opened to a parade of floats and marching units—and to traffic. In the evening, a huge community sing was held nearby, and downtown at a banquet in the Mayflower Hotel tributes were paid by Governor Martin L. Davey, civic leaders, industry leaders, and the clergy— all of whom gave thanks for Harvey Firestone's public spirit.

The next year, the World's Fair took place in New York and the Golden Gate Exposition in San Francisco, with exhibits by the company. He would have been pleased to see the millions of persons impressed with the demonstration of Firestone tire making at the Fair and the millions who viewed the life-size model farm on rubber. And in the second year of the Fair, tires being made of synthetic rubber. . . .

For the research that Harvey Firestone had stimulated in this field was far advanced. Experiments with various types of synthetics, to determine their characteristics, led the company to build tires of duPont's Neoprene in 1933 and 1934, and to become the first to supply the United States Army with synthetic rubber airplane tires. These were size 6.00-20, made with rayon plies. Passenger-car tires 5.50-17 were also built of this stock in 1934. It must be said, in both cases, that the treads wore poorly, and further research was indicated.

The company's chemical research division worked on various chemical combinations and studied samples of German and Italian synthetics in 1936, as well as American specimens. The qualities of man-made rubber had much to recommend it, especially resistance to the action of oil; hence its usefulness for hose and other mechanical goods. On the other hand, the cost of producing synthetic discouraged extensive adoption.

Batches of German Buna-S (a union of butadiene and styrene) came to this country in 1938, and Firestone made tires of this in August for road tests. Meanwhile the company had intensified research in a separate laboratory room on the fifth floor of Plant 1, where it succeeded in May, 1939, in copolymerizing the ingredients of Buna-S according to a formula of its own. A little later this "pilot plant" also produced Buna-N (a copolymer of butadiene and acrylonitrile) and studied the results for comparison with the German types. Engineers co-operated in determining the best method of processing synthetics into finished products.

On September 11, 1939, Firestone built the first tire of its own Buna-S and the next day cured it, Harvey Firestone jr. declaring: "Synthetic might come to be quite a volume. We want to be right on top of it." *

However, the Buna-S process had been patented by I.G. Farben of Germany, which held the American rights jointly with the Standard Oil Company (New Jersey). Before the year's end, Standard bought the sole rights, offered licenses to American rubber companies, and drafted an agreement with Firestone. This arrangement, first of its kind, was concluded in February, 1940, and Buna processing soon began, although in a limited way. Butadiene, a petroleum derivative, the principal ingredient, was expensive: manufactured on a small scale and difficult to procure. In April, Firestone announced that it was producing Buna-S under the license.

Indeed, there were new horizons. And on some of them, war clouds.

The cancer of totalitarianism had become virulent. Hitler's Germany formed an *Anschluss* with Austria in March, 1938 (and the same month Firestone produced ninety-six-inch airplane tires for the United States Army's giant 140,000-pound B-19 bomber). In the fall of that year the notorious Munich pact emboldened Hitler; the Sudetenland was not all that he wanted, for Czechoslovakia was further dismembered. Japanese troops marched on Canton and Hankow. The Italian

* H.S.F. jr. to W. S. S. Rodgers, president, Texas Co., Sept. 12, 1939.

Parliament was dissolved, and a Fascist state was proclaimed, soon to form an Axis with Nazi Germany.

The shadow of another world war darkened Europe
when Hitler, in September, 1939, after making a non-
aggression treaty with Soviet Russia, used this freedom
to roll a motorized army into Poland. He refused to
recall his troops, and Great Britain declared the existence of a state of war. The Nazi dictator asserted that
he wished only for peace. The Soviet dictator seized that
part of Poland which the Nazis had left for the Com-
munists.

Great Britain, with France and the dominions as
allies, waited for Hitler's next thrust. The Japanese
course in Asia was an enigma. The United States buckled
down to national defense.

Only two and a half months' supply of rubber was
held in this country at the end of 1939, based on a
national annual consumption of 575,000 tons. Drastic
cuts by the International Rubber Regulation Committee, in the exportable percentage from the Far East,
had kept stocks low. From ninety percent in 1937, when
rubber was twenty-four cents a pound, the quota was
slashed in half in 1938 as prices declined. A gradual rise
in percentage was allowed in 1939, but it proved inadequate. American industry asked for eighty percent. The
Committee decided on seventy-five.

The Administration in Washington was anxious that
rubber stocks be accumulated. The Committee, concerned more with averting an oversupply and weaker
prices, assured industry that enough rubber would be
available for its requirements. But Washington asked
during the last quarter of 1939 that the quota be lifted
to eighty-five percent. Eventually a concession of eighty
percent was made for the first quarter of 1940.

When a war of action broke out with Hitler's invasion

of Norway and Denmark, the United States government decided to build up a rubber stockpile against an
emergency. In June, the Rubber Reserve Company was
set up under the Reconstruction Finance Corporation
with the joint participation of the rubber industry. By
bartering cotton and cash with Great Britain, the Rubber Reserve Company acquired 88,000 tons; and it
dealt directly with the I.R.R. Committee for 150,000
tons to be delivered in 1940 (180,000 more in 1941), at
eighteen to twenty cents. The quota was increased to
ninety percent, but shipping facilities from the Far East
were woefully inadequate.

The Low Countries had been invaded. The Netherlands and Belgium had surrendered. The British had
been squeezed out of France through Dunkirk. Norway
surrendered. The Nazis occupied Paris, and France fell.

While planning to store large reserves of natural rubber, the Administration also perceived the value of
synthetic rubber to supplement them. Harvey Firestone
jr., with James E. Trainer, vice president in charge of
production, was invited to Washington in July to confer
with the Advisory Commission to the Council of National
Defense. President Roosevelt had suggested the study of
a program for synthetic production in case imports from
Malaya and the East Indies were cut off.

Firestone jr. recommended an immediate start on a
vast project of government sponsorship of plant construction to produce butadiene and polymerize synthetic
rubber so that a large quantity would be made available
and the cost reduced. In a radio broadcast on "The
Voice of Firestone" he apprised the public of the vital
role of rubber in national defense.

Events abroad have swept into the discard many previous con-
ceptions of military strategy and tactics. Speed is the very essence
of modern warfare. And the realization of this significant fact em-

phasizes again the vital importance of rubber, the material that makes such speed possible. . . .

The army tank, once a cumbersome, unwieldy vehicle which waddled along no faster than a man could walk, now races along its rubber track blocks at forty miles an hour.

No longer does the infantry, footsore and weary, plod twenty-five miles a day. It covers twice that distance in a single hour in its rubber-tired cars and trucks.

The romantic picture of galloping horses wheeling field artillery into position has been rudely cut from its frame. Guns many times larger and heavier, mounted on pneumatic-tired carriages, are now swiftly towed by trucks and tractors.

Since the last war, airplane landing speeds have increased sharply. Modern pursuit ships must have tires capable of withstanding the terrific impact of landings at eighty miles an hour.

And large quantities of rubber are required for gas masks, raincoats, airplane seats, and many other items of equipment needed by mechanized and motorized armies.*

But would the United States have enough rubber in the event we were forced into war? Enough not only for the armed services but for civilian transportation of their supplies? If war came, the industries of America would be the fighting men's comrades in arms.

Firestone jr. intimated in this broadcast that the government was thinking of the future course of the rubber industry—how best to serve the nation—and how to acquire rubber. Drastic conservation measures and the collection of old tires and scrap for reclaiming were proposed steps, he said. "The third step would be to start immediately on a large expansion program for the production of synthetic rubber."

Bales of Buna-S made by the company were shipped to New York for its factory exhibit at the World's Fair. They were withheld until August 3, the fortieth anniversary of the founding, and on that day the public saw for the first time a demonstration of the manufacture of

* H.S.F. jr. broadcast, July 15, 1940.

synthetic rubber tires—a preview of "the world of tomorrow." Firestone jr., removing from a watchcase vulcanizer a 6.00-16 Champion tire containing synthetic rubber, pledged the company's support to the national defense program and announced that it was erecting a plant in Akron (behind the Xylos plant) to produce synthetic rubber in commercial quantities.

In September, this strange-looking, spidery steel structure of metal tanks and open framework took its place among the more staid factory buildings, and on October 21 started its production of Firestone's Buna-S (later called Butaprene). Engineering and technical data on plant construction and operation were sent to Washington as a contribution to the grand plan.

Liberia! Of course, there was Liberia, a source of natural rubber supply far beyond the reach of the Japanese menace, now penetrating Indo-China.

The plantations in Liberia were shipping increasing quantities. With renewal of development work in 1936, new plantings had proceeded on a modest scale from year to year, for the emphasis was put on yield per acre. From 19,000 acres in bearing in 1938 came an output of 3,100 tons; from 29,700 acres in bearing in 1939 came 4,800 tons. Now in 1940, the stand planted to rubber trees had grown to 72,500 acres, three-fourths in high-yielding, budded stock, and 34,200 acres were tapped for nearly 7,000 tons.

At Harbel Landing on the Farmington River, an enlarged processing factory was built. A hydroelectric plant was begun, to furnish all the needed power. In a building on the Research Reserve, chemists studied the variations of clonal and seedling latices in relation to centrifuging. This research was of utmost importance, as half of the rubber collection on the Firestone plantations was shipped out as liquid latex.

The factory at Fall River, Massachusetts, received the latex in huge tanks from the ocean-going steamer docked at the company's wharf. Here, in addition to foamed latex products and Contro, molded and extruded rubber goods and battery separators were made, with Roger S. Firestone in charge. This plant revised its production schedules to the pressing needs of the times. Fall River made gas masks. Fall River made airplane seats. Some of its liquid latex was diverted to the composition of bullet-sealing fuel cells for British Mustang fighter planes. London had been blitzed.

All branches of the United States armed forces were getting the cooperation of Firestone and its subsidiaries at the close of 1940. This work of developing and producing equipment for defense had a long history, going back to the early 1930s, when Army Ordnance appropriations were so small that the company bore most of the initial expense. The glory of this effort was Firestone's pioneer role in the creation of rubber tracks, so vital in giving the United States the mightiest, speediest, most maneuverable military tanks in the world.

17

Early Work for Defense

A SMALL rubber bushing held destiny in its compact body. Out of the new-products engineering division this device was developed—one of numerous rubber-to-metal adhesion specialties. Since a bushing functioned to guard against friction in a moving joint, a rubberized one in place of metal bearings dispensed with lubrication. Such a flexible coupling or hinge, absorbing the movement, might be made capable of performing under heavy loads with negligible stretch and heat. The answer to these requirements was the patented Firestone bushing, first applied to automobile spring shackles.

The reason this bushing could stand the weight of a car was its fabrication as a precompressed compound. The production technique was to treat the metal core chemically, vulcanize the rubber to it, and force the unit under great compression into the outer sleeve. Tests proved its load capacity was triple that of ordinary non-compressed bushings. And it afforded a wide angle of twist; was maneuverable. Ideal, then, as an articulated joint for crawler-type vehicles—why not use this to hinge the links of army tank tracks?

The company broached the suggestion to Army Ordnance in 1933. Tank designs were in evolution. Ordnance showed quick interest but was not in a position to carry the work forward. The idea of providing bushings led naturally to the rubber blocks they were intended to connect. Firestone undertook to produce a pilot track, shouldering the cost of molds in which the rubber was bonded to steel skeleton links for a cushion tread and articulating them by means of the rubber bushings.

A tank design having been adopted in 1936 for limited production by the Rock Island Arsenal, the Arsenal sent Firestone the metal components (forged and machined) of tracks; Firestone returned them vulcanized with rubber blocks and joined with the bushings. In getting this "education" the company acquired know-how and was prepared when the drama of the accelerated defense program commenced in the early fall of 1939. After the first contract for the manufacture of this tank was awarded to American Car & Foundry, Ordnance officials recommended Firestone to them as a source of track supply.

Firestone was willing either to do a rubber job or to take the responsibility for furnishing complete tracks, as it had analyzed methods in machining and processing the components on a large scale, as well as techniques in rubberizing them. Its quotation on complete tracks that would pass the performance specifications was accepted. A few weeks later the Arsenal, on being authorized to procure a considerable number of tracks, again asked for a bid and again placed a contract. Manifestly, the company's costs compared favorably with the Arsenal's own. The two orders were carried out concurrently; the delivery dates were met.

As the needs of the mechanized army increased, more tanks, combat cars, and other crawler vehicles had to be equipped. Firestone supplied the various body manufacturers whom Ordnance called upon. Firestone financed its own plant expansions, contributed development work, and adjusted its output to changing requirements, coping with difficulties of obtaining materials and man power. Our armed forces ultimately received tanks of monstrous size and power; and precisely as the modern automobile and the titanic bulldozer had become realities by virtue of their tires, these maneuverable fortresses were made possible by the service of their tracks and flexible bushings.

But before the test of war came—on desert, in mud, yes, even in the sea—the Firestone organization familiarized itself with other articles of defense and sought to improve them.

The significant role of aviation in modern warfare called attention to one of the most vulnerable parts of a plane in combat. This was the fuel cell. Flak or machine-gun fire, striking the container, could drain it of the airplane's life substance within a few seconds. Firestone's research laboratory took up a study of the problem early in 1939.

It was not a new subject. Near the close of World War I, the executive board passed upon experimental work that had been done and considered manufacturing leak-proof gasoline tanks for the Army; and Harvey Firestone urged his colleagues then to make the company the leader in this sphere of production. At that time, the principle in use for bulletproofing was crude-rubber sheeting cemented to the outside of a metal container. Firestone's offering was tested by the Army at Wright Field, Dayton, Ohio, and was found satisfactory, but as the government technicians failed to decide on a design, no orders were placed. The holocaust ended; the matter was dropped.

When Hitler disturbed the peace of Europe, Firestone resumed experimental work—in reverse. What had been regarded as the most feasible protection was discarded, for the flaws became more obvious with the possibility of correction. A projectile emerging from an aluminum tank caused the exit hole to flower out, and the metal "petals" impeded the outer rubber coating in the sealing of the break. Now the sealant was to be placed inside the tank: rubber next to gasoline. This had not been possible with natural rubber, which would dissolve upon being exposed to the contents; but was practicable with a synthetic lining. Once the lining was pierced, the sealing material would swell rapidly on contact with the gasoline and thus close the opening to prevent escape.

Firestone developers embarked on the adventure of constructing a strong nonmetallic fuel cell with walls tough and resistant to rips and cracking; in effect, perfectly aligned and capable of serving as a container itself. Each new combination of materials improved the performance, tested on the company's own range under various calibers of ball- and armor-piercing gunfire. For a time the most successful wall construction consisted of three layers between Neoprene lining and a steer-hide outer ply; that is, a sheet of pure latex, a ply of sponge rubber, and another latex sheet. The thickness of the whole came to about half an inch.

The solid gum was the chief sealant, swelling as the bullet hole brought contact with gasoline and not going into solution, which would foul the fuel lines and motor. Extremely low temperatures did not impair the effectiveness of the gum. Sponge rubber was quicker to react to gasoline but was not so permanent as the latex sheet; these two materials supplemented one another. Sponge cushioned the bullet's impact and swelled rapidly. The fuel did not penetrate far from the wound.

Steer hide not only gave rigidity to the cell, but its fibrous nature restricted the tear of the bullet; and even if the emerging projectile tore a great hole in the aluminum tank, the leather still supported the liquid head and kept the rubber hole from stretching. The behavior of the supporting structure was of utmost importance to the working of the sealant.

In cementing the plies together, care was taken to keep out moisture and air. Neoprene cement was used, affording further resistance to the passage of gasoline. Still not satisfied, the Firestone technical staff decided to apply a resin coating to the lining, to reduce the penetration of the gasoline and check the swollen gum from bulging into the interior.

On the proving grounds of airplane manufacturers, shells of 30 and 50 caliber were fired at Firestone's newest product. The cells were unshattered, the holes sealed themselves, and there was no harmful amount of debris in the tank.

The first order came in November, 1940, from North American Aviation, which was producing P-51 Mustangs for the British government. The units were of eighty-five-gallon capacity, to be fitted several in each wing. Firestone bullet-sealing fuel cells, the first of many thousands to be made in the strenuous years ahead, for the United States and our allies, were sped from the company's Los Angeles plant to help in the magnificent air defense of England. They were superior. German cells obtained during the blitz were built up with plies of crude rubber and tread stock wrapped around a fiber inner liner, which shattered under gunfire, thus depriving the sealant of mechanical support and causing heavy leakage.

Tank tracks. Fuel cells. These were not the only prewar articles of defense in which Firestone gained experience and made contributions. For the Navy, a seadrome lighting buoy was designed in 1938 and first produced in May, 1939. This steady beacon was essentially a four-ply, thirty-nine-inch tire with yellow sidewall and tread, withstanding the elements. For the Chemical Warfare Division, on an initial order for 10,000 gas masks in December, 1939, the company set up facilities at Fall River for the complete manufacture of the rubber and plastic parts, making first deliveries the following November; the machine shop fashioned new tools to increase operating efficiency, and because of lowered costs, Firestone made voluntary refunds to the government.

In 1940 the company also made rubberized fabric pontons, shell guard facings, and bogie wheels to support the load of the tank inside of its rubber track. It began what eventually became a monumental production of metallic links to make 50-caliber machine-gun cartridges into belts. A department for barrage balloons was organized in December. A bullet-resisting tube was produced for military service, sealing itself after a direct hit instead of going flat. Airplane tires were made of racing-tire construction, using a high degree of carbon black in the stock for the two outer plies.

And there were combat tires, developed for the Army by September. They were of extremely heavy body construction so that tactical maneuvers could be continued even though the tires were punctured by bullets and were deflated.

As ninety percent of all farm tractors manufactured that year were equipped with rubber tires, Firestone's farm market likewise increased. For improved service to trucks and busses, an all-rib Transport tire was produced. Earthmover tires kept growing huger—the year witnessed gigantic 36.00-40s standing ten feet high!

These were the largest pneumatics ever produced. Thirty-four plies built on a special drum; expanded in a machine two and a half stories tall; cured in a mammoth mold. Each tire weighed 3,646 pounds with tube and protecting flap. It contained three-quarters of a ton of rubber, a bale and a half of cotton, a half ton of pigments, sixty pounds of steel wire. Mounted on a forty-inch wheel, it measured thirty-nine inches in cross section. A set of these tires could sustain twenty-five tons and float the huge earth-scraping and hauling equipment over rocky or soggy terrain.

The grand total of civilian and Army tires produced by Firestone in 1940 came to 10,900,000. Plant capacities were enlarged in Akron, Los Angeles, and Memphis.

The urgencies of national defense kept John W. Thomas and Harvey Firestone jr. constantly active in all its phases. Lee Jackson, executive vice president, presided at weekly meetings on these problems. J. E. Trainer and various department heads joined with him in exploring further avenues of government service: continuous bands to be tested for half-trac cars, a good insulating material to be found for airplane spark plugs, bogie rollers for scout cars, firing tests to be made on sample oxygen tanks for the Royal Air Force, brake-lining specifications to be checked with the Bureau of Standards, a more aggressive tread to be designed for motorcycle tires, and examination of a display of airplane parts to determine what else the company could manufacture.

In the development of civilian tires, rayon plies were used for high-speed, heavy-duty trucks to meet the problem of excessive heat. Rayon cord, produced in the company's New Bedford mill, went also into airplane tires. There were studded and wide-base Ground Grip tires. And, as a result of testing new tractor models for the makers to determine the most suitable sizes and designs, Firestone developed and pioneered the three-rib Guide Grip front tractor tire. This led to establishing a farm-tire testing station at the homestead farm the next year for the accumulation of technical data. Finally, for the motorist's enjoyment, the new De Luxe Champion tire.

In this busy year, sales amounted to $187,200,000, the largest total yet, and after adding $1,500,000 to the reserve for contingencies, the net profit was $8,600,000. More than $2,000,000 of the profits came from foreign operations. Exports to Europe had decreased, but the demand from South America and other parts of the world rose. The foreign factories were working to the hilt, in particular Brentford, Bombay, and Port Elizabeth, for their energies were in the war.

The Brentford plant had stepped up its production of heavy-duty tires. Incursions into man power, as reservists were called into service, were overcome by devising a more efficient lineup of machines and employing more women workers. All nonwar operations were shifted to this country. Brentford was serving the Commonwealth and the world as a rampart against Nazi advance. In the blitz of November but slight damage was inflicted on the factory; the personnel, safe in shelters underneath, returned to their work in a few minutes after the "all clear."

A month later, when A.R.P. spotters on the Brentford roof sounding a warning of raiders in the night, the employees found safety in good time as four high explosives struck the plant, one falling on exactly the same spot as before—the east-wing, tire-building room. Three machines were damaged, but there were no casualties.

The new factory in Bombay made 100,000 automobile tires in its first year, and a considerable number of bicycle tires. In Port Elizabeth, the production was a half-million tires by the middle of 1940, to supply British troops in the Union Defense Force, in East Africa, and in the Middle East, among others. Bullet-resisting tubes, life rafts for the R.A.F. on coastal patrol, and cement were among the products.

Firestone's Canadian plants had long been on a war basis. In evidence of the changed nature of the output at Hamilton, an increase of less than seven percent in tire units from 1939 to 1940 actually represented a jump of 36.6 percent in pounds. The cotton mill at Woodstock, serving Hamilton, kept pace and soon furnished rayon tire fabric for military needs.

With the beginning of 1941, the weekly national defense meetings at Akron headquarters considered every aspect of manufacture in which industry might express its partnership with the armed forces. As John W. Thomas said in addressing the stockholders' meeting, the first responsibility of the Firestone organization "is to serve our country by cooperating with our government in the vitally important work of national defense." The executives discussed bullet-sealing oil cells (a more difficult task than fuel cells because of the hot oil), the fabrication of molded cells, self-sealing hose for gasoline and oil, complete wheel assemblies for planes (wheels, brakes, tires, tubes), pilot seats, life rafts and vests, greater traction for tank tracks, and a steel-and-rubber combination track.

Harvey Firestone jr. visited Chairman William S. Knudsen of the Office of Production Management in January to place every sinew of this giant organization at the disposal of the defense program—"to play whatever part you feel may be useful." Sending Knudsen a list of the manufacturing plants and their capacity to make products of rubber, cotton, and steel, he wrote:

If there is any problem toward which you think our experience in management, research, development, engineering or manufacturing should be directed, I want you to know that we are eager and willing to tackle the job.*

* H.S.F. jr. to Wm. S. Knudsen, Jan. 30, 1941.

As a result, the O.P.M. made a careful study of Firestone facilities to see, as it said, "whether there are some additional ways your fine organization can participate." It did not take long. Knudsen came up with a big surprise.

Meanwhile the company shifted into gear for the mass production of tracks, half-tracs, cells, machine-gun belt links, gas masks, barrage balloons, and many other articles.

The cartridge clips, made by the steel products division, were destined for guns that would destroy enemy equipment. Precision of manufacture was the essential, for the belts must feed the firing chamber at the rate of 800 cartridges a minute; the guns would swirl on stationary mounts or on scout cars, tanks, planes. In a portion of the Fall River plant, taken over for this work, links were cut from coils of spring steel and stamped by dies, heat-treated for toughness, and rust-proofed. Each stage required accurate workmanship—for the 65,000,000 belt links turned out by the end of the year. Akron and Wyandotte were now put in readiness to add their millions to a stupendous grand total.

The gas masks, after the experimental orders of 1940, were produced in large quantities at Fall River under the direction of the mechanical rubber goods division. Plastic lenses, valve frames, and all other components were made there, with activity quickened to seven days a week by March, 1941. Seven types of masks were eventually fabricated, each for a different function. Firestone developed a one-piece mask with the canister screwed directly into the side of the facepiece, eliminating interference with the fighting man in assault or combat.

The barrage balloons were first patterned in March, first made in May. Dilatable to eighty-three feet, with

a capacity of 28,400 cubic feet, these were the D-6 type
for the protection of cities and other military objectives
from dive bombers. The balloons formed a barrier to
keep attacking planes from flying too low; each suspended a cable to tangle their propellers. The quarters
initially provided in Plant 1 proved inadequate, so that
the facilities were moved over to the Club House auditorium. Fall River also shared the honors as several types
of balloons were ordered.

Firestone needed every square inch of space. Steel
Products needed more room for the increased demand
for heavy-duty rims on combat and transport vehicles.
The Los Angeles plant, serving airplane makers on the
Pacific Coast, needed and obtained a new building for
the exclusive production of fuel and oil cells.

The Army, the Navy, and their Air Forces called for
larger quantities and wider varieties of equipment as the
flame of Nazi ambition seared the Balkans and suddenly
sprang at the throat of Russia; as England endured unmerciful blitzes. Germany, Italy, and Japan had signed
a military mutual-assistance pact. President Roosevelt
had signed the Lend-Lease Bill.

The nucleus of a flotation gear department was formed
in July. Navy life belts, the first item developed, were in
production by September, at which time a seven-man
pneumatic service boat was also being made for the
Navy. Many other items issued from the engineers'
thinking. The scope was amazing. A new subsidiary was
formed, the Firestone Aviation Products Company, with
Leonard Firestone in charge. It added many new items,
including wheels and brakes, Foamex parachute seats,
Foamex filler for airplane wings, and oxygen cylinders
for high-altitude flying.

Firestone developed a radioactive spark plug, made

with polonium, and a method of processing polonium and its alloys. The patents on these were assigned to the United States government.

Before Firestone tires and tubes were on their way to China and England under lend-lease, an improvement in the form of a channel tread enabled combat planes to take off and land on soft fields (mud- or snow-covered), where other tires bogged down. There were low-profile nose-wheel tires, also channel-tread airplane tires for carrier-deck landings. Light-gauge rayon of higher count gave plies of thinner body and cooler running; excellent for truck-bus use. Truck transport demands, greater than ever, with American industry keyed up to defense, meant higher speeds, longer hauls, heavier loads. All this spelled tires of unprecedented strength. Firestone delivered.

All-Traction tires were also introduced this year. Having the wearing quality of a highway tire and the traction quality of an off-the-road tread, they served both purposes. For improved traction in mining and excavation service, the Rock Grip tire. Nor was the motorist neglected in this abundance of improvements. For him Firestone made the Super Champion, a first-quality tire at a lower price, borrowing glamour from the fact that the 1941 Indianapolis Sweepstakes were won on Firestones without a single change.

The year's aggregate exceeded 12,500,000 tires.

Firestone was fundamentally a tire company.

But a skillful manufacturer was a manifold national resource. Thus the sweeping offer to Knudsen brought an invitation to examine a mobile antiaircraft gun. This opportunity and its sequel were spectacular.

It was in February, 1941, that the Cleveland Ordnance District asked Firestone to send representatives to the Frankford Arsenal, Philadelphia, where a Bofors gun had arrived from England—a forty-millimeter mobile cannon like those that had fought off low-flying planes in the evacuation of Dunkirk. This weapon of deadly destructiveness spun on a traversing field of 360 degrees, with an elevation arc of ninety-five degrees. It fired 120 rounds a minute, detonating on impact in little more than one ten-thousandth of a second. With a horizontal range of 11,000 yards, the Bofors had a vertical range limited to 5,400 yards, devised for defensive action. Would Firestone undertake to build the carriage and mount for this gun, and assemble it with furnished breech block and firing tube? A complex, delicate mechanism of 1,485 parts!

"Eager and willing," Firestone jr. had said.

With great speed, Ordnance emphasized.

It was a matter of space as well as time. Besides an addition to the Mechanical Building, ten acres of floor space would have to be provided—a new structure erected.

The gun originally had been designed by an armaments firm in Bofors, Sweden, and was manufactured under license in various European countries. The blueprints supplied to Firestone that February were Swedish, English, and Canadian, all in the metric system, and had to be redrawn and transposed in accordance with Ordnance standards. Draftsmen from the various engineering departments pitched into these stacks of drawings, working in day and night shifts, seven days a week, with feverish intentness so that Firestone could produce two pilot models.

Ordnance wanted this instrument of superfine tolerance in mass production. The Bofors had never before been manufactured in the United States and never anywhere except on a "hand-tailored" basis. Another difficulty: materials must be used that contained a minimum of strategically scarce alloying elements, whereas the

British used nickel-steel for many parts Ordnance asked Firestone engineers to propose any design changes that might make the construction stauncher, improve the operation of the mount, lessen manufacturing costs, or speed output. They tackled the task with relish.

Each part, each nut and bolt, screw and washer, was set up on a big display board and examined. Ideas fairly leaped from this array. The chief change was a reduction of the number of forgings, using welded elements in many instances. But most important was the elimination of riveting. The frame of the original carriage required more than a thousand rivets. Firestone redesigned it for welded construction, thereby gaining greater rigidity and saving fifty man-hours per mount. The top carriage section was also redesigned for welding; again costs were lowered, strength was unimpaired, and field care was made simpler. The chassis was strengthened at a cost lower than that of riveted construction.

The changes—all made simultaneously with the translation of the blueprints to avoid loss of time—all saved many man-hours of production. They saved expensive tool and die charges; moreover, machine tools were scarce. In many cases fabrications were substituted for costly forgings; axles for the mount, originally forged from solid steel, machined, and bored on a lathe, were made of welded tubes with cast-steel ends. The ball-bearing traverse mechanism was an intricate affair—to begin with. In this single instance, redesign saved 480 man-hours per mount. There were other changes, other economies; the plates used were half again as thick as those in the model. Less building time would mean more building in a given time. Thus, ingenuity at Firestone dispensed with about six thousand rivets and reduced the total cost to the government by twenty-five percent.

In planning for the Bofors plant, the shortage of

structural steel posed a problem. Search, however, uncovered a sufficient quantity near Toledo, lying in storage after having served the temporary purposes of the Philadelphia Sesquicentennial Exposition. On May 1 ground was broken near the Mechanical Building in Akron in ceremonies that began with John W. Thomas operating a steam shovel; the men present were solemnly aware of the vital obligation their company had assumed.

Within fifty working days a two-story structure, 630 by 324 square feet, was completed—and the engineers were ready with their pilot models, two weeks ahead of schedule.

On June 30, 1941, Firestone formally presented its first two Bofors carriages to the United States Army. They were assembled with gun tubes and breech blocks and were drawn by scout cars through the streets of Akron. Then they rolled away for testing on the Aberdeen Proving Ground in Maryland—on 6.00-20 Transport tires with bullet-resisting tubes. This was a rubber company's finishing touch.

The far cry from rubber to Bofors guns was simply a harking back to the founder's decision in 1907 to manufacture rims, for this gave birth to the Steel Products Company, which in turn had many offshoots; stainless-steel barrels, for example, which led easily to welded oxygen cylinders and now, as a proficient steel manufacturer, to ordnance.

On an initial order for 1,000 Bofors carriages, the schedule started at five a day and stepped up to ten a day. Ultimately they were made 1,500 a month. England, in dire need, received the first shipments. America, after the fateful hour had struck at Pearl Harbor, was able to blast away at kamikazes.

When we entered the war, the rubber situation was very grave.

18

Creating a Rubber Supply

SUNDAY drivers, on the day of the sneak attack on Pearl Harbor, wore out 5,000 tons of rubber, as estimated by an official of the Office of Production Management. The next day the Japanese completed their conquest of Siam, landed in Malaya, advanced toward Singapore, the key to Java and Sumatra. With tires consuming seven out of every ten pounds of rubber used in the United States, the government faced a solemn problem: how best to conserve the rubber supply for war needs.

In the effort to build up a stockpile, the Rubber Reserve Company had accumulated but 130,000 tons by the beginning of 1941. The pile grew slowly. On the other hand, the pace of manufacturing advanced, for this was a year of extraordinary auto production (3,700,-000 new passenger cars and 1,000,000 new trucks and busses would have to be equipped) and an all-high registration of nearly 34,500,000 motor vehicles.

In June, to check the scramble, the O.P.M. abolished private importation of rubber from the Far East; the Rubber Reserve Company became the sole buyer. Allocations were made to the manufacturers, their quotas cut one percent in July, twenty percent by December. The surplus of imports went into the reserve.

Only 600,000 tons were on hand—enough for one

normal year. The armed forces alone needed this much. Hence the O.P.M. directly after the declaration of war stopped the civilian sale of tires and tubes, permitting release only to doctors and essential commercial vehicles.

Singapore's surrender in February, 1942, and the occupation of the Netherlands East Indies the following month, proved the wisdom of a stockpile. America had depended upon the Far East for ninety-seven percent of its rubber; now none could be expected from there for the duration except what might trickle through from Ceylon. Conservation by rationing had already been extended to the retreading and recapping of tires. The use of reclaim rubber was ordered for new tires, but motorists were loath to give up their old tires, the greatest source of reclaim. One hope remained to keep the supply of natural rubber from disappearing. It was synthetic rubber.

Back in 1940, the Advisory Commission to the Council of National Defense had recommended—and Harvey Firestone jr., as a member of the rubber committee, strongly urged—that the Reconstruction Finance Corporation provide for butadiene and styrene plants and for polymerization plants to furnish 100,000 tons of synthetic rubber a year. Although a large expenditure for construction was authorized, the program was snagged by intragovernmental disagreements. The Firestone company, however, pursuing its own plans, enlarged its plant facilities to produce on a commercial scale in November, 1940, and before the end of the year was in regular run on Buna-S, Buna-N, and other synthetic types.

While jurisdictional disputes were still going on in government departments in January, 1941, Firestone arranged with Standard Oil for large purchases of butadiene. In August, synthetic production was accelerated to three tons a day to bring down the per-pound cost and add this output to the natural rubber quota. Rigorous Army tests of Firestone's Buna-S tires proved their worth, and hundreds of thousands of such tires were built by December.

The R.F.C. program was also under way. Firestone had signed a contract with the Defense Plant Corporation in May for the building of a plant to have 10,000 tons annual capacity, and in July an agreement with the Rubber Reserve for operating it. With three other R.F.C.-financed plants and four private ones, the country would have 80,000-ton capacity some time in 1942.

Having assumed the obligation of performing a large part of the over-all job, Firestone entered into a discussion with other rubber companies, with Standard Oil and the Rubber Reserve. This resulted in a pooling and an exchange of technical information between the companies and the government. The formula for Buna-S eventually adopted by the government was essentially the same as the Firestone formula, and it became known as GR-S, signifying government-produced general-purpose rubber of the butadiene-styrene type.

In November, 1941, the directors of the company, in a move to strengthen the organization for the greater responsibilities ahead, elected John W. Thomas chairman and Harvey S. Firestone jr. president.

The day after Pearl Harbor, Congress declared the existence of a state of war between this country and the treacherous, tyrannous forces of Japan. That Monday, Firestone jr. went on the air with the impassioned resolve of a freeborn American. He made his stand.

Tonight, in the heart of every American, there is a vibrant new spirit of unity and loyalty and the determination that the fundamental rights of all mankind shall not perish from the earth. And this evening the Firestone organization pledges anew to the President of the United States and the American people its wholehearted support and dedicates to our nation its resources, its manufacturing facilities, its engineering ingenuity, and its scientific skill that more and more defense materials may flow in an ever-increasing stream to assure final victory.*

Pearl Harbor quickened the pulse of the rubber planners. R.F.C. Chairman Jesse Jones telegraphed John W. Thomas a plea for speed and a promise of full cooperation.

In view of very grave situation in which we now find ourselves I urge that you redouble your efforts toward the construction and completion of our plant with a view to getting it into production at the earliest possible moment and if possible go on a twenty-four-hour seven-day basis.†

The synthetic-rubber program was amplified. The decision to produce 400,000 tons annually was hailed by Firestone jr. as "a practical step forward in solving the critical problem of rubber supply facing this country." He arranged for the enlargement of the Defense Plant so that it would have a rated capacity of 15,000 tons, and he received authorization to build and operate a second plant in Akron of equal size.

Speed was urgent. Speed! Under the tremendous requirements of the armed forces the natural-rubber stockpile would probably last no longer than the middle of 1942. The collapse of Singapore changed the objective to 800,000 tons of synthetic a year.

The Defense Plant rising at Firestone was rushed to completion—the first to be finished, the first to produce. On April 26, Firestone made a test run of 6,500 pounds of GR-S. It was good. The initial batch immediately went into combat tires. In a few days, the plant was in

* H.S.F. jr., *Voice of Firestone* broadcast, Dec. 8, 1941.
† Jesse H. Jones to J.W.T., Dec. 9, 1941.

regular production, to be increased to rated capacity as fast as sufficient quantities of the chemical ingredients became available.

This was the beginning of a wondrous achievement. Hitler and Hirohito were being outsmarted by American man-made rubber. It cost fifty cents to produce a pound of synthetic, but every pound meant a pounding of the enemy.

Firestone undertook a larger part of the program. In May, the company entered into a Defense Plant agreement to construct and operate two plants with 60,000 tons total capacity at Lake Charles, Louisiana, near the Texas oil fields. Its competence was again requisitioned a few months later in an engagement to build and equip a 30,000-ton plant at Baton Rouge, to be operated jointly by a group of smaller manufacturers.

In Akron the newest and strangest of the structures on the Firestone premises—a vast maze of pipes, tanks, and domed mixing chambers called "autoclaves"—housed the silent miracle of rubber creation. Tank cars arrived here, some filled with butadiene, derived from chemical fractions of petroleum such as butane and butylene, and also derived from grain alcohol; other tanks brought styrene, made from coal-tar benzene and ethylene (ethyl benzene with hydrogen removed). These two fluids, butadiene and styrene, whose molecules were to be combined into larger molecules resembling those of natural rubber, were piped to storage tanks. After redistillation to remove impurities, they were piped out to the mixing vessels, three parts butadiene to one part styrene.

Soap and water were added to form an emulsion which would facilitate molecular linking. A catalyst sped this up. The mixture was heated and agitated in the process called "polymerization." Now there was a milky mass, looking much like latex from the drippings of a rubber tree. Similarly it was solidified, washed, dried, and compressed into large bales.

The polymer Buna-N (GR-N) resulted by combining butadiene with acrylonitrile. This had its own special uses.

GR-S was excellent for replacing natural rubber for most purposes. Used in tires, it was in fact superior in resistance to abrasion, aging, oil, and skidding on wet pavements; but was less tacky and necessitated a separate cement for the plies. Also, it tore more easily, was less resilient, generated more heat. In large or heavy tires, rayon would be required in place of cotton.

The fine points were all to the good. The weak ones would have to be studied, counteracted, strengthened. Research went on. In the meantime, natural and synthetic, employed together—or reclaim and synthetic— prevented inroads on the stockpile.

In the spring of 1942, the replacement of natural rubber was not proceeding fast enough. The synthetic production program lagged behind the goal, though the 22,476 tons produced in the course of 1942 almost tripled the amount of the year before. The government's drive for scrap rubber was also limping along. Jesse Jones asked Firestone jr. for suggestions on getting car owners to part with their old tires, and was advised that "price won't bring it in," President Roosevelt should dramatize an appeal. In a few days the President initiated an intensive campaign. Every gas station became a collection depot . . . and 450,000 tons came in, converted into about 300,000 tons of reclaim.

At the Firestone Memphis factory a process of "flash" devulcanization was developed, whereby scrap was exposed to steam at a very high pressure, with a gain in both time and tensile strength. For a while Firestone offered Victory Tires, made wholly of reclaim, for essential civilian driving.

The processing of synthetic types into manufactured products was more difficult, more expensive, than processing natural rubber. It required more operations, more machinery, more man-hours. Because of the different molecular structure, the years spent in developing compounds were of little use; synthetic called for new formulas for compounding. Milling took longer. Firestone's technical men originated methods and designed new machines to speed the work, and the company made these findings available to the government and other rubber manufacturers without royalties or other payment. In August, Firestone was in large-scale production of 100 percent GR-S tires.

Dissatisfaction in Congress over the administration of rubber control, and the lack of harmony between the Rubber Reserve Company and the rubber branch of the War Production Board, led to the passage of a bill the same August, which in the President's eyes was ill advised. Vetoing it, he appointed a fact-finding committee to canvass the whole situation and recommend action to obtain "the rubber necessary for our total war effort" without disrupting other war production.

This unusual investigation is being directed solely because of the interest of the American people in the subject, because of the great impact of the lack of rubber upon the lives of American citizens, and because of the present confusion of thought and factual statement.[*]

The natural-rubber stockpile, with depletions barely balanced by imports, was under 600,000 tons. The great number of heavy combat tires, requiring six times more rubber than the typical passenger tire, would surely drain the supply. As military and other essential needs were estimated at 842,000 tons up to January 1, 1944, a deficit of 211,000 loomed if not met by synthetic rubber.

"We find the existing situation to be so dangerous that unless corrective measures are taken immediately, this

[*] F.D.R., veto message, Aug. 6, 1942.

country will face both a military and a civilian collapse."

This was one of the facts and conclusions presented by the President's committee, which consisted of Bernard M. Baruch, chairman; James B. Conant, president of Harvard University, and Karl T. Compton, president of the Massachusetts Institute of Technology. With the assistance of technical experts, they rendered their dramatic report in September, 1942.

> To dissipate our stocks of rubber is to destroy one of our chief weapons of war.
>
> . . . the country is dependent, finally, upon the production of synthetic rubber which, it is hoped, will reach its full swing in 1944.
>
> Why not earlier? Why so late? The answers to these queries lie in the past. These errors, growing out of procrastinations, indecisions, conflict of authority, clashes of personalities, lack of understanding, delays, and early non-use of known alcohol processes, are not to be recounted by us, nor shall we go into the failure to build up a greater stockpile of crude rubber. . . .
>
> If our hopes are realized, the production of . . . synthetic materials will total 425,000 tons by the end of 1943 . . . the critical year of 1943.*

Delay, the Baruch committee warned, would mean "the successful operation of our mechanized army would be jeopardized." Lack of rubber constituted "the greatest threat to the safety of our nation and the success of the Allied cause."

The committee recommended expansion of the program to 1,100,000 tons capacity a year, of which 845,000 tons should be GR-S.

Until this capacity was reached, the mileage of the nation's 27,000,000 passenger cars must be restricted by gasoline rationing, and tire life further prolonged by reducing the speed limit. The committee proposed also that new tires and recapping, largely from reclaim, be released to maintain necessary civilian driving. Collec-

---

* *Report of the Rubber Survey Committee*, Sept. 10, 1942.

tion of scrap rubber should be continuous. Large-scale planting of guayule should be undertaken. Rubber manufacturing space must be expanded to process the huge scheduled output of synthetic.

Firestone jr. expressed himself as wholeheartedly in accord with these proposals. The company helped carry out what the committee called "an ambitious technical project that must be rushed to completion at breakneck speed."

Every promise was performed. In January, 1943, Firestone's second defense plant in Akron came through with its first batch; in August, Lake Charles was in swing. As the months passed, the rate of operations exceeded expectations. The Baton Rouge plant, likewise designed, constructed, and equipped by Firestone engineers, had already been turned over to the Co-Polymer Group. At Port Neches, Texas, where Firestone operated two additional defense plants, each with an annual capacity of 30,000 tons, it pressed the first bale in November.

Knowledge gained was knowledge to be shared. Formal relinquishment of pecuniary rights in the company's formula and processes was made by Firestone jr. in a statement to the Office of the Rubber Director.

Confirming our offer to representatives of your office and of the Rubber Reserve Company, we are pleased to transfer to the government for all time and without compensation all of our patent rights on synthetic tire rubber (Buna-S type) resulting from inventions conceived and reduced to practice by our company heretofore and during the war period.

Likewise, to stimulate to the greatest possible degree the manufacture of synthetic rubber for our war effort and for the ultimate benefit of all car, truck, and bus owners, we will give the government the right to grant a royalty-free license to anyone who the government feels can make a contribution to the synthetic rubber production program, upon the understanding that such licensee will reciprocate with respect to its patent rights for a similar period.*

* H.S.F. jr. to Rubber Director William M. Jeffers, Apr. 21, 1943.

The big job remaining to the Rubber Director that year was to bring the government butadiene and styrene plants into production. The polymerization plants were as busy as could be. Firestone in Akron surpassed its rated capacity during August and brought the cost down four cents a pound below the national average.

Praise for the company's cooperation in exchanging information relative to the construction of plants and the manufacture of synthetic "to combat the problem resulting from the loss of our supply of crude rubber from the Far East" was given by Jesse Jones as the national rated capacity approached the goal.

The performance of your company in the process development, design, construction, and operation of synthetic rubber plants has been most outstanding. . . .

The success of the program to date reflects the results of the cooperative spirit which was so necessary to this effort. I wish to express my appreciation to everyone who had a part in this tremendous undertaking.*

Instead of a deficit at the end of this critical year there was a stockpile—but it was only half the size of the reserve of the year before. It owed its existence chiefly to the production of 181,470 tons of synthetic rubber. Of this amount, the various plants Firestone operated contributed 30,330 tons; in addition, in its own plant, 1,500 tons of Butaprene. Imports of natural rubber were a meager 34,500 tons, and here again Firestone played a significant role for only 17,617 tons came from Ceylon, which sent most of its supplies to the United Kingdom. The Firestone plantations in Liberia shipped 14,400 tons to the United States, including 3,790,000 pounds of concentrated latex, all turned over to our government.

"The rubber crisis has been licked!"

* Jesse H. Jones to J.W.T., Dec. 11, 1943.

Firestone jr. so declared in an address before the Economic Club of Detroit in November. The supply of rubber for 1944, being guaranteed by the rubber-company-operated plants, was no longer the major problem.

I believe it is safe to assume that America's synthetic rubber industry will be perpetuated and that a stockpile of natural rubber sufficient for all anticipated military and civilian needs will be kept on hand at all times to avoid any recurrence of what might well have been a national tragedy. . . .

There is every indication that from any economic standpoint, synthetic rubber, when produced in commercial quantities, will be able to compete in price with natural rubber. The creation of the synthetic rubber industry in this country not only makes it possible to bring this war to a victorious end, but it also will have a lasting benefit to the car owners of America by insuring the United States against a recurrence of the wide price fluctuations of the past. . . . Its very existence will bring stability to the rubber industry and annual savings of millions of dollars to American motorists.

At last Americans are producing their own rubber. They know how to make it and they know how to use it. Again America has won its independence!*

The critical question now was tire-producing capacity. The industry's peacetime ability to produce, cut in half by the nature of combat tire construction and by the laborious processing of synthetic rubber, was unequal to the challenge of 1944 for another reason: the enormous requirements of the fighting forces and home front in a crucial war year.

The industry needed more factory space, more machinery, more trained personnel. "So it is evident," Firestone jr. concluded, "that while the rubber crisis has been overcome, the tire crisis has not."

* H.S.F. jr., Economic Club of Detroit, Nov. 8, 1943.

ꓘꓘꓘꓘꓘꓘꓘꓘꓘꓘꓘꓘꓘꓘꓘꓘꓘꓘꓘꓘꓘꓘꓘꓘ

19

Every Plant an Arsenal

THE might of the Firestone organization was thrown into the war. Management, sharing with all segments of the populace the consecrated task of defending freedom, marshaled its resources. Not only factory facilities and collective intelligence and skills; what Firestone also brought to serve the nation, as in peace, was its tradition as a creative force.

Despite virtual suspension of civilian tire business, there was no lag in employment, no disruption of the dealer and service-store network. On the contrary, prevision and alertness kept the huge enterprise functioning as part of the country's economy, resilient enough to absorb the shock of war, sturdy enough to do a monumental job.

Because the company had the largest rubber reclaiming capacity in the world (adjuncts to the Akron, Memphis, and Los Angeles factories), Firestone was able to supply its various outlets with mass production of all-reclaim tires in 1942. The War Production Board permitted such sales for essential civilian driving and for replacement of old tires that could not be recapped or repaired. Under the speed restriction of thirty-five miles per hour, they were good for 5,000 to 7,500 miles.

Firestone had long recognized the merit of retreading and recapping worn tires and had developed special processes and equipment improving the quality of this work. Rubber strips, called "camelback," were supplied in GR-S synthetic through a nation-wide system of 137 recapping plants with dealers; factory control safeguarded the standards. In this way, as in others, substantial relief was given to the public's tire problem.

The government had halted the manufacture of new passenger cars and light trucks early in 1942, but cars in service required more attention, and so did their tires. Firestone advertising urged drivers to visit their dealers for periodic tire inspection and other aids to extra mileage. An organized plan was instituted for removing glass and tacks, applying a preservative to seal cracks and prevent deterioration, aligning wheels to avoid uneven wear, and rotating tires from wheel to wheel. Thus dealers helped in the rubber conservation program. Moreover, in the factories, every employee was cautioned to save every pinch of rubber possible. Floors were swept to recover the tiniest particle. In the retread shops, even buffings were collected.

In the realm of retailing and serving the home front, the principle of diversification proved a source of strength. Dealers, as well as company stores, were enabled to adapt themselves to wartime conditions and thereby survive. As in 1940, when the company made available such merchandise as housewares, farm equipment, and plumbing supplies for better-balanced sales, so in 1941 gas and electric ranges, refrigerators, washing machines, luggage and sporting goods, and in 1942 work clothing, glassware, dinnerware, paints, and phonograph records were added. This attracted many new dealers to the Firestone banner, and they obtained the complete business franchise.

Instead of retrenching on its store program, the company enlarged and modernized some of its older units and increased the total from 626 to 641 in 1941 and to

656 in the war year 1942. The stores helped build up
the annual volume and contributed profits, further to
enhance the company's financial position to assume
broader war work.*

While original-equipment tire business faded out with
the production of less than 250,000 passenger cars in
1942, and only 139 and 610 in the two succeeding years,
automobile manufacturers ordered tires for the jeeps,
armored cars, and greater number of heavy trucks they
were building. Combat tires, of tougher compounds,
were so constructed that they could run 100 miles or
more after deflation by bullets or shell fragments. They
were held secure by a divided rim which Firestone
created.

The conventional narrow, flat-base rim could not do
the job of holding a bullet-ridden tire in place. Firestone
put an extra metal band or bead lock between the inside
edges of the heavy tire and bolted this to the main section, the two parts being tapered to clamp the beads.
Good not only in small sizes for jeeps, the divided rims
were practicable also in twenty-four-inch diameters and
thirteen-inch widths for giant tires bearing heavy artillery across country. It was by means of the divided rim
that military tires could be used at low inflation pressure
for better flotation and traction in soft soils, mud, or
desert sand.

Firestone made 987,289 divided rims during the war
years.

Tubes, too, were improved to meet the order of the
day. Dual-seal tubes, with their "inner tire" of two plies,

* Company sales in 1941 totaled $268,000,000, profit $11,200,000 (4.2 percent) after the addition of $6,650,000 to the reserve for contingencies. The
annual dividend rate of $1.25 was advanced to $1.50 this year and the next.

To secure the benefits of a lower interest rate and a longer-term maturity,
the outstanding 3½ percent debentures were refunded with a $50,000,000 issue
of twenty-year 3 percent debentures.

On 1942 sales of $352,700,000 (almost double the 1940 volume), profit was
$12,500,000 (3.54 percent) after carrying $3,000,000 to the reserve.

remained inflated in the face of a blowout long enough to allow safe stopping. Punctureproof tubes, with a thick inner layer of soft, uncured rubber that was squeezed by air pressure around a penetrating object, were especially useful in areas such as cactus country.

Complete redesigning of the airplane tire line in 1941 resulted in lighter weight, greater strength, and longer tread life. The new pursuit and bombing planes could take off more quickly and withstand the impact of high-speed landings. The government wrote the Firestone construction into specifications for all Army and Navy plane tires in January, 1942, and adopted also the flat Firestone channel tread, with its wide footprint, as standard. Both were licensed royalty-free to the industry for the duration; so was the low-profile safety tire and wheel unit, which could run though deflated and which used less rubber than other nose-wheel tires.

Firestone's experience in huge, off-the-road tires was called upon for multi-ply earthmover and excavator tires in urgent demand for constructing airports and cantonments.

The company provided instruction, beginning in the spring of 1941, to armed service personnel on the care and emergency repair of tires, tubes, rims, spark plugs, wheels, and batteries. The teachers of these training courses were experts who had conducted the Firestone battery and brake school. Students came from various Army camps and naval centers, to be returned as instructors and thus communicate throughout the service branches the knowledge requisite for maintaining the nation's mechanized fighting forces.

Chairman Thomas struck the wartime keynote when the company dedicated itself to the war effort at the stockholders' meeting in January, 1942:

It is overwhelming mechanized might and not military manpower alone that will tip the scales of victory in this conflict. That is why the responsibilities of industry are so great.

He appealed to the entire personnel to "shift into high gear mentally."

We are in a race against time. The stakes are liberty, our system of free enterprise, our American way of life.*

In the general offices in Plant 1—an industrial G.H.Q. —the strategy of achieving production tasks for the government was planned. Speed on the part of research and engineering staffs was enlisted. Assignments were made to the various constituent plants. The best utilization of factory space was mapped out—with an unceasing quest for more space.

From the start, tank track production had been assigned to the Industrial Products plant in Noblesville, Indiana, skilled in turning out automotive parts and other rubber-bonded-to-metal articles. Ordnance pressed for greater production. The plant was extended and another building was erected in 1941, the company financing this expansion itself. Half-tracs for high-speed scout cars and troop carriers were needed; they must be able to resist heat and abrasive action.

Firestone's pioneering in tank tracks had earned leadership, and the calls were great. By providing the mobile land fortresses with their own rubber road, to hurtle over rough terrain and shell holes, the Noblesville workers were helping to drive wedges into enemy lines. As heavier vehicles were made, with more powerful engines, they built tracks equal to the load, and the Firestone rubber bushing assured maneuverability.

For tanks up to forty tons, track blocks were twelve to twenty-three inches wide. Finally came fifty-ton tanks; the tracks were twenty-six and a half inches wide. Changes in vehicles, variations of service requirements

* J.W.T., *Firestone Non-Skid*, Mar. 10, 1942.

in the different theaters of war, necessitated constant redesign and avoidance of overstress. A sudden switch to steel blocks was specified, though Ordnance had previously determined that rubber was not so vulnerable to shellfire as steel; the inner side of the track remained rubber for the efficient operation of the eight or more hard-rubber bogie rollers (wheels) that meshed with the track and carried the weight.

After experience in the African campaign, Ordnance was convinced of the necessity of reverting to rubber blocks to cut down maintenance, and the industry was told in 1943 to switch back as fast as possible. At this time, the rubber shortage had become less acute and GR-S was worked into the track compounds.

But the machine-tool shortage and the scarcity of metal components persisted. A Track Production Integrating Committee was formed to channel production information and speed up procurement. The diminution of available man power in the small town of Noblesville posed a constant problem. The factory had to reach to a wider radius for workers; extra supervision was installed to train unskilled personnel; a high ratio of female labor was employed. To keep the huge schedule going, seventy percent of it was subcontracted for components, and in many cases this meant merely the use of factory space and roster, for Firestone supplied both equipment and technical direction.

With the Los Angeles factory lending a hand and an assembly unit set up in Indianapolis, Firestone maintained the required rate and adapted itself to every change. There were calls for amphibian tracks, of hollow steel blocks with steel grousers that propelled the tank in water and on land; and for continuous bands of metal-reinforced rubber, for half-tracs. In unremitting production until V-J day, gratified with reports of service life, Firestone completed a monumental job of 82,283 sets of tracks. To this, Akron and Wyandotte added 2,320,455 bogie wheel or rim bases.

More than a billion belt links for machine-gun cartridges were ordered to supplement the production at Fall River. Akron divided the contract between Wyandotte and itself. Akron made room for this operation in its battery plant. Stamping presses, furnaces, grit blasters, and rustproofing equipment were installed, in readiness at the end of January, 1942. Conveyors carried the clips from the press line, where multi-station dies stamped cold-rolled steel in seven steps at the rate of 100 a minute. Conveyors took them along to the degreaser, to the furnace for heat-treating, to a tank for oil-quenching, to a draw furnace for attaining Rockwell C50 hardness, to a blaster for removal of scale, and to a Parkerizing tank. Conveyors bore them also to inspection machines. Akron shipped them by the carload, 12,000,000 the first month.

Now Wyandotte too was making deliveries. By the middle of August, it shipped 100,000,000; three months later another 100,000,000, two months more the same quantity, and by the next two months a total of nearly half a billion. Memphis, producing on a separate contract, used a section of its raw-material warehouse, renting warehouse space elsewhere in town. Memphis employees were recruited chiefly from housewives. By April, 1943, all plants had produced an aggregate of one billion links. By June, a billion and a half.

In July, Ordnance requested closer tolerances—down to two one-thousandths of an inch. Work stopped, dies were rebuilt. By September, more than 1,700,000,000 had been shipped, and by the end of the war 2,224,000,000.

The belt-link story was not entirely astronomical. There was precision and down-to-earth ingenuity. Each link had to stand inspection under a hundred-pound pull test to determine proper heat-treating. It must show no rust after a twenty-four-hour salt-spray test. Each link was inspected for size of loop and for center distance; the machine gunner trusted them not to jam on him. Firestone developed apparatus for reprocessing the rejects and thus salvaged a large percentage of them. Another saving, originating in Memphis, used four-stage dies which left no scrap strip.

A safety stop for the dies reduced breakage and permitted the stamping presses to run without operators in attendance. This was one of the "ideas for victory" contributed by employees; the man who figured it out received an award of $1,500. As a result of Steel Products research on the gauge of the steel, Ordnance authorized the proposed thickness and the links were made stronger. They did not break in loading, shipping—or firing.

Another achievement, with several remarkable aspects, was the development of oxygen cylinders for high-altitude flying. The Royal Air Force, early in the war, had found the stratosphere a safe place from which to do accurate bombing. Flying from a height of 18,000 to 35,000 feet, a crew had to wear oxygen masks or succumb to quick death. To save space in the fuselage, cylinders were designed for compactness, loaded with oxygen compressed to 1,800 pounds per square inch. This was the type first installed in Flying Fortresses—with disaster. In an encounter with a Messerschmitt, a B-17 in British service disintegrated after a burst of machine-gun fire had struck an oxygen cylinder. At least, this was a suspicion until tests determined that it was the cause: the oxygen flashed out in a torch of flame twenty feet long.

Thereafter, planes were equipped with low-pressure systems, down to 400 pounds, and the containers were enlarged four and a half times. In January, 1941, Firestone sent such fifty-liter cylinders to the R.A.F. for testing.

It was not strange that Firestone should consider itself capable of producing these supplies. Rather, it was natural. For Steel Products in Akron had been manufacturing welded stainless-steel barrels. The method was original: huge toggle presses stamped half cylinders out of sheet steel, as well as end pieces, and specially developed automatic welding machinery fused the parts by atomic hydrogen. The welded areas did not rust. In making oxygen cylinders, the presses stamped out spherical domes. Tested for leaks and ruptures, the product passed muster.

In a few months, Firestone was making the cylinders for the A.A.F. The beverage-container production line had stopped, the presses merely rearranged, and without the loss of a single day, without idleness of machines or utilization of additional ones, the 3,000 employees changed over to their new activity. The War Production Board cited this as a perfect example of conversion: no new tools, no unemployment.

But the best part of the story had not been told. Bent upon further developing safe cylinders, Firestone succeeded in the fall of 1941 in making them light-weight (sixteen-gauge stainless steel) and shatterproof. The walls were reinforced with welded spiral and longitudinal strips. Though pierced by tumbling 50-caliber machine-gun bullets, they did not explode; even the tear was restricted. This life-giving device exceeded Army standards and was in mass production by March, 1942, mostly of 2,100-cubic-inch capacity.

Extension of the Steel Products building did not suffice. A separate oxygen-cylinder plant was erected in 1943, bringing output to nearly 600,000 at the end of the year. Besides several stationary types, portable ones were manufactured so that radio operators and other crew members could move about the plane. The schedule in one case reached 1,000 a day. In all, Firestone produced more than 1,277,000 cylinders during the war. United Nations planes flew high with safety.

The plastics division provided lenses for oxygen masks. The industrial products division evolved a unique pressure-sealing bushing that made it possible to pump air into a plane without leakage around electric cables and piping passing through compartment walls.

Gas masks for the land forces constituted one of the company's great war programs after the early manifestation of confidence by the Chemical Warfare Service. It was well placed. Firestone's plastic lenses were optically correct, chemically resistant, and shatterproof. They were molded in great quantities and cost less than glass. Firestone also developed a new method for clamping down eyerings on the lens assembly; the machine for this operation was later used in all other manufacturers' gas-mask assembly plants. Firestone molded face blanks in a battery of ovens, the rubber being squeezed down over the mold and cured in a single piece. The company's experimental machine shop contrived an automatic filling device for putting charcoal in mask canisters, thus expediting production.

The major burden of this work fell on Fall River. Thousands of assemblies were being made there daily in 1941 when a fire swept the plant and destroyed nearly half of it. Other Firestone factories immediately took up as much of the task as they could, the remainder being sublet, until the plant was rebuilt. Noblesville made face blanks and shipped them to Fall River. In 1942, the latter received rush orders for civilian gas masks, to be produced at the rate of 10,000 every twenty-four hours, besides the service masks that were being made and assembled 15,000 a day. Memphis received a separate contract and, on completing it, continued to make parts: face blanks, nose tubes, and nose cups, 2,500,000 each.

Peak production was passed in 1943, when Fall River's obligations included 1,000,000 standard service masks, 1,000,000 lightweight service masks, 2,000,000 lenses in addition, and the repair of training masks. The grand total of assemblies, which made Firestone one of the nation's chief suppliers, was more than 7,393,000.

Fall River was indeed a busy workshop throughout the war. Skill in plastics led to rifle stocks (cooler, lighter, more durable, cheaper than wood) and to battery cases for walkie-talkie radios, but chiefly to Army helmet liners. It took little time to switch over the battery-case press equipment to helmet molds. The first contract for these liners, which were to be worn under the regulation metal helmets or by themselves as protection behind the front, came in April, 1942, and required 750,000 at the rate of 150,000 a month.

Although only a few ounces in weight, these helmet liners were strong enough to stand upon and capable of taking the impact of forty-five pounds to the square inch. Like many other Firestone products, they saved lives. Besides which, they were a comfort, with Foamex composing the inner suspension to cushion shocks and with proper insulation and ventilation provided. Despite a labor shortage in the summer of 1944, reducing Fall River's general production, the offensive against the Axis demanded increased quantities of this perfected headgear—and the Army got them. More than 7,500,000 all told!

For the Navy, the same plant made Foamex liners to fit into voluminous steel deck helmets. Among other good points, they improved acoustics for the telephone or radio set housed in the crown of the helmet. Foamex mattresses were supplied to Army and Navy hospitals, until latex was restricted. Foamex crash pads to line the walls of tanks and planes, Foamex parachute seats and pilot seats and backs, Air Force life belts and vests, flotation bladders, raincoats, delousing bags and clothing bags—all poured out of Fall River. And flapper valves, molded here for every manufacturer of fuel cells, to stabilize the flow of fuel in flight.

In the progress of the vast fuel-cell program, the molding of fittings from synthetic rubber in place of machining them from sheet steel was a minor revision. The war brought about two radical revisions.

Aromatic gasoline mixtures supplanted 100-octane soon after Pearl Harbor. As they had a greater tendency to penetrate the cell wall and dissolve the rubber, a new inner-liner coating must be found. All fuel-cell manufacturers were called to Wright Field to organize a permanent technical committee, and Firestone was assigned to this special problem. By substituting Butaprene-N for Neoprene as a coating and by backing it with a barrier of rubber-impregnated fabric, the deterioration was stopped.

But another thing: the critical shortage of sheet latex for the sealant. Various substitutes were tried. At first, twenty-five percent reclaim was used in the compound, and later synthetic rubber and guayule; ultimately, in the summer of 1943, 100 percent GR-S.

A construction temporarily used by the Army Air Forces early in 1942 consisted of an inner ply of nylon sheet coated on both sides with Buna-N synthetic, two plies of sealant, and three plies of gum-dipped, calendered rayon cord fabric. The stiff fabric replaced more costly steer hide in keeping the sealant in functional position.

Firestone engineers kept working to achieve a further improvement. To prevent the cracking and shattering of the liner—which happened in handling and by gunfire in extremely cold weather—a film of nylon was applied in liquid form between the liner and the sealant. This miracle not only shut out the fuel, it allowed the liner to become plasticized. The method became standard.

Still another change was effected. Self-curing cement originally held the built-up wall together. Now the assembly was molded and steam-cured. In the search for the best kind of building form, cardboard proved the most suitable. After curing, it was water-soaked and removed. Contours were various and irregular, designed to fit specific cavities in the wings of the plane or the fuselage, although in the case of jettison cells used for auxiliary fuel supply they were shackled to the belly or wings.

Jettison cells of the nonmetallic bomb-bay type could be dropped when empty or when less weight was wanted in combat with pursuit or interceptor planes. They were fastened to the bomb shackles, wooden hoops serving as stiffeners. These cells held as much as 800 gallons.

Regular fuel cells were made in sizes up to 400-gallon capacity, the larger ones put in position with reinforcement ribs. Oil cells had to be built to withstand not only severe gunfire but also higher internal pressure. These were enclosed in an aluminum shell at first, but a nonmetallic type was sought, and Firestone came through— the first to qualify—with seven plies of woven glass fabric coated with resin and two plies of rayon cord.

Apparently, there was no end to cell development. Each unit had molded rubber fittings with metal inserts for the connections—single-flange fittings. Firestone induced the A.A.F. to adopt double flanges and, besides this, overcame the tendency to crack at high altitudes by covering them with an ozone-resistant cement.

In handling this production of cells after the start in Akron and Los Angeles, assignments were given to many other cities in the urgent need for space and facilities. Subsidiaries were set up in leased buildings. The California company, however, kept expanding its operation and accounted for almost half the enormous output. As early as 1941, the Los Angeles plant had built a special addition for both fuel and oil cells (many airplane manufacturers and assembly plants preferred to buy both kinds from the same source), and in 1942, when tire production declined because of rubber and labor shortages, Los Angeles put greater emphasis on cells. Fall River was almost as heavily engaged with this item as Akron, where the technical direction remained.

A building in Dallas, to assume part of the 1943 requirements, leased at the time American marines were trying to dislodge the Japanese from Guadalcanal, was enlarged by December as the A.A.F. bombed Nazi installations on the shores of North Africa and Naples. In New Castle, Indiana, a factory was purchased to turn out more cells; it made an outstanding record.

The Memphis plant cured its first of many cells in the spring of 1943. Allied troops were then forging ahead in North Africa; Flying Fortresses and Liberators of the A.A.F. had started blasting military targets in Germany, and the offensive on Guadalcanal had secured a foothold in the Solomon Islands. Soon American formations over the industrial Ruhr would paint an omen in the sky. The cry was "Forward!" More planes must be rushed to all fronts—fully equipped, with every possible safety for our fliers.

More fuel cells! The California company opened a subassembly plant in Pasadena and another feeder at Compton Junior College; a plant in Santa Ana, California, and another in Ferndale, Washington. Production sprang up also in Coshocton and Zanesville, Ohio; in Paterson, New Jersey; and Bristol, Virginia. The subsidiary at Hamilton, Ontario, shipped another considerable amount.

Mitchell B-25 bombers, Airacobras, P-38 Lightnings, Thunderbolts, Mustangs, Helldivers, along with the

Fortresses and Liberators—all flew with Firestone cells protecting their fuel and oil supplies.

Second to the tank track, the bullet-sealing cells represented the largest war project the company accomplished: nearly 600,000 units, plus 24,500 jettison cells. Bofors gun mounts stood third.

Combat tanks carried jettison cells. For armored cars, Firestone had found the way to withstand gunfire through armor plate, a feat without precedent, and Zanesville built such cells at the rate of 1,850 a month.

Protection and destruction. They were the antithetical twins of war, a double concern best exemplified by the Firestone products for aviation. Besides the oxygen cylinders and crash pads, there were life belts, life vests, pararafts. There was backing material—lining the cavities in which the fuel cells reposed, to support and align the cell walls, and keeping out flying bits of metal. Bulletproof flak vests—made as a result of Firestone's development of this backing material, *i.e.*, plies of woven-glass fabric, spread with a special resin, laminated, cured in a platen press, and sheared to size and shape. Flak vests had as many as seventeen plies.

The crash pads, like the pilot seat cushions and back cushions, and the parachute seats and backs, were no longer made of Foamex. For this precious substance, a satisfactory substitute provided by Firestone was short cattle hair, fluffed up, packed into latticed molds immersed in some liquid reclaim rubber, and cured on racks.

Originally the company's aeronautics division had been simply a sales organization for the tires, wheel-and-brake units, and sponge Neoprene latex wing filler made by other divisions. In the course of time, it blossomed into an important manufacturer on its own. Early in 1942, negotiations with Curtiss-Wright resulted in a contract to produce wings for the C-46 Commando Transport—wings with a spread of 108 feet on which to bear paratroops, scout cars, Bofors guns, and supplies across the lengthening lanes of communication. In March, ground was broken for a wings building next to the Bofors building. A training school course was given to the new employees in blueprint reading, drilling, riveting, and production methods. In October, the Firestone Aircraft Company shipped its first set of wing panels, ailerons, flaps, and wing tips.

Twenty-four hours a day the work progressed, until 2,250 sets were finished. In Atlanta, Georgia, wing panels were made for Consolidated-Vultee PB-4Y Navy amphibians, using a new type of rivet cement. Aircraft work in Akron overflowed into the Bofors plant, with a monthly schedule that at one time encompassed 100 sets of wings, 6,500 wheels, close to 400 pilot and bombardier seats.

These seats were made of aluminum and steel, to begin with, but the metals had to be restricted, and Firestone succeeded in transferring the main features of the designs to plastic plywood. The pilot seats had remarkable adjustable mechanisms; for the bombardiers, parallel supports enabling them to line themselves up perfectly with their targets. Another aid to fliers and protection of the plane was the Firestone air-spring strut, a bellows connected to a reservoir of low-pressure air, compressed on the impact of landing; the shock was absorbed instead of being transmitted to the plane.

Still another development was a de-icer strip for propellers. Made of synthetic rubber, it distributed, with precision, alcohol or other ice-removing fluid to keep the blades clear and maintain maximum motor power as the plane navigated in icing conditions.

In the summer of 1943, the company acquired G. & A. Aircraft, Inc., at Willow Grove, Pennsylvania, makers of autogiros. This factory had a contract for thirty-five CG-4A gliders monthly, which Firestone took over.

They were troop-carrying, mortar-carrying assault gliders, to be towed two in tandem for the eventual invasion. Firestone helped prepare for it with 627 of them. In addition, helicopters were developed.

The same summer, Firestone engineers helped develop a caterpillar type of airplane landing gear, using no greater amount of rubber than a regular landing tire but providing from four to eight times the ground contact for swift and safe alighting on rough or sandy terrain. These "flying runways" had steel bracing and wire-beaded edges; they were grooved to fit aluminum bogie rollers, perfectly, without a chance of sideslip. They were especially useful for giant cargo and passenger planes.

Safety of the men—the abiding thought of the armed services—inspired a huge production of pneumatic gear, eminently in the sphere of a rubber company. Firestone had begun in 1941 to make life belts and seven-man pneumatic boats for the Navy. The belts were easily inflated by puncturing a carbon-dioxide cartridge or orally by a few quick puffs. Like the belts, the other articles of flotation gear were made of tough fabric with an inner coating of compounded rubber.

"Mae West" life vests, worn suspended from the neck, saved the flier who had to bail out. By pulling a cord, he let carbon dioxide fill the bladder. His head held above water, he was able to make use of another rescue adjunct. This was folded as a cushion in the plane and was fastened to his parachute harness. It became a one-man raft by the turn of a handle on a carbon-dioxide cylinder, also made by Firestone; a package of equipment, fastened to the raft by a rope, contained drinking water, a sail, a first-aid kit, a cup for drinking or baling, a complete repair kit, a canvas bucket-anchor, a sea marker, and fishhooks.

The whole nation learned the value of flotation gear

with the dramatic rescue of Captain Eddie Rickenbacker and his crew in the fall of 1942. They had disappeared after taking off from Hawaii. Twenty-three days later they were found in a life raft, many miles north of Samoa.

By this time, Firestone had constructed many rafts and boats for the various services. Girls and women sitting opposite each other at long tables looked like so many seamstresses on an assembly line, "stitching" sections of rubberized fabric with cement and passing the work on toward the end of the table, one more section added by the next operator, until the last woman finished the raft. There were parachute rafts with room for as many as ten men. There were pneumatic reconnaissance boats for the Engineers, life boats for the Coast Guard in the Aleutians (capacity, twenty-five men), and tending barges for Navy patrol planes to ferry personnel, bombs, fuel, and other supplies from shore.

Landing boats with outboard motors and machine guns were used by the Marines in the Solomons and helped them cross rivers in New Guinea. A ten-man boat, expanded to eight by eighteen feet, was only a ninety-inch bundle when rolled up. Floors and fenders were inflatable; the main tubes by carbon-dioxide cylinders, the cross tubes by hand pumps—a dual system that gave safety and insurance.

Where the retreating enemy blew up bridges, he was quickly pursued over pneumatic floats capable of supporting from six to fifteen tons of infantry and armored forces. The largest float, measuring four by four feet when folded, and, inflatable by compressed air to a length of thirty-three feet, had twelve separate compartments which permitted continued functioning though some might be punctured. By removing the central tubes, the ponton became a ferry boat.

And there was also the jungle bladder. It resembled a handkerchief. The soldier blew it up into a four-cornered bag, eight by ten inches, and fitted this under the arm to keep afloat while making his way across a river or lake.

Synthetic rubber was used with fabric. The early technique had been to cement the seams after curing. Now the parts were assembled in an uncured state and the unit was treated as a whole. In Akron, Fall River, and Memphis this work went on, and in a tobacco warehouse in Winston-Salem, North Carolina, taken over to produce 5,000 GR-S life belts daily in addition to pontons.

Firestone made 1,882,000 life belts, 429,000 life vests, more than 126,500 rafts, in a total of 2,471,000 items of flotation gear.

Almost as great a menace to life as the Japs, tropical insects had to be kept at arm's length. To the Solomon Islands came the hygienic safeguard, from Fall River by way of New Jersey.

Firestone Plastics Company was extruding, molding, and fabricating Velon. A remarkable thing, almost magic in its response to one's wishes—Velon came in sheet or filament, thick or thin, opaque or transparent. Firestone wove it into stainproof, wear-like-iron cloth. Firestone wove it into a mesh, and it was screening material, impervious to rot, to weather, and to insects of all kinds. Other plastics were used to form lenses for gas masks and liners for helmets.

The application of Velon to netting was thought up in the research laboratory of a plastics department established by Firestone in 1942 at the World Bestos Corporation in Paterson, New Jersey, a company taken over as a subsidiary a few years before to supply dealers and stores with greater quantities of brake lining. This was the involved lineage of the screen. In detail: the

Paterson plant cooperated with the Motor Transport Division of the War Department in setting up brake-lining standards for each type of vehicle; it became a chief source of supply and soon was wholly devoted to government work.

When a huge contract for brake lining was received in May, 1942, Paterson had just expanded its facilities to include plastic products for the retail outlets. Night shifts and new equipment sped deliveries on the order, but rather than build greater capacity the company subcontracted a part. The discovery that vinylidene chloride monofilament (Velon) would be admirable for sidewalls of tents in the tropics led to a Navy order, in May, 1943, for 1,000,000 square feet of Velon screening.

Paterson was confident it could fill this on time and still have enough screening production for distribution to the field, which could sell it in place of copper window screens. In July, the Army and Navy together wanted almost 6,000,000 square feet. Thereafter the plastics department operated 100 percent for the uniformed nephews and nieces of Uncle Sam, with an ultimate output of 31,446,000 square feet.

Sixty war products. Forty-eight factories throughout the world in 1943.* Firestone was ever alert to utilize space and available labor, diverting production from one location to another as contingencies arose. Sometimes an operation was temporarily suspended, as in Memphis, when a rush order came for pneumatic dummies of forty-millimeter guns which were to be used in deceiving the enemy. In the case of barrage balloons, for which Ordnance sought quickest possible deliveries,

---

* The factory in Bilbao, Spain, was inactive at times for lack of rubber and carbon black. Production in the Swiss plant was insignificant for the same reason. Buenos Aires could get little rubber for tiremaking and engaged in insulating telephone wire. São Paulo, Brazil, obtained all its rubber locally and started a fabric mill but was not permitted to ship to Argentina. Port Elizabeth, South Africa, had to look to the Belgian Congo for half of its rubber requirements.

permission was obtained to discontinue at Fall River and concentrate at Akron. For more than a year, balloons were pieced together in the Bofors building, then construction and assembly were transferred to an Akron garage building.

Balloons were made up of hundreds of fabric panels impregnated with Neoprene and cemented at the seams with Butaprene-N. Women in slacks did the job and stood with cans of aluminum paint beside the partially blown-up monsters to give them a weatherproof coating.

The first balloons Firestone produced were dilatable to a length of eighty-three feet and a breadth of thirty-nine feet. An internal elastic arrangement kept the envelope taut and compensated for variations in gas pressure due to altitude and temperature changes. There were smaller dilatable types and convoy balloons. Some looked like the blubbery body of a whale with the tail fins of a marlin; others had fins with the innocent appearance of quilting.

The large balloons shielded cities and other land objectives. Small ones were moored to the rear deck of a ship in convoy or towed by advancing columns of Army trucks. In the African campaign, troops pushing into battle through mountain passes were at first menaced by close fire of low-flying planes, but now our men were protected by barrage balloons raised over their vehicles.

Firestone delivered 7,762 balloons to the services. How many lives were saved, how much equipment and supplies preserved for good use, could not be estimated. But the war was making headway—for our side. Before the end of 1943, the Nazis surrendered in Africa, Sicily was wrested from the Axis, Naples next; the Italians withdrew from the war, Hitler lashed them back; the Marines landed in Tarawa, in Makin; General Dwight D. Eisenhower was named supreme commander of the American and British invasion forces.

To pay off the Axis partners in the coin of their own realms, Ordnance mustered the might of America. Firestone won an assignment to operate a government bomb-loading plant near Fremont, Nebraska, and another to keep up the flow of supplies by managing the Blue Grass Ordnance Depot at Richmond, Kentucky. Gun turrets for combat tanks—the Los Angeles factory cleared space to set up fifty at a time, assembling each turret with 663 separate parts and contributing 1,517 turrets to the great offensive. Rockets came a little later.

The Nebraska Defense Corporation was organized by Firestone in November, 1941, and while the plant was being constructed, personnel headed by Russell Firestone went out from Akron, Memphis, and Los Angeles as a supervisory staff. Green acres, 17,000 of them, gave way to a new industry: loading 500 pounds of explosive into a bomb case of equal weight. Men and women from the countryside came to do the work. Foremen and workers had to be thoroughly trained; operations were studied, changed, perfected; and efficiency was attained.

After the first bomb was produced on October 1, 1942, the grim activity proceeded behind the gates, with progressive speed. Capacity was thought realized in April, 1943, when the month's total was 23,000,000 pounds of explosive loaded. The record was broken in January, 1945, with more than 50,000,000 pounds. On a unit basis, the following June rang the bell: 240,000 bombs were loaded, the lines then including 400-, 500-, and 1,000-pound bombs, as well as ninety-pound fragmentation bombs.

British Mark V bombs that weighed 4,000 pounds apiece were filled with deadly new tritonal (TNT and aluminum powder). The Nebraska Ordnance Plant was the first to place tritonal loading into actual production (and a composition labeled "B"). Procedure techniques and equipment designed here, as amatol was declared obsolete and the nitrate line placed in stand-by, were adopted by other plants scattered through the country.

A mechanical means of manipulating booster charges was also devised by Firestone men. These tetryl pellets had been inserted in tubes by hand, one by one. Now rubber fingers on a serrated roller guided them into a dozen tubes at a time.

More than 2,840,000 bombs were loaded. More than 16,300,000 boosters. This tallied almost a billion pounds of explosive, handled by 4,900 workers at top speed. And not a single explosion.

Depots set up by Ordnance for receiving ammunition, explosives, tires and tubes, bearings, mill supplies, target material, and hundreds of other items, and for distributing them at the direction of the Army Service Forces, were turned over to private firms to get the benefit of their skill in industrial management and release military personnel for other duties. One of the largest of these depots occupied close to 15,000 acres in the luxuriant, pastoral region of Kentucky; an area with forty-five miles of railroad track and 145 miles of motor roads. Firestone took the job.

The company organized Blue Grass Ordnance, Inc., in 1943 and started operating in November. Within two years more than 1,400,000 tons of material passed through—at steadily decreasing costs, although wages slightly rose. From $6.46 per ton in the first month of operation at Richmond, the labor cost of handling ammunition, for example, declined to $1.68. With 3,000 employees, work averaged 0.92 ton per depot man-day, coming to a peak of 20.3 tons in direct handling and 5.8 tons in indirect handling.

This record was attributed to intensive training of supervisors and workers, efficiency studies for work simplification, and close attention of management to removing causes of delays, introducing better methods, procuring better equipment, and insisting upon preplanned operations.

But the biggest thrill was in manufacturing, and the greatest satisfaction in making new war products—if one could choose among one's children—was the Bofors gun mount and carriage, an undertaking lasting as long as evil wings marred the sky. The speed with which it had been initiated and the engineering skill that had redesigned this weapon set the tempo and tone for the continuing performance. Schedules were constantly stepped up. They reached more than 1,000 a month by August, 1942, and proceeded at this rate for the rest of the year. Firestone was told to anticipate 1,500 monthly during 1943. The orders came; and additional orders, for carriages to ride with Commandos and other planes and be fitted on the decks of Navy fighting ships and Liberty ships as a protection against strafing.

Firestone Bofors were dispatched to every theater of war. They defended England. They defended Allied troops in North Africa. Landed on the beachheads of Guadalcanal, Tarawa, Anzio, they gave cover for the onrushing waves of troops, supplies, and heavy artillery. They protected harbors and airfields; made our footholds secure. They were built so sturdily, they could be towed overland at more than forty miles per hour and set up for action in half a minute.

The Bofors had two distinct missions to accomplish: shoot down low-flying aircraft (a mission not considered done if the plane was forced to alter its course), and destroy water-borne targets such as landing boats and torpedo boats. This gun was to be used also against light-armored vehicles and medium tanks, not more than 700 yards distant, that were definitely intending to attack the gun batteries.

The maximum effective range of a forty-millimeter

gun against armored vehicles was only 600 to 700 yards. In its chief object of firing at a small maneuverable target moving 300 or more miles an hour, the flexibility of a Bofors, its high rate of fire, and high muzzle velocity did the trick. The speed of the plane left precious little combat time. At the command "Target!" the battery must be in firing position and get off one round within four seconds. Only five or six seconds more, and the enemy was out of range.

Small wonder that strength and precision were built into this gun. Firing accuracy depended as much on the carriage as on the breech and tube, for the elevating and traversing mechanisms formed part of the carriage and had to be manufactured to tolerances closer than a thousandth of an inch. Any lack of carriage rigidity caused by travel or actual firing would be translated to these mechanisms as a distortion. More than a conveyance for the gun, the carriage was an integral part of the operation of the gun itself. The Firestone-redesigned Bofors demonstrated its reliability.

As the design of carriage details was changed from time to time, simplifications were introduced for increased production at a lower cost. Each part of subassembly was made interchangeable with foreign models and with carriages produced at previous stages of American manufacture.* Firestone supplied Ordnance with power-driver units and a large number of spare parts, and conducted a school in disassembly and reassembly for the Army, training more than 900 soldiers to act as Bofors mechanics or as instructors to others.

Firestone was truly the United Nations' arsenal for these gun carriages by producing 20,231—eighty percent of all made in the United States. And by its re-

* "Any subassembly in the American gun can be substituted in the proper place in the English gun and still have the gun work effectively."—*Bofors Gun Manual.*

design, engineering changes, and efficiency in production it reduced the cost by at least $2,600 per gun, a saving to the government of more than $53,000,000. In addition, Firestone produced for the Navy 10,434 Bofors gun mounts, at another considerable saving. Originally the contracts had been on a basis of cost plus fixed fee; later they were changed over to a firm price.

This output had required strenuous efforts to overcome shortages of machine tools and critical metals, and to provide subcontractors with materials, in many instances, as well as drawings and fabrication methods and direct supervision. To increase and balance production, cut red tape, "make skill available to all," the War Department had authorized the formation of the Intermediate Caliber Anti-Aircraft Carriage Industry Integrating Committee; the War Department and the Department of Justice gave their blessing. The committee included manufacturers of thirty-seven- and forty-millimeter gun carriages and the suppliers of parts and components. They looked to Firestone for the engineering.

Firestone was the only company making Bofors at the time the committee was formed. Two other prime contractors (metal products firms) entered the picture; skill was shared with them. Bottlenecks were broken. Spare parts lent by Firestone to other manufacturers made it possible for them to avoid shipment delays. For distinguished service in guiding the committee, Vice President J. E. Trainer was cited by the Chief of Ordnance as having "contributed greatly to obtaining maximum production rates with minimum use of machines, materials, and manpower." The industry presented a fine example of fraternal collaboration in patriotic endeavor.

Firestone's war record, and all the nation's efforts, clearly bespoke America's immense power to produce.

20

Working Together for Freedom

WHILE thousands of employees of Firestone were away in the armed services, the remaining thousands also gave war service. The products of their labor fortified fighters on every front. These determined men and women, joined by large numbers of others who became Firestone war workers, devoted extra time, extra energy.

As Undersecretary of War Robert P. Patterson expressed it, after flying from Washington to Akron to present the Army-Navy "E" Award to the organization for excellent achievement: "This award is a symbol of that unity between the armed forces and the forces of production which is going to give us victory."

The presentation took place on the night of August 31, 1942, in the Firestone Stadium before a huge audience of workers and their families. Floodlights illumined the festooned stage; a microphone carried the voices across the field, across the nation, and overseas by short-wave radio. Said the Undersecretary:

All our ingenuity and might have been mobilized to resist an enemy who seeks to enslave the world.

Instead of producing to improve our living standard, we are obliged to produce weapons of destruction to save ourselves from slavery, starvation, and death. . . .

You men and women here in the Firestone Company have shown by your devotion to your job that you understand the stakes. You have proved your right to freedom by exerting your best efforts to defend it.

The Army-Navy production pennant was accepted in behalf of the organization by Harvey Firestone jr., less in the light of a reward than as "a challenge for the future." And yet the bestowal of this high honor, the first to be given to a rubber company, inspired the thought: "I know how proud and happy my father would have been if he had lived to be here with us this evening."

To all of us this is a very personal war. . . .

We know that the war materials we are making here may save the life of someone who is very near and dear to us. . . .

This America of ours is unique among the nations of the world. We have made it the greatest country on earth because we have jealously guarded our cherished freedom, earnestly fostered our national spirit of individual initiative, and staunchly preserved our fundamental right of free enterprise.

Here in America we as a nation enjoy advantages of liberty and justice unequaled in the history of the world. But as so often is the case, whether it be a nation or an individual, now that we have won for ourselves a better way of life, there are thieves abroad who seek to rob us of it. We are determined that they shall fail.*

In presenting the "E" pins that each of the personnel would be entitled to wear, Rear Admiral Clark H. Woodward declared, "There can scarcely be an American triumph on land or sea or in the air but that you will be able to exclaim, 'I helped produce that victory!' "

Yes, it was a personal war for each Firestone man and woman, and though the battlegrounds were remote and did not always bring news of triumph, the reminders of participation came frequently. A telegram from Brigadier General James H. Doolittle of the Army Air

* H.S.F. jr. at Army-Navy "E" Award presentation, Akron, Aug. 31, 1942. (The actual date of the award was Aug. 8, and the Fall River plant had been notified of its own citation a week earlier, its presentation ceremonies being held Aug. 24.)

Forces, addressed to Firestone employees, told them: "We bombed Tokyo in the North American bombers you helped build."* He had flown from "Shangri-La" with their fuel cells. Another Army wire told of action in the Middle East—with Firestone equipment. Again, the War Department quoted a broadcast by a Russian flier: "A German shell went through my right tank. The tank did not burst into flames. I go on flying."

An inspection visit to Akron by Lieutenant General William S. Knudsen thrilled the workers on the production lines, and he in turn was notably impressed with the expertness of women operating lathes and drill presses. The company employed approximately eleven thousand women—most of them in factory activity. Almost the entire personnel of the balloon and life-belt division was female labor. Many a housewife was engaged in tire building and in air-wing riveting. A training program took up new employees and filled the gaps left by skilled men now in arms.

Visitors from worlds of flaming action brought vividness and sharper meaning to the work. Captain Hewit T. Wheless, hero of Bataan, who came to watch airplane-wing parts take form, addressed a large and grateful audience. Three London firemen, veterans of the blitz, toured the Bofors plant; said one: "Surely, American mass production will spell mass destruction to the Jerries."

It was not only the physical immensity of the expanse of Firestone factories but equally the human spirit that marked the organization.

Women workers had been knitting for war relief early in 1941 and making surgical dressings for the Red Cross. Employees bought Defense Savings Bonds. They conserved the food supply by planting more than fifteen

* May 21, 1942.

hundred gardens on company plots. When the United Service Organization was started to provide for the religious, spiritual, educational, and welfare needs of two million boys separated from home by enlistment or selective service, Harvey Firestone jr. led the drive for Ohio's contribution; he was state chairman throughout the war. For the residents of Akron, in need of relaxation from the strain of long hours, the company gave 200 acres of its land (adjoining the Firestone Public Golf Course) to the Metropolitan Park Board as a park site.

Wartime's new customs—identification badges, share-the-ride, National War Fund campaigns, scrap drives and other drives, voluntary pay-roll deductions for war bonds as much as $15,000,000 in a year, contributions to the Red Cross and its blood bank—all these imparted a quality of conscious pride in living. On the flagstaff atop the clock tower, the broad waves of Old Glory and the flapping Army-Navy pennant and Treasury Minute Man flag reared as exciting symbols of patriotic emotion. The employees had shifted "into high gear mentally." In evidence: their numerous, worth-while suggestions for cutting costs of manufacture, speeding production, and promoting the safety and welfare of fellow workers.

The company awarded bonds and prize money for ideas for victory, on the recommendation of a labor-management committee, and the War Production Board issued special citations. One worker designed a rack that tripled the capacity of heat-treating furnaces. Another devised a gear-shaping fixture, another a method of sealing one end of the life-belt tube. A testing device for the remote-control equipment on the Bofors gun reduced inspection time by half. A new type of plating hook dispensed with adapters and pins for holding tire rims in place during plating. The lubricating system of the Bofors was improved. Another employee came up with a timesaving idea for forming de-icer caps. Another received $3,500 for improving tire-building machines.

One woman in the life-belt division scored four times and then won a fifth award: her suggestion for making dual life belts that saved twenty percent of the man-hours (and woman-hours).

These belts saved the lives of many in Solomon Islands battles. The night after a beachhead had been seized on Guadalcanal, a strong Japanese naval force slipped in between two islands and sank four American cruisers. Seaman Elgin Staples, adrift several hours until his rescue, told a radio audience two months later that a Firestone belt had kept him alive; his mother, an inspector in the life-belt division, spoke next. She said that this belt bore the date of February, 1942, and had been okayed by her.

"It was like having Mother's arms around me," said Seaman Staples.

Many a letter from former employees in combat zones arrived at the company's offices, telling how vests and pararafts and rubber boats brought them to safety after they were pitched into the sea from wrecked planes and ships.

An Air Force bombardier, formerly in the development department, related that he and his men floated in the mid-Atlantic five days in a raft before being spotted by a Navy plane and picked up by a cruiser. This lieutenant came of a Firestone family. His father worked in Plant 1, his mother in the Aircraft Company. As a result of his experience, Firestone added to the rescue accessories of every raft a bottle of cement and a piece of synthetic rubber to repair rips caused by fish and flotsam.

After the Battle of Midway, a Marine corporal on furlough came to visit his mother in the bead room in

Plant 1. He had commanded a Bofors crew in that furious Japanese assault during which a large naval armada approached the island with an advance guard of planes. His crew was credited with knocking out five Jap aircraft as our fliers soared out to cripple the fleet. Corporal Kenneth Boston told some of the story to the workers as he passed along the production line.

"It's the fightingest gun I ever saw," he said. "I sure was proud of the opportunity to operate that Bofors and knew it would deliver the goods when I noticed the stamp 'The Firestone Tire & Rubber Co.'" The serial number was 2. "You're doing a swell job." He marveled at the speed of the work. "Don't let down a minute. I can guarantee that the guns you're making are smashing those Japs plenty. A friend of mine is captain of another Bofors crew and he has credit for thirty-eight Jap planes."

The good work was kept up. Firestone's eight plants in Akron won a white star on their "E" flag for continuing to maintain high standards* and subsequently a second and a third star. Stars fell on Fall River and Los Angeles, on Gastonia and Nebraska Ordnance and the synthetic-rubber plants; wherever Firestone operated, the record was one of high achievement. For protecting the plants against sabotage and espionage, the Firestone military police at Akron received the Auxiliary Military Police Guidon Award, conferred by the Commanding General, Fifth Service Command.

Management's skillful role was leavened by generous gestures, such as the gift of a Liberty carillon to the embarkation center at Camp Patrick Henry, Virginia, in honor of the 9,000 men and women of Firestone in

* Maj. Gen. L. H. Campbell jr., Chief of Ordnance, War Department, to H.S.F. jr., Nov. 5, 1943: "On behalf of all personnel of the Ordnance Department of the Army, I send heartiest congratulations to all the employees of your eight plants for adding a star to their Army-Navy 'E' pennants. It is a good sign that victory is on the way."

uniform (October, 1943). This number was continually augmented (a total of 16,382 by the war's end), and the Firestone Veterans' Service Bureau was established to help returnees improve their former status.

Through a Military Service Bureau, the company maintained a letter-writing team of cheerful young women who answered mail and filled requests—from 13,000 correspondents. Chairman Thomas personally corresponded with thousands. The house organ, *Firestone Non-Skid*, regularly went out to all, to make fast the life line of their peacetime interests. "Voice of Firestone" broadcasts were beamed abroad to take the music that Americans loved to them in their rest camps. Packages each Christmas and other remembrances were mailed by the company they left behind.

Millions of copies of booklets prepared by the National Recreation Association—*Fun En Route, More Fun En Route,* and *World o' Fun*—were made available by Firestone to military and naval personnel on transports, landing craft, hospitals, submarines, and faraway posts. And 65,000 albums of music records enriched the hours on leave at the USO.

Key men—many chemists, engineers, and other technicians—were lent to the government to serve in important capacities, and some assisted in foreign countries under Lend-Lease programs. To overseas bases of the Army Air Forces men went to train thousands of ground crews in the maintenance of equipment, and by their observations of combat performance were instrumental in indicating improvements.*

The three younger Firestone brothers entered the

---

* Maj. Gen. Oliver P. Echols, Assistant Chief of Air Staff to H.S.F. jr. Aug. 22, 1944: "Many of them have performed this essential service at great personal risk to themselves. The Army Air Forces regards these men as an indispensable element in the all-American team of fliers, mechanics, technicians, and production workers who are helping us to destroy the military and air power of Germany and Japan."

armed services early in 1942. Leonard, a lieutenant in the U.S.N.R., left his post as president of the Aircraft Company and was assigned to the procurement and materials division of the Navy. Raymond, in charge at Memphis, an artillery officer in the Reserve, was transferred to the Army Air Forces, helped set up headquarters technical training center at Knollwood Field, North Carolina, and finally served as a major in the ferrying service of the Air Transport Command. Roger, who headed the Fall River plant, was commissioned in the U.S.N.R. as lieutenant j.g., was assigned to the Naval Bureau of Aeronautics, and later to the Office of Chief of Naval Operations, advancing to lieutenant commander as administrative assistant of the Over-All Logistic Plan Committee.

Constant reminders were brought home to the Firestone workers of their direct connection with the shooting war. One day the crew of the *Memphis Belle*, a bomber that had flown twenty-five missions over Germany and other Nazi-held territory, landed at Akron Airport to thank Firestone personnel for their large output of war equipment. Tiremakers who examined one of the plane's big landing-wheel tires exclaimed that they had built it —they knew by the casing number. The pilot grinned: "It took a rough beating."

A B-19 tire that came back to the factory for inspection —ninety-six inches across—had sustained sixty landings. Such was the running story. A telegram to the workers from the Navy's Chief of Aeronautics related:

Your pneumatic tires on high-altitude Corsair fighter planes take a terrific beating yet stand up under punishing South Pacific take-offs and landings. . . . You who provide important pneumatic tires for this vital plane should continue your fine work in meeting your schedules.*

* Rear Admiral D. C. Ramsey to the men and women of The Firestone Tire & Rubber Company, Nov. 12, 1943.

The fact was, that though Firestone was delivering a great variety of steel, plastic, and rubber products, the company's paramount production was in tires and tubes.

Tires for Lend-Lease—to China, the United Kingdom, the Soviet Union, to New Zealand, India, French North Africa. Tires to roll back the enemy wherever he was. In the beginning, Firestone imported molds of special British tread designs to meet the specifications, but as the need for quantity superseded traditional preference, the Lend-Lease countries accepted the standard American military tread design. Even so, two difficulties remained: the procuring of an adequate number of tire-building machines and the proper factory scheduling to utilize the available curing facilities.

One of the sizes required by the British in large quantities was 10.50-16, an oddity in this country; Firestone had to obtain the necessary equipment. Then again, the British used a rubber bead lock for the heavy-construction combat tire; they were persuaded to adopt a metal bead lock similar to the type used by the United States Army. And the shipping instructions to wrap tires and tubes separately were changed at Firestone's suggestion that tubes be inserted in the tires partially inflated, thereby saving cargo or deck space and wrapping materials—and providing good life-saver units.

Of more than 1,268,000 Lend-Lease tires (besides tubes) shipped by Firestone, 646,000 went to the British and 474,000 to the Russian armies on the eastern front.

Tires—for a war of speed. In World War I infantry covered thirty miles in a day's forced march. Now, riding in trucks and half-tracs, it took them less than half an hour. Horse-drawn, steel-tired artillery carriages that once moved at five miles an hour were supplanted by motorized artillery flung into battle ten times faster. Instead of lumbering tanks that joggled along on steel tracks, today's tanks of monstrous size smashed through defenses with quadrupled speed—on rubber.

Airplanes no longer required hard fields; thanks to low-pressure channel-tread tires, they could take off and land on rough or soggy ground. Airports used to take months to build with old-fashioned wagons and rubberless tractors. The time was cut down to weeks by using modern giant tire-equipped earthmovers.

While the nation's synthetic-rubber capacity was being built up, better methods of using synthetic in combination with natural rubber or alone were desperately sought. The stockpile declined. Requirements overreached supplies. The W.P.B. set mandatory schedules for stepping up synthetic content.

Industry cooperated with Ordnance in exchanging data on the compounding and fabrication of synthetic-rubber tires. In this, the chief instrument was the Synthetic Tire Construction Committee, composed of chemists and engineers of the tire companies, brought together by J. E. Trainer in December, 1942. For two years, the committee maintained a test fleet of trucks in the Southwest. They pooled their skills and experience; improved their techniques and improved the tires. They quickened the conversion from natural rubber. Every pound of synthetic was used as fast as it was made.

Within a year, the industry was more than fifty percent converted to synthetic rubber. Compounders had learned to achieve the proper blends of carbon black, zinc oxide, accelerators, and antioxidants. Methods were likewise devised to compensate for the lower tackiness of GR-S by increasing adhesion and thus preventing tread and ply separation. GR-I (butyl) was employed for inner tubes—ten times superior to natural rubber in containing air pressure. At the end of 1943, synthetic production was being stepped up at a rate which would soon pass the rate of natural-rubber consumption in any year before 1941.

But the need was greater. The invasion was coming.

The supply of natural rubber stood slightly higher than the danger line. It was imperative to use it in very large military tires. Prospective imports for 1944 would equal merely one-tenth of our requirements. And a quarter of this amount was coming from Firestone's plantations in Liberia.

The cord fabric situation was just as dramatic. A combat tire consumed five times the fabric in most passenger-car tires. But the cotton supply remained stationary; the mills were short-handed. Rayon cord, to make synthetic rubber cooler running: not all the capacity of the prewar viscose rayon plants could satisfy the present demands of the tiremakers. Expansion of the rayon industry was essential, and was promised. The synthetic-tire program depended heavily on it.

Firestone had increased the output of its New Bedford and Gastonia mills in high-tenacity rayon cord for combat and airplane tires and had found the way to spin yarn for weavers of cotton shelter-tent duck when the Army urgently needed it. Gastonia also processed nylon cord; it had lighter weight and greater strength.

More weaving space and spindles had to be obtained. In March, 1943, the company bought a cotton mill in Fort Worth, Texas; small in capacity but very useful at a critical period. The same year, quarters were leased in Roanoke, Virginia, and Worcester, Massachusetts, and an extension was built to the mill at Woodstock, Ontario. In September, Firestone organized another subsidiary and acquired the Marlboro Cotton Mills at Bennettsville, South Carolina, bringing the total number of mills to seven and winning another "E" flag and star. As each hit its stride, the aggregate amount of cord

fabric that Firestone processed came to 1,700,000 pounds
a week.

There was enough synthetic rubber in view: a national
rated capacity of 850,000 tons a year; Firestone-operated, 150,000 tons. And the cord situation looked better.
But a tire crisis threatened. The tire industry, confronted
with the demands of the great offensive and the W.P.B.'s
call for 30,000,000 essential civilian tires in 1944, must
have more machinery for mixing, calendering, building,
and curing; more factory space; more trained workers.
Synthetic took longer. Military tires were bigger.

On the W.P.B. authorization to the industry to
proceed with the necessary increase in manufacturing
facilities, an expansion program costing $75,000,000 was
laid out. Firestone agreed to undertake a large portion
of this and spent $15,000,000 to enlarge the Akron,
Memphis, and Los Angeles plants.

In addition, Firestone built a factory in Des Moines,
Iowa, which it leased from the government; for large
military tires only. To meet the corresponding demand
for rims, the Akron and Wyandotte rim plants provided
greater capacity. In Milwaukee, Wisconsin, a factory
was leased and equipped to make tractor rims; tractor
lines were moved here from Wyandotte to free labor for
truck rims needed by Ordnance.

Of such itemized activities were the nation's preparations for victory comprised. With such energy, mastery,
devotion of management and personnel to the greatest
cause in history, was the cooperative effort sustained.
Working together, united Americans would not fail.

21

Liberia and the Offensive

EACH year, on the Firestone plantations in Liberia, about 5,000 additional acres reached the tapping stage. Rubber oozing from trees covering almost 39,000 acres became available by 1944. Precious natural rubber—and the yield increased more than proportionately, for these were heroic times and *Hevea brasiliensis* also strained in the war effort.

The strategic position of the Firestone Plantations Company bestowed upon it an unexpected role. After the fall of France in 1940, Pan American Airways, acting under a secret agreement with the United States Government, sought the aid of Harvey Firestone jr. in bringing about the construction of an airport in Liberia with the utmost haste. President Roosevelt also took an eager interest. Liberia was at the back door of French West Africa (Dakar only 700 miles away), and Liberia's coast line lay opposite the tip of Brazil at the narrowest span across the South Atlantic.

After several months' lapse, chiefly due to the uncertain relationship of West Africa to Vichy France, the matter was reopened by Army Intelligence.

What we wish to know (if it becomes necessary in the very near future in the national interest), is whether it would be possible for the Firestone Plantations Company to construct one or more large landing fields in Liberia of such size as to permit the landing and takeoff of the heaviest and largest-type airplanes. . . .

Your company is the only large American organization with proper contacts capable of doing this job in Liberia.[*]

[*] Capt. Merian C. Cooper to H.S.F. jr., June 25, 1941.

In July, 1941, Firestone was authorized to negotiate with the Liberian government. Preserving the strictest secrecy, no one connected with the project referred to its military nature. Ostensibly the purpose of the field was to serve as a spur for the airline's New York-Lisbon run. Nor were contracts signed between them. On merely oral understanding, Firestone set to work at once and expended $1,700,000 in the first stages.

Caterpillar tractors and bulldozers were rounded up and shipped out. Operators were recruited and flown across. In Liberia, after several sites were examined, the company manager at Harbel Plantation selected one agreed upon by the Liberian government and Pan American as the most accessible for construction material. This area was south of Harbel, along the Farmington River and north of the rubber seaport of Marshall, mainly low bush and sparse in population. Soon palm trees went crashing down under the determined push of bulldozers.

President Roosevelt met with Prime Minister Churchill in August. They jointly announced the Atlantic Charter, and a few days later the President released this news:

An important step has been taken to speed the delivery of planes direct to the British in the Middle East.

Agreements have been concluded under which the Pan American Airways system will ferry aircraft from the United States to West Africa and then will ferry them on to the Middle East.*

Firestone engineers kept speeding the construction work, in step with day-to-day radio direction from Akron headquarters.† A steady stream of supplies came up the surf in Firestone lighters. The company's experience with native labor stood it in good stead, for with a force of

* Aug. 18, 1941.

† H.S.F. jr. to G. H. Seybold, Aug. 21, 1941: "This is a large, urgent, and very important project that will involve some degree of personal inconvenience to many of our own employees for its duration."

several thousand workers approximately 2,500 acres were quickly cleared and graded; hangars and other buildings were erected. Hardly was one runway of 8,700 feet paved than the bombers began to land in January 1942, while another runway was being built. And none too soon. Germany's General Rommel was threatening Alexandria.

Now great transports zoomed in on Roberts Field— named for Joseph Jenkins Roberts, Liberia's first President. This became the principal landfall for the flights that brought reinforcements to the Near East, the Middle East, and over the hump to China. It was also a base for Royal Air Force planes on the prowl for Nazi submarines menacing the South Atlantic sea lanes. It was one of the few fields outside the United States that did not require change to accommodate the huge B-29s. At the height of traffic, Roberts Field handled thousands of planes a month.

The task of construction had fallen on Firestone's overburdened staff whose technicians were at the same time in the process of building hydroelectric works. Plantation structures were converted to house Army arrivals. Food was supplied to them from the company stores, and medical facilities were freely extended. The radio station was put at the service of the strategists in Washington. In short, Firestone was a partner of the armed forces.

As part of the Allied plan to make the whole of West Africa secure, American troops were landed in Liberia under a pact of mutual assistance. Dakar's doubtful political status would remain doubtful not much longer. In November, the United States Army took over the ferrying service from Pan American.

With Roberts Field functioning in the over-all strategy, General Eisenhower was able to pour troops into Casablanca, Morocco, and numerous other places in North Africa. They sped along the rim of the Mediterranean and applied the pincers on Marshal Rommel as the British under General Montgomery, bolstered by Allied supplies in Egypt, pushed toward Tunisia.

On the wings of the North African campaign's progress, President Roosevelt held his historic conference with Churchill near Casablanca in January, 1943, and then flew to Roberts Field. Riding a jeep with Harry Hopkins and President Edwin Barclay, he toured the adjacent Firestone plantation at Harbel. For the best part of an hour, Roosevelt observed the rubber trees in Division 2 and inspected Labor Village 45. He expressed pleasant surprise at the physical appearance of the workers and their living conditions, remarking on the contrast this presented with native labor he had seen in North Africa.

The same month, to the music of a United States Army band, the Hydro was dedicated—the first hydroelectric project in Liberia. The company's own engineers built it, with native hand labor. Concrete for the diversion dam (1,100 feet long) and the spillway (500 feet long) and nearby structures had been made of crushed rock obtained nearby, sand at the mouth of the river, cement from the United States and England. Brick for the power house came from the company's local yard. The Hydro provided power for Roberts Field, the plantation factory, the hospital, research laboratories, and other plantation buildings.

Under a Port Agreement signed at the end of the year, the United States Navy directed construction of a harbor at Monrovia to serve as a naval base. It cost $19,000,000 in Lend-Lease funds. However, the war was over before the harbor was completed (officially opened in 1948).

Liberia's economic life received considerable stimulus

from the war, with a quarter of the government's revenues directly provided by Firestone in export taxes, land rent, import duties, and the payment of the "hut tax" for every native whom the company employed. Indirectly, Firestone was responsible for much more of the revenue, through duties paid on increased imports consumed by the people on its payroll. The daily working force on the plantations usually totaled 26,000, sometimes 30,000.

Most of the workers were employed the year round, and incentive bonuses augmented their pay. The company provided them with land for gardens. Its stores sold them food at prewar prices—all-important rice, for example, at two and a half cents a pound instead of the current import price of ten cents. The Liberian government urged natives to gather wild rubber, to be sold to the Rubber Development Corporation, an arm of the Reconstruction Finance Corporation. The government and Firestone acted jointly as agents for this R.D.C. program.

The company's Loan Agreement with Liberia was amended in 1944, lowering the interest rate from five to four percent until 1950, when the rate was permanently set at four and one-half percent. The company had agreed in 1939 to take its interest in bonds instead of cash in any year that the government's revenues were under $565,000.

Firestone was not the only rubber grower in Liberia. The company had provided seedlings and high-yielding budded trees to 100 or more Liberians—among them Ex-President King, President Barclay, and the future President, W. V. S. Tubman—as well as the services of trained men to open up their plantations. They had nearly 2,500 acres under cultivation.

At the time the war spread to Africa, experiments

had been started in the various divisions of the Firestone plantations to determine the effects of different tapping systems. A score of units of planted rubber were given over to research workers, with another area for selection planting of new, locally developed clones. A permanent research building housed a staff of botanists and chemists; they had a well-equipped laboratory and operated a small pilot factory with their own drying sheds.

Even when the military and political situation was uncertain, the expansion program continued, and further investments were made. The researchers' investigations went on. Under the botanical program, besides studies in the development of better planting material and the breeding of clones, others were conducted in the suppression of diseases, improvement in culture practices, tapping, and the use of fertilizers. The chemists analyzed latex from each clone for reactions to centrifuging, storing, bulking, transportation, and milling. As the war progressed and more natural rubber was imperative, the company further increased its efforts for more production.

The first step was to institute double-panel tapping. The normal practice was to tap a tree for fifteen consecutive days and let it rest the next fifteen. Now a tree was "asked" for extra effort. With two half-circumference cuts, one at forty inches from the ground, the other (on the opposite side) at eighty inches, the tree was tapped daily; fifteen days one panel, fifteen the other. In consequence, the yield was sixty to seventy percent greater.

Full-spiral tapping, another new method, was applied to the oldest clonal trees, tapped but once in four days. The amount of latex thus obtained equaled that drawn in the usual way, but this technique freed about a third of the labor force to attend to the seedling plantings on the double-cut daily basis.

Intensive tapping was hazardous to the health of the trees, for their productive life depended mainly on the bark and its renewal. But the demands of the emergency overrode caution, and even immature trees were tapped.

As a result, Firestone was able to produce more than 11,000 tons for the United States stockpile in 1942.

The next year Firestone harvested close to 15,000 tons, an average of 740 pounds of dry rubber to the acre. Besides this, 100 tons were shipped from other Liberian plantations. In 1944, the total rose again. The fighting machine of the United Nations needed it badly. Our stockpile, as 1944 drew to a close, was critical: below the 100,000 mark.

Ceylon's production, given mostly to Britain and the Soviet Union, had reached its peak and was falling back a bit. As for South America and Central America, not all the inducements offered by way of higher prices (rubber from these regions averaged 60 cents a pound as against 28½ cents, the set price for Ceylon and Liberia) and free transportation brought forth any great quantities for export to us.

Firestone Plantations were the only wartime source of liquid latex for the United States and our Allies. Firestone possessed the equipment, the machinery, the trained personnel, and made this its main drive. Liquid latex was used chiefly for field telephone wire, assault wire, blood-plasma tubing, high-altitude oxygen masks, surgeons' gloves, other surgical products, and meteorological balloons.

In 1945, Firestone tapped as many as 57,000 acres and shipped at a rate of nearly 20,000 tons a year, thereby providing a supply vital to our nation's—and the United Nations'—survival.

The pioneering venture, on which Harvey S. Firestone had embarked two decades before, thus unfolded its wisdom during the war years; even as the early experiments he had fostered on synthetic rubber were vindicated.

In operating the government plants in Akron, Lake Charles, and Port Neches, the company brought the cost below that of any other producer. For the needs of the crucial year 1944, Firestone contributed 118,303 tons of GR-S to the country's output of 670,268 tons. The government had spent $700,000,000 in creating this industry, and in the twinkling of two years "two new and complicated manufacturing arts were developed— the making of synthetic rubber and the manufacture of this material into finished products." So Harvey Firestone jr. summed up the achievement.

It is just about the best national investment that we have ever made. No other insurance policy begins to match it, for it absolutely guarantees us rubber freedom.*

Enough synthetic rubber was produced this year and the next to spare considerable amounts for shipment to the United Kingdom.

At Sarnia, Ontario, Firestone operated jointly with three other firms a synthetic-rubber plant furnishing its own power, butadiene, and styrene. It had begun producing rubber in February, 1944.

By being the first to mix carbon black with synthetic-rubber latex, Firestone had shown how to avoid long hours of milling and mixing and the procurement of extra equipment. Firestone also blended synthetic latex with natural latex. A new development issuing from its laboratories was a compound that gave synthetic rubber better cohesive quality. Now medium-size truck tires contained seventy percent GR-S, and increasing propor-

* H.S.F. jr. in *The Saturday Evening Post*, Mar. 4, 1944.

tions were being used in combination with natural rubber for larger tires.

More and more man-made rubber came out of the government plants in 1945. In June, the Firestone-operated plants in the United States struck a stride of 14,000 tons a month in final defiance of the Japanese encirclement of the groves in the Far East. (Later these plants did 17,000 tons a month.) Of the year's national total of 820,373 tons of all types of synthetic rubber, GR-S accounted for 719,404 tons, and Firestone delivered 171,148 tons of GR-S, close to twenty-four percent.

Considering that the 1945 rubber consumption in the United States came to 105,300 tons of natural and 693,600 tons of synthetic, the Firestone Company had the distinction—though basically a manufacturer—of contributing effectually to both these categories of raw materials.

The severest pinch in the natural-rubber shortage occurred in March, 1945. Imports would have balanced the rate of consumption but for the Army's exceptional demands for very large tires. Our troops were in Nazi Germany.

Plants 1 and 2 in Akron had almost doubled their pre-war personnel to more than 9,000 men and women tire builders in feverish preparation for D day. In all other Firestone tire factories, the story was similar: full production, speed, not a minute to lose. Memphis switched fuel-cell work to other localities in order to concentrate on tires and tubes. Akron shifted fuel cells to rented quarters in the city. None of the aspects of war work was sacrificed: the company's 1944 fuel-cell output increased enormously, and its total of 69,000 employees in this country met schedules on every one of the products entrusted to them.

In England, the Brentford factory, using GR-S from

the States, was building tires for the British Army, the R.A.F., and the A.A.F.; for Lancaster and Halifax bombers, tires five and a half feet high and two feet in cross section; for D day transport, a spring-type bead lock developed by Firestone to enable British army vehicles to negotiate the beaches.

Cleveland Ordnance summoned Firestone to work on a secret device. It must be ready in ninety days. It would surprise the enemy and save many lives in the invasion. Before the work started, the time-limit was cut to sixty days; then again to forty-five. No one could miss the sense of urgency. The quantity was to be 350; Firestone would be the prime contractor.

While workers in thirteen different plants in the Ordnance district made parts, such as canvas, propellers, sprockets, rubber tubing, and metal frames, hardly a soul knew what the assembly would be. At Firestone only a handful of men harbored the mystery. Out of Akron, the materials were shipped to Lima, Ohio, under cover, from the end of January, 1944, to a day in March when the secret task was done. The "D-D device" met boat-side schedules.

June 6—up from an empty sea, onto the shores of Normandy, Sherman tanks emerged with guns blazing. They had been lowered, the night before, from LCT boats, miles out, their tracks submerged. They had been masked as harmless trawlers by a canvas structure which was also the flotation mechanism. Twin motors propelled these hidden thirty-five-ton tanks closer to shore. Pneumatic controls lowered the canvas from its framework of vertical tubes and horizontal slats. Mars, not Venus, rose from the sea.

Along 100 miles of Normandy beach, troops landed from England and dug in under a great panoply of planes. Supreme Commander Eisenhower held the narrow strip grimly. The news from other theaters was heartening: Rome had fallen to the Allies; new bases had been wrested from the tenacious Japanese in the South Pacific to take their war nearer home. Not until late July did Eisenhower break through. He pierced the line at St. Lô.

The race across northern France, the heavy loss of vehicles, the inexorable needs of tomorrow—abruptly brought a tire shortage. General Somervell sent out an appeal: tires for the trucks that supplied the men.

The road to victory in Europe ends in Berlin. Each day of advance by our armies shortens the road in front of us but lengthens the road behind us, and the road behind us must be filled with trucks at all times, carrying ammunition, food, and supplies to our combat troops.

Four million tons shipped overseas each month. Much of it unloaded over the beach. Virtually all of it forwarded by truck. Our Air Forces and Army had destroyed railroad bridges, rolling stock, and track to prevent German reinforcements from coming up, and German demolition covered retreat by finishing what was left, General Somervell said. Not only were our supply lines lengthened, but additional troops had entered into action.

He quoted a wire from General Eisenhower, to send more field transportation.

Trucks and tractors are needed and are consumed in prodigious quantities. Earnestly hope that no consideration of any nature will be allowed to interfere with the steady flow of these items to this theater through the months to come. The demands exceed our present ability to supply.

The Allied Armies had covered ground faster than they thought they would. If they were not handicapped now, the war would end sooner. Somervell put another punch into his appeal:

These trucks can be provided only if tires are made available. The immediate supply situation with respect to heavy truck tires is serious.

General Clark used 34,000 tons of heavy artillery ammunition in breaking the Nazi lines in Italy in one month. It had to be carried to the front in heavy trucks.

Trucks without tires are useless. We ask for your best effort. Please give us the tires to keep our trucks rolling on the road to victory.*

The tire industry needed more man power. Industry leaders assembled in Washington to confer with War Production Board officials and Lieutenant General Lucius D. Clay of the Army Service Forces, on means of intensifying production. The War Department directed the release from military service of men over thirty with experience in heavy-duty military-tire construction.

General Alexander Patch jr. now landed on the southern coast of France with American and French troops and forged northward. The supply problem was the same. Trucks laden with cargoes of tires ranged the convoy routes. The Russian armies were advancing from the east, transporting by truck.

Under Lend-Lease that summer, Firestone shipped large quantities of tires to Algiers, supplementing airplane tires sent up from its South African factory at Port Elizabeth for use in North Africa, the Mediterranean area, and India. The plant in Bombay, responding to the call of the A.A.F., was also building airplane tires and helping to keep aloft the life lines to Burma and China. In Los Angeles, Leonard Firestone, having been placed on inactive duty in the U.S.N.R. to take charge of the plant there because of the death of its manager, was also solving problems of war production. To Memphis, Raymond Firestone returned from the A.T.C. in October to direct this factory's flow of giant tires and

* Lieut. Gen. Brehon Somervell to H.S.F. jr., Aug. 5, 1944.

tubes into the reservoir of 6,500,000 needed for the first quarter of 1945.

"Two big paws frozen to the steering wheel of a heavy-duty truck twenty-four hours a day. This is our secret weapon." So wrote a combat correspondent in the overseas edition of *Yank*.

"The rubber industry has put forth a tremendous effort since August 1," acknowledged J. A. Krug, head of the War Production Board, on a visit to Akron late in November. "But we are still running a million tires short of our minimum requirements for the next quarter."

It was the day that the United States First and Ninth Armies and the British Second Army punctured the Siegfried Line. Trucks running from Cherbourg and other beachhead harbors—the "Red Ball Express," the men dubbed it—had been burning up tires at the rate of one per vehicle per day. In three months, this express service had delivered more than 500,000 tons of supplies across 700 miles of treacherous terrain. General Eisenhower, in his good-humored way, thought back on the first Army Transcontinental Motor Convoy of 1919 and its fledgling attempt to demonstrate the practicability of trucks.

Here again Harvey Firestone's foresight and conviction, expressed in the "Ship by Truck" movement and activated by unceasing development of truck tires and rims, bore fruit.

Now Production Chief Krug asked that current tire production be stepped up twenty-five percent to fill Eisenhower's bill.

The workers were apprised of the critical situation. At the instance of John W. Thomas they received copies of the Somervell appeal. The industry pledged all-out effort and went on a seven-day week for four months with a goal of 21,000 extra tires a day.

The deed was as good as the word; so good that the accelerated production outstripped the supply of carbon black and other ingredients. In March, 1945, the workers were temporarily released from their pledge. However, military operations proceeded on all fronts, chewing the enemy and chewing up rubber.

The same month, Firestone introduced a new construction with slightly thicker rayon cord (34/1,000-inch gauge instead of 24/1,000-inch), which more than doubled the tensile strength and made fewer plies feasible. It sped up production.

Meanwhile a windowless, air-conditioned plant of 1,000,000 square feet had been set up in Pottstown, Pennsylvania. This was a former engine factory belonging to the government. The materials, prepared in Akron, were sent there and converted into 7.00-20 six-ply tires.

Firestone's output of 8,877,000 tires in 1944 and 10,716,000 in 1945 represented a vast increase over the first two years of the war, not merely in units but, more importantly, in weight.

In the events of those two years, the Firestone workers had taken part: the recapture of Guam, the entry into Paris, the return of General Douglas MacArthur to the Philippines; the renewed raids on Tokyo, this time by carrier-based planes; the Battle of the Bulge, with the Germans halted by lethal rain from 6,000 bombers and pushed back; the general withdrawal of German forces on the western front, the relentless day-and-night bombing of Berlin, and the sweep of thousands of planes across Germany to blot out gun emplacements and industrial plants.

"Hitler—Stay Clear of These If You Want to Live."
"We're on Our Way—to Tokyo."
These inscriptions and many more were written by

employees on a Bofors gun, Firestone's 25,000th, after it was rolled off the production line and out into the sun in a brief celebration between shifts. A woman worker wrote: "Betty A. G33. Hi, Son." Another mother: "I hope that this gun and all like it will protect you, Angelo."

They helped silence the Luftwaffe. They provided, according to a letter from the Navy Department, the most effective answer to Japanese suicide planes.

Into the Bofors building moved another Ordnance project: 40,000 rocket launcher clusters for aircraft firing. Three launching tubes to the cluster, primarily an assembly task, they were ordered early in 1944, before V-1 robot flying bombs began landing in England. Willow Grove received a similar assignment but sent the work first to Jenkintown, Pennsylvania, while it was busy with gliders, and later completed the order itself. Atlanta, too, while building airplane wing panels, was put on rocket launchers and on rocket motors, as well as a quarter of a million five-inch rockets. Both Willow Grove and Atlanta produced bomb aimers by the thousands.

Prowling over Japanese shipping lanes a few hundred miles from Tokyo, Navy planes fired these rockets. Rear Admiral Hussey sent Firestone workers an official report.

Using aircraft rockets of the type you manufacture, a squadron of Navy PBJ bombers last week damaged three Japanese destroyers and two cargo ships in attacks on convoys in the Bonin and Volcano Islands. . . .

This action typifies the increasingly important role of rockets in the Pacific offensive. The Navy urgently needs tremendous quantities of these projectiles and counts on your best efforts to keep them coming. *

The commander of the Third Fleet, Rear Admiral W. F. Halsey jr., also reported to the men and women of

---

* Rear Admiral G. F. Hussey jr., Chief of Navy Bureau of Ordnance, to the men and women of The Firestone Tire & Rubber Company, Feb. 7, 1945.

Firestone, telling of the "terrific job" rockets were doing on the invasion beaches.

They eliminate lurking Japs and thereby help to keep our own casualties at a minimum. Thousands of rockets are expended in a short time in every amphibious operation. We need every rocket you can produce. We can't have too many or have them too soon for the tough battles ahead.*

Flying bombs were falling daily in London and in the neighborhood of the Brentford plant. There was many a close call. One day a V-2 rocket scored a direct hit on a factory across the road, with severe casualties. The Firestone factory shook, but its blast walls and window protection averted serious damage; a number of workers, however, sustained minor injuries.

The routing of the enemy, wherever he might be, was a welcome command in 1945. Fifty-seven millimeter high-explosive shells. Ninety-millimeter-guns (M-3) for mobile weapons. For this work a defense plant in Burlington, North Carolina, was assigned to Firestone. And in Akron the company produced sixty-millimeter trench mortars and seventy-five-millimeter gun mounts. A woman working on the mortars received a letter from her staff-sergeant son in Germany, saying that he was using them in his division of the First Army headed for Berlin.

That was its specific destination. American troops reached points along the Rhine in March, and after air-pommeling the Germans' rear, they made several crossings on ponton bridges. One surprise landing on the east bank, near Karlsruhe, was accomplished by that gay masquerader, the "D-D device." Penetration of the heart of Germany came swiftly. One city fell after another. In a few weeks, the Elbe was crossed.

Meanwhile the American flag had been planted on

* Telegram, Mar. 21, 1945.

Iwo Jima, and we had landed on Okinawa. In Italy, the offensive of General Mark W. Clark overran Bologna and so weakened the Nazi-Fascist hold on northern Italy that the Germans gave the country up. It was the end of April. Street fighting in Berlin. Allied Armies from the west, Russians from the east, had closed in on the only military resistance remaining in Germany. On May 7, unconditional surrender. Next day, the articles signed, the forces of democracy celebrated V-E day.

Rejoicing was tempered by realities. The end of the fighting in Europe did not mean that the home front could relax, General Somervell reminded.

There will be continued huge requirements for tires to fill the demands of both Asiatic Pacific and European theaters. As long as our troops are overseas we must keep the supplies rolling to them on the tires you produce.*

The tires, the tank tracks and bogie rollers, the tank turrets and billions of machine-gun belt links, the Commando wings that carried thousands of tons of precious cargo and the gliders that carried airborne troops behind enemy lines, the fuel and oil cells and shatterproof oxygen cylinders, the pontons, gas masks, life belts, and life vests, the Bofors gun and other war products that hastened victory and saved lives. For these Harvey Firestone jr. gave thanks to the members of the organization. In a broadcast on the eve of the company's forty-fifth anniversary, he paid them tribute for their services.

And tribute came also after the last Jap outpost had been wiped out, and closer bases secured, and the naval might of the Orient rendered ineffective by Admiral Chester W. Nimitz; after atom bombs blasted Hiroshima and Nagasaki, and the ensuing silence expanded the small voice of Emperor Hirohito on August 15, accepting defeat. Then General Somervell wrote:

* Somervell to J.W.T., May 5, 1945.

Your company has played a very important part in producing the equipment and supplies which have been such a decisive factor in winning the war.

You and your associates and employees must have a deep sense of satisfaction as you look back upon your accomplishments on the war production front. Now that the war is won, I want to express to you the gratification and appreciation of the Army Service Forces for the magnificent achievements of your organization.

The energy, initiative, and efficiency which industrial concerns like yours have demonstrated in the war effort give me complete confidence that the problems of transition to normal peacetime production will be met with the same effectiveness as those of war-time and will be as swiftly and successfully solved.*

* Somervell to H.S.F. jr., Sept. 7, 1945.

22

Transition to Peace

"POSTWAR," during the war, was a theme of American thinking. Our undaunted citizenry looked forward not only to peace but to peace and plenty. On the production side this meant planning—which products to make, in what quantities, in which factories, with how much employment, and how speedily the conversion could be achieved on each class of goods. To gear the immensely expanded Firestone organization to the estimated needs of a pent-up demand, for an era of relaxed restrictions, economic analyses were essential. Hence Firestone designated its marketing research department as the hub of the program.

As early as May, 1943, the company's postwar planning committee went into action, calling upon the managers of various departments and other key men to present a picture of their individual goals. These separate plans were freely discussed before the committee, which in turn diagnosed and sometimes improved on them before making recommendations to the management. Marketing Research further proposed procedures for efficient distribution.

Through this funnel and by this catalytic agent, the company charted a course for maintaining employment, production, and sales at a high level. New products— to keep the steel and industrial goods factories humming.

But above all, tires—for a tire-hungry public and the new automobiles that would soon be manufactured again. Thanks to forethought, the new tire plants were situated in Des Moines and Pottstown, where they could serve the Middle Western farm area and the Eastern market after the war.

The objective of Firestone Industrial Products Company was to attain a volume in the fourth postwar year equal to five times its 1939 total. This ambition could be realized only by getting approval of additional capital equipment to make, in particular, the new plastic and synthetic-rubber products that were coming out of Firestone laboratories in the wartime quest for alternatives to rubber. This was merely one of the plans.

Some reshuffling of plant operations must take place after ordnance machinery was moved out. Noblesville, however, was slated to resume specialization in molded goods for the automotive industry and trade sales, as well as fan belts, radiator hose, and wringer rolls. On the other hand, Paterson could not be enlarged sufficiently to handle all the pending brake-lining business, and it was decided to transfer the work to New Castle, where fuel-cell schedules were about to be completed. This war plant at New Castle, which had been purchased in 1942, was now marked as the Middle Western factory for extruded goods, a category hitherto concentrated at Fall River with a consequent gain in Eastern accounts. Now better service could be rendered to the market radiating from Indiana; Foamex too might be made here for the Western trade.

"We will manufacture anything and give delivery on anything that you men can sell"—a sales conference of this division was told at the beginning of May, 1945. The collapse of Nazi defenses seemed imminent. "Postwar" was almost at hand.

Electronic vulcanization had already reached the production stage. Tank tracks required only twenty-eight minutes in the steam mold after two minutes of electronic preheating, instead of sixty minutes by the all-steam method. Foamex could be vulcanized in four minutes by electronics, instead of thirty, and dried in one hour instead of sixteen hours. No longer was it necessary to wait for slow heat to permeate the rubber to the core; by placing the object between two metal plates supplied with high-frequency alternating current from an electronic generator, almost instantaneous uniform heating was effected throughout. This saving of time and cutting of cost bore promise of greatly increased output in application to other articles. Some day electronic vulcanization might be successful with tires.

In winning approval of a new building for Fall River, to double the Foamex capacity, the planners also obtained authorization for an electronics unit to be installed there. Another Fall River product in increasing demand was Contro elastic thread for various types of apparel. The presses used here for plastic gunstocks and helmet liners would easily be reconverted to battery cases and radio cabinets, just as Steel Products could swing back from oxygen cylinders to stainless-steel beverage containers.

Another project recommended by the planning committee was quantity production of resins, particularly a synthetic resin developed by Firestone plastics researchers that was eminently suited for brake lining. The wartime search for rubber substitutes had revealed that vinyl resins, properly plasticized, exhibited rubberlike qualities. By making its own vinyl resins, the company could cut costs considerably. Pottstown was destined to get such a plant. A great future was mapped out for Pottstown to handle the huge market for Velon products.

"The fields of application of rubber and of plastics," the sales conference was informed, "can no longer be separated."

As for synthetic rubber, already proved better than natural rubber in the manufacture of most industrial products and mechanical rubber goods, the ability to "tailor" it to a specific job opened up fairly unlimited uses.

Thus a continuous flow of products—improved products—was assured. The corporate charter had been amended, giving Firestone authority to "manufacture, produce, buy, sell and otherwise deal in rubber, cotton, rayon, plastics, synthetics, chemicals, metals, and petroleum, and products which are made from or partly from any one or more of the said materials."*

Akron, centralizing all sales, remained the mother of development, in the engineering laboratories that were currently experimenting with a tapered rim to eliminate bead wobble, among other activities, and in the very latest edifice, Firestone Research.

"Science and engineering have made our civilization possible," said Harold W. Dodds, president of Princeton University, at the dedication of the Research building.

> They have wonderfully expanded man's power to enjoy and to appreciate the good things of life. They throw new light on the nature and purpose of life and help point out how we can realize a new world.†

By authorization of the government, whose cognizance of research in chemistry and physics was secretly manifested in atomic energy studies, Firestone had procured materials and man power for building construction in the midst of the war. Ground was broken in 1943, the structure opened in March, 1945. Enthroned on a hill overlooking a ten-acre expanse at the edge of the factory

---

*Authorized by stockholders' meeting Oct. 28, 1944.
† H. W. Dodds, Akron, Sept. 18, 1945.

grounds, Firestone Research presented the most modern
hall of science: not a house of miracles but a painstaking
laboratory devoted to the unlocking of mysteries. As
President Dodds observed in September, the scientific
method called for "ruthless logic linked to imagination
and the creative instinct."

> This laboratory we dedicate today will make a distinguished
> contribution to that flowing stream which constantly enriches the
> field of human endeavor and human satisfaction. It is the embodi-
> ment of a living faith in the power of ideas.
>
> We predict great success for it in the ceaseless adventure of the
> advancement of knowledge. *

Among the first items on the agenda had been the
improvement of synthetic rubber for military tires, investigations in glass fabric for lighter flak vests, and
studies for the wider application of electronic vulcanization. Now that the war was over, wider research in
plastics, textiles, and metals was in progress, besides the
quest for new GR-S monomers to make better rubber.

Presiding over Research, John W. Thomas, the company's original chemist and recent recipient of the gold
medal of the American Institute of Chemists,† had
directly supervised the construction of the new $2,000,000
building. Two-man laboratory units, twelve by twenty-
four feet, were enclosed in prefabricated, insulated steel
walls that were removable for rearrangement of the
space or for the entry of large equipment. On three
floors comprising 100,000 square feet, there was room
for a hundred such units in addition to offices, library,
and dispensaries. Service shafts, with a central supply of
distilled water, steam, gas, compressed air, and electric
current, supplied each nest of four laboratories.

Many of the testing instruments set up in Research

* *Ibid.*

† This award was presented at the Institute's meeting in Columbus, Ohio,
May 11, 1945, in recognition of achievements under Mr. Thomas's direction
in the development and production of synthetic rubber.

were designed by Firestone's own engineers: a forced vibrator, to measure the dynamic properties of rubber stocks; low-temperature bending modulus apparatus, to determine stiffening effect upon rubber stocks and plastics; a relaxometer, to find the resistance of rubberlike materials to oxidation while under strain; and an infrared spectrograph for the study of molecular structure.

An electron microscope with a magnification of 100,000 diameters was installed. An ultraviolet spectrograph and a recording microphotometer identified and registered impurities. An X-ray diffraction unit determined the fibrous and crystal structures of materials for their adaptability to new purposes.

One of the first developments coming from Research was an accelerator—Isocyclex—which bore promise of effecting a substantial saving. Another was a wetting agent for cotton cord; it increased tensile strength. Another, a vapor-proofing agent for Velon Film.

The biggest triumph of the first year was the polymerization of GR-S for a highly concentrated latex, superior in several respects to natural rubber latex. Despite its percentage of solids, it had excellent fluidity; it possessed age resistance, was colorless and stable. A basic compounding ingredient in adhesives, in glove dipping, and in Foamex—that foe of fatigue—the new latex was already being produced in quantity at one of the government plants operated in Akron by Firestone.

Now it could be revealed, with War Department sanction, that more than 100 Firestone physics researchers and production workers had been engaged during 1944 and 1945 on work for the Manhattan Engineer District. Under a special research contract, they had devised and tested hundreds of compounds in aid of the plants that were producing the atomic bomb.

Operation of the company's own Butaprene autoclaves was given over to the Xylos subsidiary, which now produced the new latex as well as GR-S reclaim. Xylos' output was so large, vast amounts were sold to the trade. On the other hand, the company was unable to supply the full volume of automotive mechanical parts and adhesives in demand, for lack of sufficient manufacturing equipment. While reconversion proceeded on schedule in most instances, some raw-material and labor shortages still obtained.

Postwar planning had envisaged full employment. A canvass was taken of each plant to learn how many war workers wished to continue on the roster. To this number was added an estimate of veterans returning to their jobs. Enough production was assigned to the individual factory to take care of the total. Actually, the stepped-up schedules projected into the future contemplated a growing personnel including displaced workers from other fields.

The company's Veterans' Service Bureau had called upon all department heads to list the names of their men in the armed services so that reemployment might be anticipated. The bureau's task was to make sure that every qualified man received at least his old job, or one of like seniority and pay, and to recognize his special aptitudes and leadership developed in service. If he was not yet ready for a better position, the standard procedure provided for a course of training. At each plant a veterans' reemployment division was instituted. For the disabled, a program of rehabilitation. Placements for "limited service" required the approval of both the medical examiner and the safety director.

Thanks to this careful mobilization for peace, the company's plans were well articulated when the happy day came that hostilities ended. Pessimistic armchair economists—and even many practising ones—had predicted an immediate depression across the country with the cancellation of war contracts and the rapid return of millions of men to civilian status. Firestone's state of readiness accommodated the demands of the public and of industry quickly and smoothly. By the end of 1945, close to 3,000 veterans were reemployed plus 9,700 men formerly in uniform but not formerly in Firestone employ.*

In another year, Harvey S. Firestone jr. was able to report that the company had doubled its working force and tripled its wage payments in the period 1940-1946. After granting new wage increases in 1946, he noted that the average annual earnings of employees in the domestic factories had advanced 81.2 percent over 1940. This compared with an average rise of 73.6 percent for all United States manufacturing industries. On an hourly basis, rubber workers continued to be among the highest paid industry employees in the country.

In reaching and surpassing postwar goals, the company's fiscal operations played an important part. Back in December, 1943, a special meeting of the common stockholders had authorized $60,000,000 of new preferred stock. At the same time they voted to increase the par value of the common stock from $10 to $25, which resulted in capitalizing about half of the consolidated earned surplus, then totaling approximately $65,000,000. In January, $45,000,000 of the new preferred bearing a dividend rate of four and a half percent was offered to the public and the proceeds were applied to the redemption of the outstanding six percent preferred, which amounted to $45,400,000.

During 1944, the company made voluntary price reductions on goods produced for the government, the

* As of July, 1947, the tabulation was: 9,327 Firestone veterans reinstated and 11,797 other veterans employed.

pursuit of efficiency having borne fruit in lowered costs. To take care of financial requirements while the war lasted, through the period of war contract settlements, and into the time of production for civilian needs, an arrangement was effected in August with the National City Bank of New York. This was for a three-year, unsecured revolving credit of $75,000,000 at interest rates of two to two and a half percent. Because of the prompt settlement of terminated contracts, the availability of these funds soon proved unnecessary, and in October, 1945, the arrangement was canceled.

In the war years 1942–1945, the company added a total of $11,000,000 to the reserve for contingencies. Net income was 2.41 to 2.78 percent of sales. The first postwar year afforded an addition of $5,000,000 to the reserve. Firestone was in the strongest financial position in its history, with an earned surplus of more than $70,000,000 that was destined to keep climbing.

Volume of $545,300,000 in 1943, yielding a net income of $15,100,000, had risen to $651,400,000 in 1944, with a net of $16,300,000, and to $681,000,000 in 1945, net $16,400,000. In the full year of peace, 1946, sales were well maintained at $577,800,000. The net for this year was $27,680,000, or 4.79 percent of sales, and the common dividend rose to $4.25; yet in this year as much as $23,800,000 was expended for additions to plants and their improvement and equipment—to create more jobs and produce more goods. *

To continue the fiscal story: early in 1947, as favorable interest rates prevailed, the company sold $25,000,000 worth of twenty-five-year 2⅝ percent debentures and with the proceeds redeemed 250,000 shares of outstanding 4½ percent preferred stock. Sales this year mounted

* Common dividends were $2 in 1943 and 1944, $2.50 in 1945. Since 1946, the annual rate has been $4.

to $638,400,000, net income $26,970,000 or 4.23 percent of sales, and expenditures of $24,400,000 additional were made for plant expansion and improvement. The demand for Firestone products hit a new peacetime high.

On the administrative side, several changes had occurred. For his financial skill John J. Shea, treasurer, had been further honored by his election to the additional post of vice president in 1941. Harold D. Tompkins, a member of the sales department since 1919 and sales manager since 1940, became vice president in charge of sales as Lee R. Jackson moved up to executive vice president. Harvey H. Hollinger, comptroller since 1928, was elected secretary in 1943, succeeding Stacy G. Carkhuff, who retired after more than forty years with the company, but continued as a director until his death.

Mr. Carkhuff's immediate successor had been Bernard M. Robinson, a director, former assistant secretary and general counsel, who had served the company with distinction for twenty-five years. He died six months after his election as secretary.

Long years of service distinguished the officers. Mr. Shea had joined the Firestone accounting department in 1907, Mr. Hollinger in 1913.

All five sons of the founder were now on the board of directors. Roger S. Firestone, on his release from the Navy in October, 1945, joined his brothers Harvey S. jr., Russell A., Leonard K., and Raymond C. Firestone. Each had a definite executive role. Their fellow directors included Lee R. Jackson, executive vice president, and James E. Trainer, vice president in charge of production, besides Mr. Shea, Mr. Hollinger, and Chairman Thomas.

John W. Thomas announced his retirement in January, 1946, but remained as a director and honorary

chairman. Harvey Firestone jr. became the active head
of the company to steer the vast organization in the era
of peace.

The Firestone Tire & Rubber Company, with subsidiaries domestic and foreign, had progressed into the
ranks of the world's most influential industrial enterprises. Each activity undertaken had reflected new honor
on its name. And this was the chief satisfaction derived
from the free competitive system: while profit acted as
the incentive, the cup was full only as it measured service
to society.

23

Production and Social Values

FIRST in the order of objectives, the accumulated demand must be filled. This was a clear matter of production. Then, when the backlog was exhausted, the greater test would come. For with the return of a buyers' market the country was going to face the problem of sustaining employment and national income. This called for creative business—how to continue production at a high level under conditions of competitive selling. In the first period, price inflation must be checked lest it prove a boomerang and incur a recession. In the second, lower prices were essential for the reanimation of demand.

A spokesman for this economic philosophy, Harvey Firestone jr. declared before the National Industrial Conference Board in 1946 his confidence in the American standard of living.

Markets must be broadened by making more and better products available at lower prices. . . .

In the unfilled needs of our own people we have all of the new "economic frontiers" we can handle for many years to come. Even though our living standards have been far higher than any other nation's, many of our citizens have lived under substandard conditions. If we can find a way to distribute the good things of life to this portion of our population, we shall have a market which in size and permanence will far exceed the present huge war-born backlogs.[*]

That other lusty offspring of the war—America's

[*] H.S.F. jr., New York, Nov. 19, 1946.

synthetic-rubber industry—provided a basic means of enabling the motor economy of the nation rapidly to resume its functioning. Not only was a supply of rubber at hand, the supply was adjustable to the tire industry's and the auto industry's requirements; no longer subject to control by cartel price manipulation. Similarly, rayon cord for tire plies assured stability in place of the price fluctuations of cotton. And Firestone was producing both of these man-made components.

In the government plants operated by Firestone, 129,400 tons of synthetic rubber were polymerized in 1946, representing 86 percent of their rated capacity as against 114 percent the year before. The reason for this reduction was twofold. The revival of natural-rubber imports from the Far East, slow at first, gained momentum during the year; and when a shortage of butadiene occurred, the Office of Rubber Reserve raised the maximum percentages of natural-rubber content to total rubber content of tires to avoid limiting production.

The government continued to set percentages both to maintain the natural-rubber stockpile and to preserve the synthetic-rubber industry, for reasons of defense. On the same grounds, the government remained the exclusive importer of natural rubber and regulated its disposal.

In passenger-car tires, the natural-rubber content was advanced from two percent to twenty-six. In truck-bus tires it rose to seventy-nine percent. The year saw an unprecedented consumption of rubber in the United States, totaling 1,040,000 tons, seventy percent going into tires. Synthetic made up 761,700 tons of the total. If automotive manufacturers had been dependent upon natural alone, tires would have been few and inordinately expensive. As it was, synthetic rubber was obtainable at the government price of eighteen and a half cents a pound, natural at the government price of twenty-two and a half cents.

The proportion of natural to the total used in the Firestone factories had dipped to its lowest point of 13.7 percent in the last quarter of 1945. The increase in 1946 was manifested in the company's tonnage of 45,234 natural, 83,979 GR-S, and 14,241 other synthetic. Reconversions from GR-S brought the natural rubber percentage up to 49.5 in the final quarter of the year, to 52.5 in January of the next year.

These figures reflected the national picture of a steady climb in the quantity of natural rubber entering manufacture. Most of the tire producers favored government retention of the import monopoly, and allocation. They expressed fear that the price, in an unrestricted market, would be shot up high by the growers while a strong demand lasted; after which, they fancied, the growers might wage a price war against synthetic and knock the rival out.

Harvey Firestone jr. disagreed. As long as domestic controls obtained in the specification of synthetic rubber in finished products, there was safety. His company was historically opposed to interference with the free flow of supplies. He denied the existence of any reasonable justification for what was virtually a buying cartel. Hence he favored adoption of the Crawford Resolution, then before Congress, for the return of private buying of natural rubber.

This measure, introduced by Representative Fred L. Crawford of Indiana, provided also for the continued operation of the government plants. Synthetic rubber, Firestone said, should be produced in the most efficient plants.

As the cost of synthetic rubber goes down and the quality is improved, it is reasonable to expect from an economic standpoint that the price of natural rubber will be reduced in order to compete.*

At hearings on the resolution before the House Armed Services Committee, he emphasized the provisions with regard to the synthetic-rubber industry.

It is the best paid-up insurance policy which this country ever had. Its maintenance is vital to the national security and economic independence of this country.†

Upon the adoption of the resolution by Congress as of April 1, Firestone hailed the return to a free rubber market as an important step in the reversion of the United States "to a normal peacetime economy based on the system of free enterprise which has made our country the greatest nation on earth." In the synthetic-rubber industry we had a great asset and bulwark. There would be no necessity for paying an excessive price for natural rubber.

True enough. While natural momentarily advanced a few cents as manufacturers descended on the open market, it was only a matter of weeks before the price slumped under that of synthetic—to fourteen cents— and thereafter continued to be attractive. In the middle of 1947, the graph curves of consumption crossed, and the year ended with the ratio of natural to synthetic headed for one and a half as to one, a ratio since maintained. Firestone was using more than sixty percent natural rubber at the close of 1947.

In September of that year, the Firestone-operated synthetic plant at Port Neches had been placed in stand-by condition, having run, with the others, at sixty-five percent of rated capacity. Their output was 102,300 tons of a national total of 447,200 tons. Firestone was still one of the world's largest producers of synthetic rubber.

* H.S.F. jr., quoted in *The Wall Street Journal*, Feb. 24, 1947.
† H.S.F. jr., Feb. 26, 1947.

In discussions on permanent legislation, Firestone urged piecemeal disposal of the government plants to private industry. Congress provided by the Rubber Act of 1948 that the facilities ultimately be sold or leased, but until June 30, 1950, there should be retained, as a matter of national security, in addition to natural-rubber stockpiles, 600,000 tons capacity for GR-S and 65,000 tons for other synthetics, with the production to be at least one-third. Mandatory minimum percentages ensuring consumption of this amount would be established.

It is further declared to be the policy of the Congress that the security interests of the United States can and will best be served by the development within the United States of a free, competitive synthetic-rubber industry. In order to strengthen national security through a sound industry it is essential that Government ownership of productive facilities, Government production of synthetic rubber, regulations requiring mandatory use of synthetic rubber, and patent pooling be ended and terminated whenever consistent with national security as provided in this Act.*

The new minima, under an amended rubber order, were lower than those which had prevailed, but in actual practice the tire industry used higher percentages, for experience proved the merits of synthetics in various phases of construction. Another order, in July, 1949, further eased the requirement of synthetics to encourage manufacturers to take advantage of the low cost of natural rubber, which was about sixteen and a half cents. Synthetic stayed fixed at eighteen and a half.

Tire prices were already below their prewar level— what other industry could make such a claim in a time of general chafing at the high cost of living? But more significant, a development took place that betokened greater mileage. It was the "cold process" of producing synthetic rubber, evolved as a cooperative, industry-wide project sponsored by the Office of Rubber Reserve.

* Public Law 469, Eightieth Congress.

For a long time it had been known that polymerization of butadiene and styrene at a temperature lower than the customary 122 degrees Fahrenheit had a beneficial chemical effect. As the temperature was reduced, the molecules tended to line up in a more orderly arrangement and thus make rubber that offered more resistance to abrasion. But by the same token, this process took longer. Scientists knew these facts when the government's synthetic program began; they had a refrigeration method that took several days instead of twelve to fourteen hours.

During the war, time was of the essence. After the war, experiments in cold GR-S proceeded, with a search for chemicals that would satisfactorily speed the reaction. The right catalyst, the right activator, the right reducing agent, and the right stabilizer were found in 1948. By circulating a refrigerant between the double walls of the autoclaves, the mixture was cooled to forty-one degrees. Linkage was achieved in twelve hours. The cost was but a quarter of a cent higher per pound than by the usual method.

Firestone obtained O.R.R. approval in September to equip a small section of the Lake Charles plant with machinery for the cold process. A hundred pounds of the new GR-S were used experimentally. It was almost as easy to mill as natural rubber. Popular-size passenger-car tires made in Akron Plant 2 were given treads of the new rubber and underwent road tests. They showed remarkable superiority over regular GR-S—were even fifteen percent more durable than natural-rubber treads. And an avenue for still further improvement lay in the use of superfine furnace black as a reinforcing agent.

Firestone had chosen Lake Charles because this, of all the government GR-S plants, had maintained the lowest production cost during and after the war. In May,

1949, half of the plant's capacity was changed over to cold-process rubber, and plans were laid to adopt it in all synthetic tire treads when the supply permitted.

Greater safety. More mileage. This was in the Firestone tradition. Improvements had been under way all through the period of straining to replace tires for motorists who had been nursing their old ones for five or six years; and to provide tires for the new cars at last allowed to be manufactured. Many of the tires were made with rayon cord bodies, whereas before the war only the Imperial brand and truck tires had used rayon, constituting merely six percent of Firestone's fabric consumption. In 1946, the percentage rose to forty-six and a half, and the trend was vigorously upward.

The Indianapolis Sweepstakes, resumed in 1946, gave vent to America's undying excitement in the challenge of speed and endurance. As at all other major automobile races and the annual Pike's Peak Climb that year, the crowds saw Firestone De Luxe Champion tires ride to victory.*

In the two postwar years, Firestone exceeded all previous production records, an accomplishment resulting from expanded facilities and heightened efficiency. The factories ran full tilt: Akron, Memphis, Los Angeles, as well as Des Moines and Pottstown, both leased from the government to help supply the country's needs and both later purchased.

The Firestone textile mills rolled out more than a million pounds weekly of rayon and cotton cord at New Bedford, Gastonia, and Woodstock, cotton at Bennettsville, and rayon at Roanoke and Worcester. Inventories remained low; maximum operation was required.

---

* These tires bore Bill Holland on his record-smashing whirl of 121.377 miles per hour around the 500 miles at Indianapolis in 1949. A new track record was made in the 1950 classic by Johnnie Parsons, who averaged 124.002 miles per hour for 345 miles, after which the race was stopped because of rain.

Enough fabric was produced to supply the company, to ship to foreign subsidiaries, and to sell in considerable quantity to other companies. Outside of the industry, few people realized that fabric amounted to almost one-third of a tire's weight.

High-tenacity rayon gave the new passenger-car tires super strength. By using 2200/2 gauge with twenty-six ends in the two inner plies and twenty ends in the two outer plies, tread plies were dispensable; the thinner casings were stronger and lighter. "Cord fatigue" was further averted by an improved dip and by substitution of rayon filler threads for cotton filler.

Gastonia made nylon cords for the new Imperial premium tire in 1947: an extra ply between the tread and the rayon cord body. The tread itself was redesigned for greater traction quality and eye appeal, with nine ribs and thousands of sharp-edged angles. For 1949 the nylon operation was transferred to New Bedford in preparation for the introduction of an all-nylon truck tire.

But as for cotton—so entrenched was public acceptance of its rival rayon that the decreased demand for cotton cord tires resulted in the discontinuance of cotton production at New Bedford. Mass production of rayon cord had brought the cost below cotton. Apart from the government-supported price of raw cotton, fifteen operations were necessary to convert cotton into cord, as against four for rayon: ply twisting, respooling, cable twisting, and weaving. By early 1949, less than half of Firestone's fabric consumption was cotton.

In each of the company's tire factories a quality training class was instituted for the production workers and their supervisors, even while a sellers' market obtained. The theme was this: the customer is interested only in service for his money. Firestone products, the men and women were told, would continue to be of superior quality only if each worker did his job in accordance with the specifications. It made sense to them.

An inkling of the competitive days ahead came in 1947, when mail-order houses cut prices and the tire manufacturers reduced their list prices despite wage increases. Later in the year part of the cut was restored. Tires still sold for less than prewar tires and gave better performance.

In the Firestone line that year, the De Luxe Champion passenger-car tire was made with an improved eight-rib design. The company resumed manufacture of white sidewalls and of Life Protector tubes with inner chambers capable of retaining two-thirds of the air in case of a blowout. The new curved-bar Champion Ground Grip tractor tire, recently introduced, was taking so well that the Des Moines factory was expanded, and room was made there also for the new Champion Spade Grip which gave tractors maximum flotation and traction in watery cane and rice fields.

Earthmover tires, with 21.00 cross section and larger, were built by Firestone with a tapered fit between the bead and the rim—an innovation that became standard for the industry. Firestone Steel Products had developed this improvement on the wartime divided rim in 1946, redesigning the base and side ring to attain a full five-degree taper under both beads. It eliminated the rocking and shifting of heavy tires on their bead seats and prevented premature bead failure; only one bead had been anchored before. Tests showed that ten percent more wear was obtained by eliminating the wobble.

For on-the-job changes of giant earthmover tires— some of which weighed a ton and a half apiece—Firestone fashioned a bead loosening tool. Such casings had a way of getting "frozen" to the rim flanges after months of wear, and the long lever easily pried the beads from their seats. Another development, a large dynamometer, determined the horsepower requirements of huge construction equipment. Firestone engineers had taken two years to complete this, but it was time well spent for it saved incalculable energy otherwise lost because of poor evaluation of vehicle capacities. And it tested the tractive ability of heavy-duty tires.

In the realm of automobile tires, the public received a big and pleasant surprise. A casing with a larger footprint—long and rectangular instead of elliptical—and a wider cross section, was developed late in 1947 by Firestone engineers. The size was 6.70-15 in place of the conventional 6.00-16. The smaller rim diameter enabled some car manufacturers to lower the center of gravity of their new models for easier steering. Most important, the cushion of air contained 115 cubic inches more volume, carried at twenty-four pounds pressure instead of twenty-eight. It was the Super-Balloon.

It provided a smoother ride. The broader width gave greater flexing action in absorbing road shocks. It provided a safer ride. The lower pressure meant cooler running and greater protection against blowouts. The long foot-print meant driving stability, quicker stopping, better non-skid.

The tread of the Firestone Super-Balloon was heavy and flat, with high sloping shoulders. Aside from its practical virtues, it was in aesthetic harmony with the svelte lines of the forthcoming beauties. Many automobile manufacturers ordered the new tire as original equipment for their 1948 models.

Launched with the general public in January, 1948, the Super-Balloon rendered pillowy comfort, but some skeptics fretted about tread wear until they became accustomed to keeping the pressure low, as indicated, for overinflation could injure the sides of the treads. As always, mileage varied with individual care. To supply motorists while they were waiting, impatiently, for the delivery of their new cars, Firestone made special sizes fitting their present cars. That year the assembly lines glowed with Super-Balloons. Another milestone had been reached in the evolution of the pneumatic tire. And it was to be capped with long-wearing treads of cold-process rubber.

Motor-vehicle registration now topped 40,000,000, and cars were doing more miles on the road than formerly. The progressive mechanization of farms and the increasing tonnage of highway trucking opened wider markets for tires. Although replacement sales of the tire industry declined from the exceptional totals of 1946 and 1947, the fact that the figure was as high as 50,500,000 in 1948—on top of the 76,000,000 tires sold as original equipment during the three years past—attested to the persistent demand. Far in excess of prewar demand, this probably represented the postwar normal.

Firestone's tire factories worked full force in 1948. The hectic days of tire selling had calmed down, but the company increased its tire and tube inventories, which had been abnormally low in relation to the volume of business done. In 1949, the cautious tone that prevailed in business generally, though auto production reached an all-time high, affected replacements, and the restless industry gave the public another cutback in prices.

The fertile minds of research engineers, insulated from the vagaries of economics, concentrated on creating better service. The Polar Grip tread, brought out by Firestone in 1947, received a thorough testing on ice and snow the following winter. Tires recapped with this tread had more than a million "isocel" particles milled and molded into them, acting as an abrasive, and as each particle wore away it left a tiny suction cup with biting edges that gripped the roadway. For extra traction on winter roads, the company later introduced Studded Ground Grip Super-Balloons. Another advance was tubes of improved butyl that eliminated buckling and cold-weather cracking. Still another was the new tractor tire, with its open-center curved bars.

Steel wire plies had long appealed to the engineers. From the wish to the thought, the leap was like lightning, but the journey from concept to realization was a painstaking row. The theory was that metal would conduct heat away from areas of internal heat build-up and dissipate it before the rubber stock could deteriorate. In the Firestone development department, a tire of flat braided wire had been fashioned early in 1941. Scarcity of steel deterred much further venturing. In 1944 four constructions of wire were made for heavy-duty tires to withstand the rough terrain in logging and strip-mining work. Fine wires of extremely high tensile strength were twisted into cord and bonded with rubber to form stretchless plies—even nylon stretched—and thus lessen the tension of the tread surface and prevent tread separation.

In the final experimental stage in 1945, having come through field and laboratory tests with flying colors, wire cord plies were considered by Firestone as worthy of their work in the world. The plies proved five times stronger than the strongest fiber cord. Four of them took the place of fourteen of rayon. With thinner walls, the tires ran cool; with cooler tires, the treads lasted longer.

Ideal for heavily loaded trucks at high speed, these tires were put into freight service the next year and did as much as 80,000 miles. No blowouts. In 1947, Firestone publicly pronounced them the most rugged pneumatics

ever built. The company's experience in making count-
less items of mechanical rubber goods had furnished the
know-how in bonding rubber and steel. The engineers
further strengthened the adhesion by brass plating and
the use of special compounds. By 1949, thousands of
these perfected tires had been doing service on busses
and trucks.

For dealers who held a Firestone franchise, all these
product improvements made the franchise more valuable.
Their interests had been watched over through the war,
for the company had always relied on independent tire
sellers for the bulk of its distribution and therefore nurtured this network to keep it in good financial shape.
Dealers' business in recapping and sales of home and
auto supplies—which were pretested in the company's
merchandise laboratory and tried out in sixty stores
before winning a place in the catalog—brought gratifying income. The planning committee had prepared to
route war-scarce durable goods their way as soon as
refrigerator, washing machine, and other manufacturers
acquired the materials and man power with which to
make them.

In this manner, the dealers entered 1946 stronger,
better financed, and more aggressive. Both they and the
company's own stores sold such a large volume of merchandise, besides tires and tubes, that postwar goals were
already surpassed at the year's end. In 1947, despite
general shortages, they experienced another successful
year. The planning division offered helps in modernizing
their stores and relocating them where this was possible.
Techniques in retailing worked out in company stores
—numbering 705 in 1948—were passed on to the 35,000
dealers for another year of profitable operation.

More traffic, more business with every customer. This

was the principle for dealers and stores. No seasonal peaks and valleys. Firestone had a powerful system of retail distribution.

II

Harvey Firestone jr. was elected chairman and chief executive officer of the company in January, 1948. Lee R. Jackson succeeded him as president, and the board also elected J. J. Shea vice president in charge of finance and Harvey H. Hollinger treasurer. Joseph Thomas, the assistant secretary and general counsel, and for twenty years a legal aid, became secretary.

Management allocated $21,600,000 for improvements and factory additions in 1948 and $19,157,000 in 1949, Firestone Industrial Products Company sharing in this with Firestone Steel Products Company, Firestone Plastics Company, and the tire plants. Industrial Products doubled the already doubled production of Foamex at Fall River as more makes of cars adopted this cushioning material and more manufacturers of furniture and bedding responded to popular demand. For its latex requirements, this division had the benefit of millions of pounds of natural rubber received in latex form from Firestone Plantations Company in Liberia.

At Fall River, Industrial Products increased its output of Contro, the elastic yarn, for weavers and knitters of apparel accessories. Improved as a nonpinking thread, it was widely used in corsets and girdles. At Noblesville and New Castle a myriad of items were made to manufacturers' specifications, from vibration dampeners for heavy machines to delicate laboratory apparatus, requiring rubber-to-metal bonding; this notably included motor mountings, wringer rolls, brake lining, bumpers, tubing, tie plates, and bushings. Loxite adhesive compounds and Loxite compounded latex dispersions, created by Firestone, issued from Pottstown and Akron to a great variety of industries, the basic formulas being adapted to their specific needs.

The brake lining operation at Paterson was moved to New Castle in 1948. Plastics research and development had already shifted from Paterson to Pottstown, and now Velon went to Pottstown. This city became the headquarters of Firestone Plastics Company, organized in September, 1947.

The plastics division introduced new forms of Velon, that marvelously adaptable filament which could be extruded in any diameter desired, with suppleness or firmness, in any color, design, or finish. In its appeal to architects and interior decorators, Velon supplemented Foamex-cushion furniture. But home furnishings and public seating were not its only outlets. Much of the woven Velon was channeled into automobile seat covers. It was beginning to be used for original automobile upholstery as well as wall covering, and continued strong as drapery and insect screening. Plastics were definitely entrenched in the textile business. Velon was being woven also in combination with natural and synthetic fibers in jacquards and brocatelles.

As Velon Film, it constituted the major portion of the plastics production—for shower curtains, table covers, draperies, bedspreads, and yard goods having embossings with textured effects. Heavier gauge Velon Flex, in varied grains, was taken up by the luggage, handbag, and furniture upholstery trades. The newest thing was lightweight Velon garden hose.

Plastics molding and fabricating took place at Fall River. Technicians gave advice on custom molding service: fittings for automobiles, airplanes, refrigerators, electrical and other household appliances. Here was another virtually unlimited range of applications that kept these plants busy. Pottstown expanded its production of basic resins and supplied other plastics manufacturers.

Firestone Steel Products continued to be the world's largest manufacturer of truck and tractor rims and stainless-steel barrels, the rims produced in Wyandotte, the containers in Akron, where wheels and auto body stampings also were made. A new, lighter barrel that was easier to ship, handle, and clean, contributed to record-breaking sales. Ten-gallon, stainless-steel milk cans, designed for free pouring and sanitation, were already in mass production.

Besides producing this abundance for the amenities of peace, Firestone was called upon to take an active part in the nation's defense program. Industrial Products still made tank tracks. Now came improved tires and tubes for all types of military vehicles, new fuel cells, a development of track-type landing gear for Superfortresses, and ordnance—the manufacture of artillery rifles. These 57- and 75-millimeter guns, lightweight and recoilless, gave the infantry the striking power of field artillery. The fuel cells were so large that six of them in a B-36 plane were able to contain 21,116 gallons.

The variegated activities of the company and its subsidiaries brought aggregate sales of $633,800,000 in 1948. After the addition of $4,000,000 to the reserve for contingencies, net income was $27,600,000, or 4.37 percent of sales. This was equivalent to $13.83 earned per share of common stock outstanding.

Net working capital at the close of the fiscal year 1948 exceeded $160,700,000. It rose to $168,500,000 in 1949, after $17,800,000 was netted on $579,600,000 sales and $5,000,000 was provided for reserves.

Exports, once restrictions had been lifted, increased substantially. During each of the war years, the foreign subsidiaries had yielded several million dollars in dividends, but because of dollar shortages, dividends since 1947 were much lower than profits, part of which was plowed back for expanded volume.

The foreign factories all operated at full capacity in 1948. Hamilton, enlarged in the fall of 1945, was well past the million-tire-a-year mark. A building extension to augment truck tire facilities was authorized there for 1949. Brentford's capacity too was increased, with steady postwar gains each year; this plant made a jump of thirty-five percent in 1948 over 1947, thanks to heavy truck and tractor tire expansion. Brentford was enjoying its greatest employment and in 1949 obtained a further extension of production facilities.

Buenos Aires, starved for rubber during the war, and finally receiving synthetic from the United States late in 1945, and natural rubber in mid-1946, embarked on record production with modernized equipment and factory expansion. A textile mill was built here in 1949. São Paulo had a mill since 1946. There in Brazil, the home of *Hevea brasiliensis*, GR-S had been used all through 1945. São Paulo worked at capacity after the war, adding tractor tires, and after acquiring additional factory space the plant increased it further and installed earthmover tire equipment.

Although the plant in Bilbao, Spain, with which Firestone had an operating arrangement, reconverted to natural rubber late in 1947, government allocation and the lack of foreign exchange for the purchase of carbon black held a checkrein on the rate of advance in production. On the other hand, the output of the Swiss factory at Pratteln increased rapidly. Another European arrangement, made in Sweden, provided a plant at Viskafors, near Göteborg, in 1946; the schedules were stepped up regularly.

Port Elizabeth, South Africa, having distinguished

itself during the war in supplementing tire supplies for the allied armies, grew extensively thereafter and added bicycle tires in 1949. For still another factory in the British Commonwealth, land had been purchased at Christchurch, New Zealand, in 1945; the first tire was built in June, 1948, and growth was rapid. Bombay was also booming, with De Luxe Champion heavy-duty tires and Rock Grip excavator tires for the needs of modern India.

In Liberia all was sunny. At the height of intensive tapping in 1946, more than 62,000 acres of mature trees furnished 22,148 tons. Normal tapping was restored next year, but as 5,000 new acres came into bearing, the yield reached as high as 21,700 tons. The planting of 3,500 acres in 1947 and additional acreage in the rainy season of 1948 gave a total of 77,800 under cultivation besides the 1,040 acres on the original plantation at Mount Barclay. Shipments—the proportion as latex growing greater with the company's own needs—now reached 24,380 tons; next year, 25,695 tons.

Looking toward the centennial of Liberia's existence as a republic, Harvey Firestone jr. marked the progress of that country and spoke at a dinner in New York of its contribution to the United Nations during the rubber crisis.

In the enterprise of supplying the world with an indispensable commodity, Liberians and Americans have now worked together harmoniously and for mutual benefit for nearly a quarter of a century.[*]

Stressing the republic's human values, he noted the free schools, the churches and hospitals, the missions in the hinterland, and the company's concern in the aspirations and opportunities of the Liberian people. One

[*] H.S.F. jr., Liberian Centennial Dinner, Waldorf-Astoria, New York, Sept. 20, 1946.

long-standing interest of the United States was that
Liberia be assisted in medical research, particularly in
tropical diseases.

To perpetuate the ideals of my father and as a contribution to
the program which the Liberian people are planning in commemo-
ration of their one hundred years of freedom, it has been our wish
to establish in Liberia an institute for research in tropical medicine.*

Firestone thereupon made a gift of $250,000 to con-
struct and equip such an institute—hospital and research
laboratories—to serve as an international study center
under the direction of the American Foundation for
Tropical Medicine. President William V. S. Tubman,
of Liberia, accepted this gift as a memorial to Harvey
S. Firestone, and the government donated a site near
Roberts Field.

It is my firm belief that this generous offer on your part will bind
more closely the ties of friendship and sympathetic understanding
which have characterized the relationship of the Firestone Plantations Company with the Government and people of Liberia.†

For the century ahead, Harvey Firestone jr. saw
greater economic self-sufficiency for Liberia with the
training of more of her citizens in farming, forestry,
botany, plant pathology, biochemistry, mechanics, engineering, medicine, dietetics, and education—human
progress based on the riches of Liberia's fertile land.

Firestone Plantations' own researchers were busy col-
lecting tropical commercial plants, studying food crops
and fruit trees, breeding domestic animals, and introducing other animals. The news in 1949 that cortisone,
a substance of remedial value in arthritis therapy, was
obtainable from a native Liberian vine, *Strophanthus sar-
mentosus*, at once prompted Firestone Plantations to offer
its facilities to the United States government mission

* *Ibid.*
† Pres. Tubman, cable to H.S.F. jr., Aug. 8, 1946.

that went to Liberia to investigate the cultivation of this plant for the relief of millions of arthritic sufferers. Subsequently, an arrangement was made whereby Firestone introduced and propagated various *Strophanthus* plants in its research gardens in Liberia.

III

In the present-day world, when the peace and progress of most nations hinge on the continued healthy functioning of American economic life, Firestone persists in the pursuit of benefits for society. Economies in manufacturing, passed on to the public; betterment of products, enhancing dollar values; a high level of employment, sustaining consumer buying power. To these is added an acute awareness of the social implications of a great corporation's acts. Just as the spirit of the company's Liberian policy has animated our new national policy of promoting the growth of underdeveloped areas, Firestone's traditions at home have been maintained in the difficult period of postwar adjustment.

"In America we pay heed to human values," Harvey Firestone jr. stated on various occasions.

To meet the higher cost of living, the company granted wage increases covering, in a single contract with the United Rubber Workers, 23,000 employees in eight plants. This set the pattern for the industry and cost Firestone an annual extra expenditure of more than $5,000,000, equivalent to more than half the year's dividends.

There was significance in the fact that one out of every four workers at Akron had been with the company for twenty years or more, and approximately half of them for ten years or longer.

In 1950 a special meeting of the stockholders approved a pension plan already adopted by the board of directors. This plan provided hourly-wage employees with a $100 minimum monthly pension (upon retirement at the age of sixty-five with twenty-five years' service), including Social Security benefits. The company announced that each worker would also be insured for $1,500 to $4,000 life insurance, depending upon earnings, and would receive upon retirement a paid-up policy of $1,000 to $1,500 in value. The entire cost is borne by the company.

Salaried employees too were covered by a noncontributory pension plan. Increased benefits were provided under the existing contributory retirement income plan. At the same time, a new group insurance program (joint contributions) was instituted, providing life insurance and weekly accident and sickness benefits; also hospitalization and surgical benefits for employees and their dependents.

In the phrase "Safety is our business," the organization observed a basic principle, ultimately to protect its customers by quality of product, but in the first instance to protect the personnel in their factory operations. These safeguards paid off. All the twenty-one plants in the United States and Canada shared in the National Safety Council's Award of Honor for distinguished service to safety, bestowed in 1949 for the fourth consecutive year on a company-wide basis. They made outstanding records in reducing the frequency and severity of accidents; the rates were sixty-seven to seventy-seven percent lower than the industry's averages, marking the factories as among the safest in the country. It was a tribute both to management, which affixed devices to the machines and kept up educational campaigns, and to the 36,000 workers themselves.

Another award in 1949, received in recognition of another aspect of human values, was a medal given to

Firestone by the National Garden Institute for sponsor-
ing industrial gardens. This was the thirty-third year of
the program, and now 2,400 workers in Akron cultivated
plots in communion with nature, besides those who had
gardens at the subsidiary plants.

In a further program to afford employees an opportunity for a fuller life, the company encouraged them to
take courses at the University of Akron related to their
work and reimbursed them for their tuition fees.

Mankind's quest of knowledge and understanding,
and the treasures of research and reflection embodied in
books, were given homage in the Firestone family's participation in a great new library for Princeton University.
All five sons had been graduated from Princeton, and
they joined with their mother in making a gift of more
than a million dollars. The cornerstone was laid in June,
1947, by Harvey Firestone jr., a member of the university's board of trustees, and in April, 1949, as representative of the numerous donors at the official opening,
he presented to President Dodds a symbolic key to the
Harvey S. Firestone Memorial Library.

> I trust that this treasure house of knowledge, which bears the
> name and memory of my father, will inspire all who enter its
> portals to carry to the farthest ends of the earth those precepts
> which will help to preserve the peace of the world.*

One of the curses of an imperfect world was the
uneradicated blot of war. With communist hatred for
the American system expressed as an armed hatred, a
large defense establishment continued, and as a counterpart to this the United Service Organizations became
reactivated in 1949. The agencies comprising USO
elected Harvey Firestone jr. president. He accepted the
designation, not as a nominal honor but as a call to
active duty and devoted much time to organizing the

* H.S.F. jr., Princeton, N. J., Apr. 30, 1949.

groundwork for the many centers and lounges, veterans hospital camp shows, and coordinated community activity for the service men and women.

On the international scene, the dollar crisis of Western European nations and the coincidental abundant supply of Far East rubber figured in the discussions of the International Rubber Study Group which met in London in the spring of 1949, Harvey Firestone jr. attending as a delegate of the Department of State. Returning, he reported world-wide recognition of the American synthetic-rubber industry as a powerful and permanent factor in the rubber market. The preservation of this industry would not be impaired. Security required it; moreover, industry generally had adopted synthetic rubber voluntarily and widely.

On the other hand, Far East rubber was the greatest single source of dollars for the British Commonwealth. New uses would help supply exchange not only to Britain but to the Netherlands and France as well. At economic conferences held in Washington in September, American and Canadian government officials guaranteed greater purchases of natural rubber for strategic stockpiles.

Firestone had already announced a new use. Following laboratory and highway tests of a mixture of asphalt with a rubber powder (both natural and synthetic), a section of rubber roadway had been laid in August on the heavily traveled route past the Firestone Homestead near Columbiana. The rubber powder bound the asphalt more tightly to the roadbed, retarded melting in hot weather and cracking in cold weather, improved traction, and made the surface more resilient.

Meanwhile experiments were continuing toward the further improvement of synthetic rubber, including the development at Research of a polymer for Arctic use. Each year more than a hundred technical reports issued from Research, of value in the solution of many problems. The significance of this phase of the business was emphasized by the election of Raymond Firestone as vice president in charge of research and development in 1949, to administer the company's accelerated program in these fields.

New and better materials. New and better products. For a new and better world.

"An integral part of the American character is forever to seek improvements," Harvey Firestone jr., said in an address before the Executives Club of Chicago. "That is one reason why we have been such a progressive and successful nation." He referred to more than economic life: to the unfolding of spiritual and political ideals. "We Americans have always held that the only real security lies in liberty and opportunity."

24

Fiftieth Anniversary Year

AMERICA'S industrial strength and love of liberty
again proved to be the reliance of the free nations of
the world in the eventful year 1950. Communist aggression in Korea and the menacing Red shadow over Europe
caused the democracies to turn to the country whose
tradition of free competitive enterprise had preserved the
will and the ability to resist. The call made upon American resources found Firestone's facilities mighty sinews
of production ready for the new emergency.

This need to strengthen the barriers of defense summoned the skill and capacity of the company to produce
military tires, tubes, and rims; to produce tank tracks and
bogie wheels, Flying Runway landing gear; radomes to
protect Air Force radar installations; Airpak cushioned
containers for jet engines; gas masks, life vests, bullet-
sealing fuel and oil cells for airplanes; rocket motors,
90-millimeter tank guns, and recoilless rifles—for immediate action in Korea.

The ability of the Firestone organization to help keep
the nation's wheels—military and civilian—rolling, had
been built up through the years. It rested on the creative
genius of the man who, half a century before, had founded
this great enterprise on the principle of public service.

The year 1950 was a year of continued building.
Indeed, it was the period of greatest achievement in the

company's history. Manufacture and distribution of goods proceeded on a record-breaking level.

Rubber, the country's most critical raw material shortage of World War II, was furnished by Firestone in increasing quantities. But it had taken strenuous effort to arouse the government to the new danger of inadequate supply. Year by year, since the war's end, the output of government synthetic-rubber plants had been curtailed. The annual rate of GR-S production had sunk to 220,000 tons, and the government-fixed price of 18½ cents a pound failed to serve as a corrective of the mounting price of natural rubber early in 1950.

When spring came, the tire industry was in the midst of a boom resulting from unprecedented production of motor vehicles—and there was turmoil in Southeast Asia. Terrorism in Malaya made life on rubber plantations perilous. There were disturbances in the new Republic of Indonesia which reduced shipments. In Indo-China, communist war suspended peaceful pursuits. Not only were Far East speculators withholding stocks from the market, but the United States government was rapidly building up a stockpile and the rest of the world was buying rubber heavily.

Greatly accelerated use of rubber by the armed forces was anticipated. Harvey S. Firestone jr. advocated stepped-up output of synthetic rubber, both for national security and for economic stability. Returning from a conference of the International Rubber Study Group held in Brussels in May—which he had attended for the Department of State—he declared that synthetic had established itself firmly in the transportation field by its satisfactory performance. However, of thirteen GR-S plants, only eight were operating and five were in standby condition.

A few days later, in Washington, he urged Congress to direct the government explicitly to lease its plants to private companies for private operation. A competitive climate would encourage the development of improved synthetic rubber. To a Senate committee he said:

> The obligation to furnish the synthetic rubber requirements of the rubber industry in peacetime and to bear the costs of operating such an enterprise should not continue to be assumed by the government any longer than is necessary. Our company is prepared to take over from the government our share of these responsibilities and, furthermore, to accept the conditions of the government security agencies with respect to the national security . . . *

Congressional deliberations on the expiring Rubber Act of 1948 took place in an atmosphere of communist threat to the major part of the world's natural-rubber supply. Finally, the law was extended for two years, with the prospect of ultimate private control postponed, but meanwhile synthetic-rubber production would be increased.

President Harry S. Truman approved the law on a Saturday in June. On the very next morning came the crossing of the 38th Parallel in Korea—a challenge to the United Nations' strength to resist.

The authorized rise in the rate of synthetic-rubber production could only be attained gradually. Civilian demand, already high, surged that summer in a wave of scare-buying of tires. Not even the release of large quantities from the Far East was able to put a brake on the advancing price of natural rubber or relieve the grave uncertainty of future supplies.

"It is impossible," said Firestone jr., "to predict how far the Korean problem may spread. Any situation which threatens to interfere with our rubber supply is of vital importance to the security of the United States."

*H.S.F. jr., statement before Senate Armed Services Subcommittee, June 6, 1950.

At a meeting in the Pentagon with the Munitions Board, he and other industry representatives joined in urging that all remaining standby plants be put into readiness; every effort must be exerted to obtain greater tonnage from the going plants. In a matter of hours, after the Munitions Board had decided that more rubber was essential, the President ordered swift action. The stockpile must be increased, and synthetic-rubber production further raised.

A new period of restrictions began. First, the National Production Authority directed a cutback in civilian manufacture, to build up government inventory and provide for defense orders. Soon other controls followed. The Authority imposed tighter curbs on consumption of natural rubber. Reactivation of standby facilities would in time bring the output of synthetic rubber to a rate of 900,000 tons.

And still the price of natural rubber rose. Its soaring ambition carried it from 69½ cents in October to 86 cents in November, and was not checked until the President declared a state of national emergency in December, whereupon more severe controls were instituted. All rubber buying and allocation were taken over by the General Services Administration. The government lifted its price of synthetic to 24½ cents in view of prevailing costs of production.

Accepting rubber-control orders as essential in the emergency, Firestone jr. declared that they had his company's wholehearted cooperation. The Firestone buying organization and its Singapore preparation mills were placed at the government's disposal.

Firestone-operated plants in Akron and Lake Charles in 1950 produced 84,150 tons of GR-S, an amount greater than that of any other company. Nearly half of this output was in "cold rubber," whose toughness made it superior to natural rubber in tire treads. In addition, Firestone turned out 3,000 tons of other types of synthetic rubber that year in its own Butaprene plant.

From the Firestone plantations in Liberia came a new record yield during the fiscal year 1950—more than 28,500 tons of finest-grade natural rubber. The percentage shipped as concentrated latex was vastly greater than before; the military needed latex for such purposes as aviation tires, tire-cord dipping compounds, foam-rubber crash pads, oxygen masks, blood plasma tubing, and surgical gloves.

Research and development, directed by Raymond C. Firestone, evolved further contributions to civilian and military progress. Experience in rubber compounding made new synthetic-rubber products possible. A special laboratory was set up to improve road-surfacing material —and succeeded. A new rayon gum-dip was perfected, providing a greatly strengthened bond for rayon cord and increasing the flexing life of the cords; also, a synthetic-rubber latex for water-base paints, and new stabilizers for vinyl resin plastics, opening still another door to economy and plenty. The first puncture-proof all-butyl tube came from Firestone. It was rugged enough to outlast several tires. Then came another development, a more startling one. It was a revolutionary new tire, blowout-safe, puncture-proof, and tubeless, the realization of every tiremaker's lifelong dream. Appropriately it was named the Firestone Supreme.

This was a big year for plant additions and improvements, costing more than $28,000,000. The Foamex plant at Fall River was again enlarged, the Des Moines tire factory too, and the Pottstown plant, which was purchased from the government, was likewise enlarged.

This was a big year for sales. In the fiscal period ending

October 31, 1950, they reached the all-time high of $690,500,000. (For the calendar year 1950 they were $736,900,000.) Net income of $33,200,000 was another record high, equivalent to $16.75 earned per share of outstanding common stock.

Employees received $167,000,000 during the year. Weekly earnings of Firestone factory personnel in the United States were approximately eighty percent higher than they had been at the close of World War II. With concern for employees' safety, the company won for the fifth year the Distinguished Service to Safety Award, bestowed by the National Safety Council for the lowest accident frequency and severity rate in Firestone's world-wide factories. The company established a new pension program and extended its insurance plan to assure additional benefits without cost to the workers.

Such was the nature of an America business in a time of intensive upbuilding of the country's defenses against disturbers of the peace. Work, hard work, lay ahead for everyone. And sacrifice—for those who were capable of it.

Many of the executives assumed civic responsibilities in their communities on top of their day's regular duties. Similarly, the nation itself looked beyond home interests to pursue a program for improvement of the world's underdeveloped areas. At the request of President Truman, Firestone jr. served as a member of the International Development Advisory Board, which was charged with the responsibility of producing a plan to strengthen the economies of underdeveloped countries and to raise their living standards. Here was global mobilization for peace.

A thousand men and women employees, answering the call to defense, left to enter the armed forces, and the Military Service Bureau was re-established to maintain contact with them. The USO, revived this year, was again headed by Firestone jr.

In a testimony of faith, the Crusade for Freedom was conducted in the fall by the National Committee for a Free Europe. Signatures were inscribed on scrolls, pledging resistance to tyranny in the preservation of the sacredness of the individual. In Akron alone, 9,200 Firestone employees participated; in other cities, additional thousands. Their names accompanied the replica of the Freedom Bell sent to the shrine in Berlin to peal on United Nations Day.

This was the voice of Firestone, the voice of all America, singing clearly: Let Freedom Ring!

II

The industrial eminence of The Firestone Tire & Rubber Company stands out as a great American story. Here, in a country which abhors cartels, which encourages initiative, provides opportunities, and rewards those who perform their social function well, the vision and vigor of a single man have created a tower of strength for all the American people.

The company to which he gave his name is keeping the faith. The sons and associates of Harvey S. Firestone, and the men and women whom they in turn have trained, have by their works given assurance that this name will persist as a symbol of service to mankind. With rubber and steel, textiles and plastics, they have welded nature's gifts and man's ingenuity into instruments for the fullness of daily living.

As the measure of a person is what he gives to society, so the worth of a company is not to be found in an auditor's report but in the extent of its contributions to the enrichment of the people it serves. Firestone's catalog is long—as the history of the first fifty years reveals.

In the realm of transportation, Firestone has enabled men and women and their families to travel with safety, comfort, and economy; to extend the radius of their contacts with other people in other places. Firestone has helped make possible the present era of truck transport, affording greater mobility and lower operating costs to industry in the distribution of goods from mill, factory, and farm.

To agriculture Firestone has given relief from the back-breaking labor formerly endured in the field, and impetus to the mechanization of farm work. Matching the fertility of the soil is the heightened efficiency of the man at the wheel of a rubber-tired tractor. The American farmer sows and harvests for a hungry world. His produce is carried to market with greater dispatch, fresh for the consumer's table.

Firestone's history is a saga of pioneering. Good roads have issued from its endeavors. And the national asset of a synthetic-rubber industry. The creation of this new industry in the midst of World War II was described by President Truman, in a message to Congress, as "one of the great achievements of our war effort."

By the courageous undertaking of plantations in Liberia, economic life was given to a remote country which the United States had originally sponsored. Firestone provided the means whereby long-thwarted aspirations of a sister republic could find expression in a world that was meant for liberty. The record in Liberia is notable. It exemplifies the international role of a modern corporation bent on public good.

To the purchasers of Firestone products, the attainment of more economical methods of manufacture has brought greater values. The quest for stronger materials and constructions has brought longer service. These twin results materially contributed to a constantly improving standard of living.

To the many thousands of people employed by Firestone, the company has given more than a paycheck with which to buy necessities and comforts of life. Firestone has thought of their happiness at work. "*We are all one,*" the founder said of his organization. Their welfare was his concern. A social-minded business exists as much for its employees as for its customers, and measures have been taken that carry out this philosophy.

While the Firestone philosophy has never been formulated in a code—and it should not be so fixed, for this would make it static—the standards and goals that the founder lived by are the ones that permeate the company today.

One of Harvey S. Firestone's principles was freedom from restrictions on supplies. Another was freedom to compete in the distribution of products. By adhering to these traditional American ideals—and fighting for them —he was a strong force in keeping the channels of commerce open and thus benefited all industry and the public.

He believed also that to stand still was to stagnate. Thus he was never satisfied with today's achievements but spurred himself and his colleagues to do still better tomorrow. With such a generating force the Firestone company has constantly sought, through research and critical self-examination, to improve its products and the methods of producing them.

This freshness of spirit, giving each new day's work a spark of eagerness, enthusiasm, and thoughtful direction, assures that Firestone will keep growing as a great American institution.

To honor the memory of Harvey S. Firestone, the dedication of a massive bronze statue of the founder climaxed the fiftieth anniversary celebration of the company on August 3, 1950.

On this inspiring occasion many thousands of persons attended the ceremonies held on the lawns outside the Research Building. They saw the founder's five sons— Harvey S. jr., Russell A., Leonard K., Raymond C., and Roger S.—pull the cord to unveil the enduring tribute to their father. The impressive sculpture by James Earle Fraser, mounted on a huge granite pedestal, high on the terrace, looked beyond that summer day and into an era of greater usefulness to mankind.

The memorial was a thing of beauty in a setting of greenery, with its semicircular granite exedra and three towering, sixty-foot Scotch pine trees watchful over the statue. Here the assemblage, eager for an unfolding of the life of the man whom they had come to honor, heard his old-time associate, John W. Thomas, speak of him as "a master-builder in the world of industry."

In Harvey S. Firestone the urge to create was an irresistible force. It was not only the inexhaustible source of his own matchless determination, dynamic energy, and contagious enthusiasm, but also the never-failing spark which served as an inspiration and an incentive to all who worked with him.

To me, one of the most outstanding characteristics of Mr. Firestone was his indomitable courage. He was absolutely fearless; through faith he conquered fear. He was never happier than when he was called upon to meet a challenge. He infused into all of those around him this same fighting spirit, and he was always ready to lead his men to victory in the never-ending battle of competition.*

The participants in the dedication ceremonies also heard the Reverend Doctor Walter F. Tunks, rector of St. Paul's Episcopal Church, acknowledge that the statue was "an excellent likeness, a worthy tribute to a great man," but he reminded them:

If you would see his real memorial, look around you! Great enterprises are more than brick and mortar and steel. Over them one always finds "the lengthened shadow of a man." . . .

*Full text of Mr. Thomas's address in Appendix, p. 401.

On the memorial we are dedicating today is this inscription: "He believed what the centuries said as against the years, and as against the hours." Only as we continue to serve ideals that will stand the test of time can we keep our nation brave and strong and free. As we honor the memory of our beloved friend, let us share his faith that we live in a moral universe where the ultimate value is not matter but spirit. May God raise up men like Harvey S. Firestone who possess the wisdom, courage, and faith to lead our troubled world into the ways of righteousness and peace!*

In the brief but poignant talk given by Harvey S. Firestone jr., the assemblage caught the tender feeling of a loving son.

"My brothers and I are gathered here with you," he said, "to pay honor to the man whom we were privileged to have as a father. And today I should like to speak of him as a father.

"In this relationship, he possessed those qualities of greatness which distinguished him throughout the course of his life.

"Much of father's lifetime was, of necessity, spent in building the company which bears his name. When he founded the company on August 3, 1900, just fifty years ago today, he entered upon an enterprise that called for vision and courage and an unswerving confidence in the future. The struggle for survival was constant and ever-present. The weeks and the months and the years took their steady toll of time and effort. His every waking moment must have been filled with a sense of heavy responsibility.

"His was the burden of the never-ending resolve to go forward; the determination to create for his company a position of leadership. These were goals of attainment which of themselves would seemingly occupy his thoughts and time to the exclusion of all other things, perhaps even of his family.

"Yet, looking back over those early years and later

*Full text of Dr. Tunks's address in Appendix, p. 403.

triumphs, the picture uppermost in my mind is of a father whose devotion and attachment to his family was not one whit diminished by the business responsibilities that rested upon him.

"I remember my father as a man of infinite patience. He always had time for his children. He exercised an affectionate discipline over our childhood. He helped us in our school work and tried to make us see the difference between learning and merely being taught. He gave us responsibilities and, along with them, the kindly advice and welcome encouragement needed to fulfill those responsibilities. He imparted to us the simple, fundamental precepts of honesty and integrity which guided his life and which, God willing, will always serve to guide the Firestone organization throughout the years to come.

"His memory, and the memory of all he stood for, shall inspire us to continue to build upon the firm foundations which he built so soundly and so well."

EVERY useful occupation gives ample opportunity for service. The happiest men in the world are those who are making their jobs mean more than simply an endless routine of work and wages. The whole structure of business is based upon making useful things for others—this is service.

HARVEY S. FIRESTONE

Appendix

Bibliography

COMPANY SOURCE MATERIAL

1. Company records, annual statements, scrapbooks, diaries, photographs and maps.
2. Periodicals:
   The Firestone, 1915–1918.
   The Firestone Non-Skid, 1916–date.
   The Firestone Dealer, 1929–1936.
   The Firestone World-Wide, 1930–date.
   The Firestone Non-Skid (Brentford, England), 1934–date.
   The Firestone Californian, 1934–date.
   Firestone de la Argentina, 1936–date.
   Boletín de Información, Firestone-Hispania, 1945–date.
   Firestone Southerner (Memphis), 1946–date.
3. Other Printed Sources:
   A Visit with the Firestone Organization, Its Men, Its Factory, Its Branches, 1916.
   Things That Interest Stockholders, 1920.
   Rubber: Its History and Development, 1922.
   FIRESTONE, HARVEY S., *America Should Produce Its Own Rubber*, 1923.
   Firestone Twenty-fifth Anniversary, 1925.
   FIRESTONE, HARVEY S. JR., *The Romance and Drama of the Rubber Industry*, 1932.
   FIRESTONE, HARVEY S. JR., *The Story of Transportation*, 1933.

GENERAL SOURCES

BIOGRAPHY

FIRESTONE, HARVEY S., in collaboration with SAMUEL CROWTHER, *Men and Rubber*. Doubleday, Page & Co., Garden City, N. Y., 1926.
GRAVES, RALPH H., *The Triumph of an Idea: The Story of Henry Ford*. Doubleday, Doran & Co., Garden City, N. Y., 1934.
LIEF, ALFRED, *Harvey Firestone: Free Man of Enterprise*, McGraw-Hill Book Company, Inc., New York, 1951.
SIMONDS, WILLIAM ADAMS, *Henry Ford*. Bobbs-Merrill, Indianapolis, 1923.

EARLY AKRON

BRADEN, JAMES A., Ed., *A Centennial History of Akron, 1825–1925.* "Rubber," by Ralph C. Busbey. Summit County Historical Society, Akron, 1925, p. 313.

DOYLE, WILLIAM B., Ed., *Centennial History of Summit County, Ohio, and Representative Citizens.* Biographical Publishing Co., Chicago, 1908.

KENFIELD, SCOTT DIX, *Akron and Summit County, Ohio, 1825–1928.* S. J. Clarke Publishing Co., Chicago and Akron, 1928. Three volumes.

LANE, SAMUEL A., *Fifty Years and Over of Akron and Summit County.* Beacon Job Department, Akron, 1892.

OLIN, OSCAR EUGENE, *Akron and Environs.* Lewis Publishing Co., Chicago, 1917.

RUBBER INDUSTRY

BAUER, P. T., *The Rubber Industry: A Study in Competition and Monopoly.* Harvard University Press, Cambridge, 1948.

Congressional Record, Vol. 67, 67th Cong., 4th Sess. Rubber Investigation Appropriation, *passim.*

FIRESTONE, HARVEY S. JR., "What About Rubber After the War?" *Saturday Evening Post*, March 4, 1944.

HOLT, E. G., "Outlook for Rubber Latex Supplies and Products," *Domestic Commerce*, May, 1947, p. 35.

————, "Rubber Tire and Inner Tube Materials from 1944 to 1946," *Domestic Commerce*, June, 1947, p. 42.

KNORR, K. E., *World Rubber and Its Regulation.* Stanford University Press, 1944.

LAWRENCE, JAMES COOPER, *The World's Struggle with Rubber, 1905–1931.* Harper & Bros., New York, 1931.

McFADYEAN, SIR ANDREW, Ed., *The History of Rubber Regulation, 1934–1943.* George Allen & Unwin, London, 1944.

RUBBER SURVEY COMMITTEE, *Report*, September 10, 1942; Bernard M. Baruch, James B. Conant, and Karl T. Compton. Washington, 1942.

SMITHSONIAN INSTITUTION, *Annual Report, 1939–1940*, "The Rubber Industry, 1839–1939," by W. A. Gibbons. Washington, 1940, p. 193.

U. S. DEPARTMENT OF COMMERCE, *Rubber*, First Annual Report by the Secretary of Commerce, April 1, 1948–March 31, 1949. Government Printing Office, Washington, 1949.

U. S. DEPARTMENT OF COMMERCE, BUREAU OF FOREIGN AND DOMES-

TIC COMMERCE, Trade Promotion Series No. 2, *The Plantation Rubber Industry in the Middle East*, by David M. Figart. Government Printing Office, Washington, 1925.

——, Trade Promotion Series No. 55, *Marketing of Crude Rubber*, by E. G. Holt. Government Printing Office, Washington, 1927.

——, Trade Promotion Series No. 181, *Rubber Statistics, 1900–1937*, by P. W. Barker. Government Printing Office, Washington, 1938.

——, Trade Promotion Series No. 197, *Rubber History of the United States, 1839–1939*, by P. W. Barker. Government Printing Office, Washington, 1939.

——, Trade Promotion Series No. 209, *Rubber: History, Production and Manufacture*, by P. W. Barker. Government Printing Office, Washington, 1940.

U. S. SENATE, Investigation of the National Defense Program. Hearings before a Special Committee Investigating the National Defense Program, 77th Cong., 1st Sess., Part II: Rubber, March. 1942, Washington.

TIRE INDUSTRY

CIVILIAN PRODUCTION ADMINISTRATION, *Report to the President*, December 6, 1946. Tires, p. 40; Automobiles and Trucks, p. 42; Rubber, p. 68.

DuCROSS, SIR ARTHUR, *Wheels of Fortune*. Chapman & Hall, London, 1938.

FEDERAL TRADE COMMISSION, *Trade Practice Rules for the Rubber Tire Industry*, October 17, 1936.

HALE, J. E., "Shoeing a Car with Low-Pressure Air," *Journal of the Society of Automotive Engineers*, July, 1923, p. 41.

LEIGH, WARREN W., *Automotive Tire Sales by Distribution Channels*. Bureau of Business Research, Study No. 5, Akron, 1948.

NATIONAL RECOVERY ADMINISTRATION, Consumers Division Report No. 2, *The Price of Automobile Tires*, by Albert Abrahamson. Washington, November 1, 1934.

NATIONAL RECOVERY ADMINISTRATION, DIVISION OF REVIEW, Evidence Study No. 36, *The Rubber Tire Industry*, by W. H. Cross, Washington, October, 1935.

——, Evidence Study No. 35, *The Rubber Industry*, by W. H. Cross. Washington, December, 1935.

NATIONAL RECOVERY ADMINISTRATION, Work Materials No. 41, *The Rubber Industry Study*, by W. H. Cross, G. S. Earseman, J. H. Lenaerts. Washington, February, 1936.

PEARSON, HENRY C., *Rubber Tires and All About Them*. India Rubber Publishing Co., New York, 1906.

——, *Pneumatic Tires*. India Rubber Publishing Co., New York, 1922.

TEMPORARY NATIONAL ECONOMIC COMMITTEE, *Investigation of Concentration of Economic Power*, Hearings, Part 5-A, March 2, 1939, Federal Trade Commission Report on Monopolistic Practices in Industries (Goodyear-Sears, Roebuck case, p. 2311). Government Printing Office, Washington, 1939.

TEMPORARY NATIONAL ECONOMIC COMMITTEE, Monograph No. 1, "Price Behavior and Business Policy," by Saul Nelson and Walter G. Keim (tire manufacturing industry, pp. 65, 93, 258). Government Printing Office, Washington, 1940.

——, Monograph No. 21, "Competition and Monopoly in American Industry," by Clair Wilcox (tires and tubes, p. 48). Government Printing Office, Washington, 1940.

THOMAS, JOHN W., *Rubber—An Epic in Research*. Newcomen Society of England, New York, 1946.

WOLF, HOWARD, and RALPH WOLF, *Rubber: A Story of Glory and Greed*. Covici-Friede, New York, 1936.

AUTOMOBILE INDUSTRY

CLYMER, FLOYD, *Floyd Clymer's Historical Motor Scrapbook*, Nos. 1 and 2. Los Angeles, 1944–1945.

DOOLITTLE, JAMES R., *The Romance of the Automobile Industry*. Klebold Press, New York, 1916.

KENNEDY, E. D., *The Automobile Industry*. Reynal & Hitchcock, New York, 1941.

LEWIS, EUGENE W., *Motor Memories*. Alved Publishers, Detroit, 1947.

TEMPORARY NATIONAL ECONOMIC COMMITTEE, *Investigation of Concentration of Economic Power*. Hearings, Part 2, Patents: Automobile Industry, December 5, 1938 (testimony of Edsel Ford, p. 256). Government Printing Office, Washington, 1939.

LABOR

Journal of the Ohio State Senate, 1913. Report of the Green investigating committee, Appendix, p. 205.

Proceedings, Special Committee of the Ohio Senate, In the matter of the Investigation of Conditions Relative to the Strike in the Rubber Industries at Akron, 1913.

ROBERTS, HAROLD S., *The Rubber Workers*. Harper & Bros., New York, 1944.

U. S. DEPARTMENT OF LABOR, BUREAU OF LABOR STATISTICS, Bulletin No. 358, *Wages and Hours of Labor in the Automobile Tire Industry, 1923.* Government Printing Office, Washington, 1924.

————, Bulletin No. 585, *Labor Productivity in the Automobile Tire Industry.* By Boris Stern. Government Printing Office, Washington, 1933.

————, Bulletin No. 634, *Characteristics of Company Unions 1935,* Division of Industrial Relations. Government Printing Office, Washington, 1938.

————, Bulletin No. 651, *Strikes in the United States 1880–1936,* by Florence Peterson. Government Printing Office, Washington, 1938.

————, Bulletin No. 737, *Wages in Rubber Manufacturing Industry,* August, 1942, by H. M. Douty. Government Printing Office, Washington, 1943. (From *Monthly Labor Review,* February and March, 1943.)

————, Serial No. R. 950, *Negotiation of Collective Agreements in the Rubber Industry,* by Harold S. Roberts. Government Printing Office, Washington, 1939. (From *Monthly Labor Review,* June, 1939.)

————, Serial No. R. 1000, *Collective Bargaining by United Rubber Workers,* prepared by Harry Cannon. Government Printing Office, Washington, 1939. (From *Monthly Labor Review,* September, 1939.)

WOOLLEY, EDWARD MOTT, "Firestone and His Organization," *Printer's Ink,* April 18, 1918.

LIBERIA

BROWN, GEORGE WILLIAM, *The Economic History of Liberia.* Associated Publishers, Washington, 1941.

BUELL, RAYMOND LESLIE, Liberia: *A Century of Survival, 1847–1947,* African Handbooks: 7. University of Pennsylvania Press, Philadelphia, 1947.

Planter's Punch, Harbel, Liberia, various dates. Staff house organ, Firestone Plantations Co.

SPANGLER, GILBERT P., *Introduction, Development and Experimental Investigation of Natural Rubber in Liberia, West Africa.* Thesis, February, 1946, Pennsylvania State College, Graduate School Department of Forestry.

U. S. DEPARTMENT OF STATE, *Report* of the International Commission of Inquiry into the Existence of Slavery and Forced Labor in the Republic of Liberia, 1930. Government Printing Office, Washington, 1931.

VILLARD, HENRY S., "Rubber-Cushioned Liberia," *National Geographic Magazine*, February, 1948, p. 201.

WILSON, CHARLES MORROW, *Liberia*. William Sloane Associates, New York, 1947.

YOUNG, JAMES C., *Liberia Rediscovered*. Doubleday, Doran & Co., Garden City, N. Y., 1934.

LITIGATION

Goodyear Tire & Rubber Co. v. *Rubber Tire Wheel Co.*, 116 Fed. Rep. 363 (1902). Solid rubber tires, Grant patent.

Consolidated Rubber Tire Co. v. *Firestone Tire & Rubber Co.*, 151 Fed. Rep. 237 (1907). Grant patent.

Gormully & Jeffery Tire Co. v. *Pennsylvania Rubber Co.*, 155 Fed. Rep. 982 (1907). Clincher tires.

Perlman v. *Standard Welding Co.*, 231 Fed. Rep. 453 (1915), affirmed in 231 Fed. Rep. 734 (1916). Demountable rims.

Perlman Rim Corp. v. *Firestone Tire & Rubber Co.*, 244 Fed. Rep. 304 (1917). Demountable rims. Trial record: In Equity 14-103, U.S. District Court, Southern District of New York, June term, 1917.

Seiberling v. *Firestone Tire & Rubber Co.*, 234 Fed. Rep. 370 (1916), reversed in 257 Fed. Rep. 74 (1918). Tire-building machinery.

Universal Rim Co. v. *Firestone Steel Products Co.*, 289 Fed. Rep. 884 (1923). Split rims.

United States Rubber Co. v. *Firestone Tire & Rubber Co.*, Equity 3646, U. S. District Court, Northern District of Ohio, Eastern Division (1934); reversed in 79 Fed. Rep. (2d) 948 (1935). Flat-band process of tire building.

Federal Trade Commission v. *Goodyear Tire & Rubber Co.*, Docket No. 2116, March 5, 1936; 304 U. S. 257 (1938). Price discrimination.

MISCELLANEOUS

Newspapers: *Akron Beacon Journal, Akron Press, Akron Times-Press;* dailies in Cleveland, Chicago, Detroit, New York, and other cities.

Periodicals: *Commercial & Financial Chronicle, Foreign Commerce Weekly, Hoosier Motorist, Horseless Age, India Rubber & Tire Review, India Rubber World, Motor Age, Motor Way, Motor World, Rubber Age, Tire, Battery & Accessory News, Tires.*

MILLER, DR. JOHN L., "The Redesigned 40-Mm. Anti-Aircraft Gun Carriage," *The Welding Journal*, February, 1943, p. 99.

ЛЛЛЛЛЛЛЛЛЛЛЛЛЛЛЛЛЛЛЛЛ

*Highlights of the Years**

1900   The Firestone Tire & Rubber Company, Akron, was organized August 3 and introduced the solid-rubber sidewire tire.

1902   The company operated its first factory, at Miller and Sweitzer Avenues, Akron.

1904   First addition to the original plant was built.

1904   Firestone developed the first mechanically fastened straightside pneumatic automobile tire, introducing it in 1905.

1906   Firestone's first delivery of tires to the Ford Motor Company; this was the largest single order for pneumatic automobile tires that had ever been placed.

1906   Firestone introduced the universal rim to accommodate either the straightside or the clincher tire.

1906   Annual sales total exceeded $1,000,000 for the first time.

1907   Firestone developed the first commercial demountable rim.

1908   Firestone pioneered the first angular "Non-Skid" tread.

1909   The company began its own rim manufacture.

1910   Annual profits exceeded $1,000,000 for the first time.

1911   "Plant 1" in South Akron was completed.

1911   The first 500-mile Indianapolis Sweepstakes was won on Firestone tires.

1912   Machine building of tires commenced.

1915   The Club House was built.

1915   Annual production exceeded 1,000,000 tires for the first time.

1916   The eight-hour day was inaugurated.

* Dates of expansion to other cities and countries are indicated under Firestone Factories on page 411.

1916   The Xylos Rubber Company (reclaim plant) was organized.

1916   The Firestone Bank was started (originally called Rubber City Savings Bank).

1916   Firestone Park, a new community for company employees, was opened.

1917   Employees' garden program was initiated.

1917   "Plant 2" construction was completed.

1917   Firestone succeeded in breaking a rim monopoly.

1918   Harvey S. Firestone organized the "Ship-by-Truck" movement.

1918   Free life insurance for employees was instituted.

1918   The Firestone Steel Products Company was organized.

1918   The tire-building machinery monopoly was successfully contested by Firestone.

1919   The Army Transcontinental Motor Convoy proved the efficacy of motor transport and pointed up the need of good roads.

1920   Good Roads college-scholarship essay contests were inaugurated by Firestone.

1920   Firestone perfected its gum-dipping process of insulating tire cords against internal heat.

1922   Firestone created the first low-pressure balloon tires.

1922   Harvey S. Firestone organized a campaign of protest against the Stevenson Rubber Restriction Scheme and advocated "Americans Should Produce Their Own Rubber."

1924   The company began its Liberian plantation operations.

1924   The company began its own manufacture of cotton for tire plies.

1925   Building tires by the flat-band process began.

1925   Firestone Stadium and Athletic Field was dedicated.

1926   The Firestone One-Stop service store program was initiated.

1928 The company's first overseas tire plant, in England.

1928 "The Voice of Firestone" radio program was inaugurated.

1932 The first practical, low-pressure tractor tire was created and introduced by Firestone (Ground Grip design 1935). This was the beginning of Harvey S. Firestone's efforts to put the farm on rubber.

1932 The company's mechanical rubber-goods division was started.

1933 Firestone first used rayon cord in tire construction.

1933 The company manufactured stainless-steel barrels.

1933 Firestone built airplane tires of synthetic rubber.

1935 The flat-band monopoly was overthrown by Firestone.

1935 Firestone developed tank track blocks for the government.

1937 The first contract with the United Rubber Workers, C.I.O., was signed.

1938 "Foamex" production was begun, using liquid latex from Firestone's plantations in Liberia; also "Contro" elastic thread and plastic products.

1938 Firestone introduced racing-tire construction in regular passenger-car tires.

1939 Firestone built Buna-S tires.

1939 Tank tracks, airplane fuel cells, gas masks, and other items were manufactured by Firestone in the defense program.

1940 Firestone developed combat tires; also began production on metallic belt links for machine-gun cartridges.

1940 Firestone's synthetic-rubber plant went into commercial production.

1941 The channel tread for airplane tires was developed by Firestone.

1941 Firestone redesigned and began the manufacture of Bofors 40-mm. anti-aircraft gun carriages; also produced barrage balloons, life belts, life rafts, pontons, and oxygen cylinders before Pearl Harbor.

1941 Firestone constructed Roberts Field in Liberia as a base for air transport to African and Asian theaters of war.

1942 Firestone created the divided rim for military tires.

1942 Firestone completed in Akron, and put in operation, the first of the government's defense plants for the production of GR-S synthetic rubber.

1942 The company constructed wings for transport planes and operated a bomb-loading plant.

1942 Firestone was the first rubber company to win the Army-Navy "E" award for achievement in war production.

1942 Firestone was the first to mix carbon black with synthetic rubber latex.

1943 The company's war work extended to the operation of an Army ordnance depot.

1944 Firestone's large production of natural and synthetic rubber and its output of tires met the grave emergency of the war.

1944 The secret "D-D" device was produced by Firestone in time for the Normandy invasion.

1945 Firestone Research building in Akron was dedicated.

1945 Electronic vulcanization began.

1947 Firestone developed the Super-Balloon tire with larger footprint and lower pressure.

1948 "Cold" process of GR-S production was perfected.

1949 The open-center curved-bar tractor tire was developed and introduced by Firestone.

1950 The Firestone Tire & Rubber Company celebrated its fiftieth anniversary.

Memorial Addresses

DELIVERED BY JOHN W. THOMAS AND

REV. WALTER F. TUNKS, D.D.

AT THE DEDICATION OF

THE HARVEY S. FIRESTONE MEMORIAL

AKRON, AUGUST 3, 1950

A GREAT BUILDER

By JOHN W. THOMAS

Today, as we look in admiration upon this beautiful memorial and the statue which will soon be unveiled, we give thanks that Divine Providence has bestowed on mortal man the skill and the ability to create such glorious works of art. It is altogether fitting and proper that we should turn our thoughts to creative ability because the man whom we honor here was a creator, a master-builder in the world of industry and a master-molder of men.

In Harvey S. Firestone, the urge to create was an irresistible force. It was not only the inexhaustible source of his own matchless determination, dynamic energy and contagious enthusiasm, but also the never-failing spark which served as an inspiration and incentive to all who worked with him.

To me, one of the most outstanding characteristics of Mr. Firestone was his indomitable courage. He was absolutely fearless; through faith he conquered fear. He was never happier than when he was called upon to meet a challenge. He infused into all of those around him this same fighting spirit, and he was always ready to lead his men to victory in the never-ending battle of competition.

Another priceless quality which Mr. Firestone possessed to an unusual degree was amazingly accurate foresight. In addition to his unique ability to solve intricate problems of immediate urgency, he always managed to find time to plan ahead. And his forward thinking was astonishingly correct. He seemed to sense what was coming and he had the rare ability to plan for the future developments as he foresaw them.

If there was one thing which Mr. Firestone deplored it was stagnation. Therefore, his supreme policy was constant change whenever change meant improvement. As Mr. Firestone used to say: "Nothing much happens in a calm." And he, personally, saw to it that the trade winds of progress kept his ship of industry sailing steadily ahead.

It was this insistence on continuous progress which made him so keenly aware of the importance of research and development. He was never satisfied with things as they were. He believed that nothing was so good that it could not be made better. And on the walls of the Firestone Research Building you will find his belief expressed in the motto "Best Today, Still Better Tomorrow." Indeed, it is most appropriate that this memorial is located so close to the heart of Firestone research.

Great as Mr. Firestone's achievements were in building and expanding the factories, he was always far more interested in people than in plants. Every time a new factory was built he thought of the expansion more in the terms of additional employment than in the square feet of floor space. He believed that loyalty was a two-way street. To those who were loyal to him, he felt a deep and abiding sense of gratitude and he was always looking for ways in which to express his appreciation. The building of Firestone Park and the provision of recreation, restaurant and banking facilities for the men and women of Firestone are a direct result of Mr. Firestone's concern for the welfare and happiness of Firestone folks.

Mr. Firestone always had in mind the future of the company after he had gone. Therefore, one of his most important considerations was the development of men who could carry on the work and the traditions of the company. Throughout his life he tried and tested, proved and improved the personnel of the company, seeking always for better men and promoting to better jobs those who showed their ability and their fitness to tackle greater responsibilities.

Mr. Firestone was an earnest student of human nature and a master of psychology, even though he never studied it. His native ability to judge character and to bring out the latent abilities of a man showed genius. He was a stickler for accuracy. Many times I've heard him say: "It's easier to do a job right the first time than to explain why you didn't."

Whenever he found a man of exceptional ability, he gave that man particular attention because he saw in him a potential leader for the future. As a result, when he passed away, he left behind him an organization of people trained for leadership, a group of men who believe wholeheartedly in the policy which Mr. Firestone expressed so often in the words: "Keep your sights up. Accept the challenge to get up there."

May his ways and his words and his wisdom continue to inspire us and those who will follow us in the years to come!

A GREAT HUMANITARIAN

By The Reverend Walter F. Tunks, D.D.

When a visitor in St. Paul's Cathedral, London, inquired where he might find the memorial to its builder, Sir Christopher Wren, he was told, "Look around you!" The bronze statue we have unveiled today is an excellent likeness of Harvey S. Firestone, and a worthy tribute to a great man. But if you would see his real memorial, look around you! Great business enterprises are more than brick and mortar and steel. Over them one always finds "the lengthened shadow of a man." It was Mr. Firestone who founded and developed this organization whose name is honored around the world.

Genius always defies analysis. You can never trace it back to its sources. How is it possible for one man to see so much farther, and so much more clearly than his associates? What is the source of courage that enables a man to "rise from a threat refreshed" and bring forth his best in a crisis? What is the secret of the amazing energy and endurance some leaders possess? How is it possible for men who have had little formal education to develop such highly trained minds that they can get at once to the pertinent part of any problem? What is this gift we call "personality" that has such magnetic influence? Questions like these always lead us back to profound mystery. "One star differeth from another star in glory."

It was evident to anyone who knew Mr. Firestone at close range that he had remarkable qualities of leadership. For one thing, he had an eager, searching mind, always exploring new possibilities. He came from pioneer stock that was used to blazing new trails. The century in which he was born had seen amazing changes. It came in lighted with tallow dips, and went out illumined with the incandescent lamp created by the genius of Mr. Firestone's friend, Thomas A. Edison. At the beginning of the century, men were still traveling by stage or horseback at a top speed of six or eight miles an hour. Then came the railroads, later the canal boats, and finally through the genius of Mr. Henry Ford, another friend of Mr. Firestone's, transportation entered a new era through the development of the automobile.

Mr. Firestone was no less creative and progressive than his illustrious friends. He was quick to see the possibilities in the field of rubber. With quiet courage he founded the company which from small beginnings quickly assumed leadership in a fast-growing industry. Mr. Firestone was never content to follow old trails. When an associate asked him one day if he would like to know how a certain operation was performed by another company, Mr. Firestone replied, "No. We can never progress unless we think for ourselves, and develop our own methods." To the day of his death, he was still doing his own thinking, and constantly searching for ways of improvement.

Another mark of Mr. Firestone's leadership was his decisiveness. He knew how easily great enterprises fail when "resolution is sicklied o'er with the pale cast of thought" and action is delayed by someone's inability to make up his mind. Decisions are sometimes difficult and costly. But hesitation and delay can prove even more costly. Mr. Firestone placed great confidence in the men he chose as his associates. He leaned heavily on their advice and counsel. But when the time for action came, he went ahead with vigor and courage, assuming full responsibility for the final decision, and knowing that no man can always be right. On many occasions where lesser men would have hesitated in a fog of uncertainty, Mr. Firestone went boldly ahead. Time vindicated his wisdom. David Starr Jordan used to say: "The world turns aside to let any man pass who knows where he is going." Such a man inspires confidence. He may make mistakes, but men will follow him because they recognize that he knows where he is going, and why.

Spurgeon once said of Mr. Gladstone, England's Prime Minister: "It is restful to feel sure of one man's integrity." There is no greatness apart from simple honesty. The world admires specialized ability, but in the long run it remembers and honors only men it can trust. Mr. Firestone was a hard fighter for what he believed to be right. No man could have given a lifetime of such distinguished public service without encountering opposition. But friend and foe alike found in him a basic honesty which compelled their admiration. His integrity was beyond question. A simple, sincere man, he never deviated from the principles he had accepted as his ideals. He had a taste for excellence, and a high sense of responsibility. If he made a promise he kept it at whatever the cost. Any demands he made upon his associates he rigidly enforced upon himself. He desired the best for others. He sought continually to improve himself. He never ceased growing. With clear vision he saw that the strength of any nation is not its material resources alone, but the moral fibre of its people. No man ever sought more conscientiously to do what was right. With real humility he turned to religion for guidance and help. To the church of which he was a member he gave generously of his time, his ability, his substance, never asking that his money be accepted as a substitute for personal service. He had the deepest respect for all churches and befriended them in every possible way. Here undoubtedly was the source of his courage and his unbounded faith in the future. He never ceased to believe that, with God's help, men's highest dreams for themselves and for their world can find fulfillment.

It was my privilege for many years to know Mr. Firestone as a close personal friend. One found in his home a kind of greatness that is a survival of pioneer days, when families were bound together by the closest ties of affection and loyalty. Mr. Firestone found his greatest joy in the companionship of his fine family. No pressure of business ever kept him from being with those he loved most in the important events of their lives. Anyone who visited his home found there the kind of comradeship that lives "one for all, and all for one." Material values are notably fragile. Love still remains the greatest gift of life, and its only imperishable wealth.

America today needs more than ever the wise leadership of men like Mr. Firestone, who live "above the fog in public duty and in private thinking." Our gravest dangers come not only from enemies that threaten us from without, but also from selfishness and dishonesty that can destroy us from within. Much of the world's unrest grows out of the fact that our moral consciousness lags so far behind our mechanical skill. Science has taught us the technical "know how." It remains for religion to supply us with the moral imperatives that "know why." Much of our boasted progress is what Thoreau called "improved means to an unimproved end." We have unlocked the secret of atomic power. Will it bless us or destroy us?

When will we learn that we live in one world—God's world—and that what happens to the least of us must be the concern of all?

On the memorial we are dedicating today is this inscription: "He believed what the centuries said as against the years, and as against the hours." Only as we continue to serve ideals that will stand the test of time can we keep our nation brave and strong and free. As we honor the memory of our beloved friend, let us share his faith that we live in a moral universe where the ultimate value is not matter but spirit. May God raise up men like Harvey S. Firestone who possess the wisdom, courage, and faith to lead our troubled world into the ways of righteousness and peace!

Directors

HARVEY S. FIRESTONE	1900–1938
	Treasurer—1900–1902
	President 1902 1932
	Chairman—1932–1938
JAMES CHRISTY JR.	1900–1902
	President—1900–1902
JAMES A. SWINEHART	1900–1903
	Vice President—1900–1903
F. W. DODGE ⎫ GEORGE GALL ⎭	1900 (For the purpose of incorporation only)
AMOS C. MILLER	1900–1925
	Vice President—1912–1925
A. P. CLEAVELAND	1900–1901
FRANK O. SAWYER	1901–1905
LOUIS E. SISLER ·	1902–1925
	Secretary—1900–1905
	Treasurer—1902–1910
WILL CHRISTY	1902–1916
	Vice President—1903–1912
ROBERT J. FIRESTONE	1905–1919
	Vice President—1916–1918
JOHN W. THOMAS	1916–date
	Joined company 1908
	Vice President—1919–1932
	President—1932–1941
	Chairman—1941–1946
	Honorary Chairman—1946–date
STACY G. CARKHUFF	1916–1945
	Secretary—1905–1943
HARVEY S. FIRESTONE JR.	1919–date
	Joined company 1920
	Vice President—1929–1941
	President—1941–1948
	Chairman—1948–date

A. G. PARTRIDGE

CARMON A. MYERS
THOMAS CLEMENTS

JOHN J. SHEA

HARRIS CREECH

LEE R. JACKSON

BERNARD M. ROBINSON

HARVEY H. HOLLINGER

EDSON A. OBERLIN
RUSSELL A. FIRESTONE

FRANK H. HOBSON
LEONARD K. FIRESTONE

JAMES E. TRAINER

RAYMOND C. FIRESTONE

ROGER S. FIRESTONE

1919–1921
Vice President—1919–1920
1919–1930
1919–1923
Vice President—1919–1923
1923–date
Joined company 1907
Treasurer—1922–1948
Vice President—1941–date
1925–1932
1936–1941
1929–1930
1937–date
Joined company 1912
Vice President—1929–1941
Executive Vice President—1941–1948
President—1948–date
1929–1943
Assistant Secretary—1919–1943
Secretary—1943
1930–date
Joined company 1913
Comptroller—1928–1943
Secretary—1943–1948
Treasurer—1948–date
1930–1935
1932–date
Joined company 1922
Assistant Treasurer—1943–1948
1932–1936
1939–date
Joined company 1931
1942–date
Joined company 1939
Vice President—1940–date
1942–date
Joined company 1933
Vice President—1949–date
1945–date
Joined company 1936

Officers

CHAIRMAN	Harvey S. Firestone	1932–1938
	John W. Thomas	1941–1946
	Harvey S. Firestone Jr.	1948–date
PRESIDENT	James Christy Jr.	1900–1902
	Harvey S. Firestone	1902–1932
	John W. Thomas	1932–1941
	Harvey S. Firestone Jr.	1941–1948
	Lee R. Jackson	1948–date
EXECUTIVE VICE PRESIDENT	Lee R. Jackson	1941–1948
VICE PRESIDENT	James A. Swinehart	1900–1903
	Will Christy	1903–1912
	Amos C. Miller	1912–1925
	Robert J. Firestone	1916–1918
	John W. Thomas	1919–1932
	A. G. Partridge	1919–1920
	Thomas Clements	1919–1923
	Harvey S. Firestone Jr.	1929–1941
	Lee R. Jackson	1929–1941
	James E. Trainer	1940–date
	John J. Shea	1941–date
	Harold D. Tompkins	1941–date
	Raymond C. Firestone	1949–date
TREASURER	Harvey S. Firestone	1900–1902
	Louis E. Sisler	1902–1910
	James G. Robertson	1910–1922
	John J. Shea	1922–1948
	Harvey H. Hollinger	1948–date
ASSISTANT TREASURER	Frank R. Talbott	1907–1909
	Mark E. Moffett	1919–1921
	H. K. Dexter	1919–1920

	Dwight Y. LaFever	1917–1918
	Ralph E. Wolcott	1917–1919
	Ralph S. Leonard	1919–1942
	Homer C. Campbell	1922–1930
	William D. Zahrt	1930–date
	Russell A. Firestone	1943–1948
	Elton H. Schulenberg	1945–date
SECRETARY	Louis E. Sisler	1900–1905
	Stacy G. Carkhuff	1905–1943
	Bernard M. Robinson	1943
	Harvey H. Hollinger	1943–1948
	Joseph Thomas	1948–date
ASSISTANT SECRETARY	Bernard M. Robinson	1919–1943
	C. M. Hamill	1919–1920
	Joseph Thomas	1943–1948
	Henry S. Brainard	1943–date
COMPTROLLER	Thomas Clements	1918–1923
	Harvey H. Hollinger	1928–1943
	Claude A. Pauley	1943–date
ASSISTANT COMPTROLLER	Horace C. Miller	1932–1939
	Timothy F. Doyle	1932–date
	Laurence A. Frese	1939–date

Firestone Factories

Plant	Major Products	Date[1]
Akron (Ohio)		
Miller & Sweitzer Aves.	[Original factory]	1902
Plant I	Tires and tubes	1910
Xylos	Reclaim	1914
Plant II	Tires and tubes	1917
Steel Products	Rims, wheels, beverage containers, stampings	1919
Mechanical Building	Molds and machinery	1920
Synthetic Pilot Plant	Synthetic rubber	1940
Gun Mount	Bofors gun assembly	1941
Synthetic Plant I[3]	Synthetic rubber	1941
Synthetic Plant II[3]	Synthetic rubber	1942
Airwings Building	Airplane wing panels, barrage balloons	1942
Atlanta (Georgia)[2]	Airplane wing panels, rocket launchers	1943
Bennettsville (South Carolina)	Textiles	1943
Bristol (Virginia)[2]	Fuel cells, life belts	1944
Burlington (North Carolina)[2]	Gun tubes	1944
Coshocton (Ohio)[2]	Fuel cells	1943
Compton (California)[2]	Fuel cells	1943
Dallas (Texas)[2]	Fuel cells	1942
Des Moines (Iowa)[5]	Tires and tubes	1944
East Palestine (Ohio)[2]	Rocket launchers	1944
Fall River (Massachusetts)[4]	Textiles	1924
Fall River (Massachusetts)	Plastics, Foamex, Contro, Velon	1937
Ferndale (Washington)[2]	Fuel cells	1943
Fort Worth (Texas)[2]	Textiles	1943
Fremont (Nebraska)[2]	Bomb loading plant operated for U.S. Government	1942

Plant	Major Products	Date[1]
Gastonia (North Carolina)	Textiles	1935
Hudson (Massachusetts)[4]	Footwear	1920
Indianapolis (Indiana)[2]	Tank tracks	1942
Lake Charles (Louisiana)[3]	Synthetic rubber	1942
Los Angeles (California)	Tires and tubes, industrial rubber products	1927
Xylos	Reclaim	1929
Fuel Cell Plant[2]	Fuel cells	1941
Memphis (Tennessee)	Tires and tubes	1936
Xylos	Reclaim	1938
Milwaukee (Wisconsin)[2]	Steel products	1944
New Bedford (Massachusetts)[4]	Textiles	1927
Belleville Warehouse[4]	Cotton storage	1929
New Castle (Indiana)	Industrial rubber products	1942
Newburyport (Massachusetts)[4]	Textiles	1929
Noblesville (Indiana)	Industrial rubber products	1937
Pasadena (California)[2]	Fuel cells	1943
Paterson (New Jersey)[4]	Brake lining, plastic screening	1938
Port Neches (Texas)[3]	Synthetic rubber	1943
Pottstown (Pennsylvania)[5]	Tires and plastics	1944
Richmond (Kentucky)[2]	Arsenal operated for U.S. Government	1943
Roanoke (Virginia)[8]	Textiles	1943
Santa Ana (California)[2]	Fuel cells	1943
Willow Grove (Pennsylvania)[4]	Rotary wing aircraft, rocket launchers, gliders	1943
Winston-Salem (North Carolina)[4]	Flotation gear	1943
Worcester (Massachusetts)[4]	Textiles	1943
Wyandotte (Michigan)	Steel products	1937
Zanesville (Ohio)[2]	Fuel cells	1943

FOREIGN

Bilbao (Spain)[6]	Tires and tubes	1932
Bombay (India)	Tires and tubes	1939

Plant	Major Products	Date[1]
Brentford (England)	Tires and tubes, industrial rubber products	1928
Buenos Aires (Argentina)	Tires and tubes, industrial rubber products	1930
Textile Plant	Textiles	1949
Christchurch (New Zealand)	Tires and tubes	1946
Hamilton (Ontario)	Tires and tubes, industrial rubber products	1919
Liberia (West Africa)	Rubber plantations and preparation plants	1924
Port Elizabeth (South Africa)	Tires and tubes	1936
Pratteln (Switzerland)[6]	Tires and tubes	1935
São Paulo (Brazil)	Tires and tubes	1939
Textile Plant	Textiles	1944
Singapore (Malayan Union)	Rubber preparation and shipping	1919
Viskafors (Sweden)[7]	Tires and tubes	1945
Woodstock (Ontario)	Textiles	1936

[1] Date construction began, or date acquired if purchased.
[2] World War II production only.
[3] Government owned; Firestone operated.
[4] Closed out.
[5] Operated for account of government during World War II; operated for Firestone account since 1945.
[6] Partial ownership.
[7] Manufacturing arrangement.
[8] Firestone equipment in leased space.

Statistical Tables

SQUARE FEET OF FLOOR SPACE

1900	*	1926	3,345,407
1901	*	1927	3,709,842
1902	11,250	1928	4,840,011
1903	11,250	1929	6,225,395
1904	11,250	1930	6,376,634
1905	13,100	1931	6,865,827
1906	43,600	1932	6,716,163
1907	82,800	1933	6,823,823
1908	108,700	1934	6,824,699
1909	139,400	1935	7,900,513
1910	154,800	1936	7,406,558
1911	554,700	1937	7,552,566
1912	559,000	1938	10,572,683
1913	610,600	1939	10,572,683
1914	817,000	1940	11,052,222
1915	924,500	1941	10,441,776
1916	1,462,000	1942	11,065,239
1917	1,621,100	1943	11,998,162
1918	2,051,100	1944	12,275,376
1919	2,072,600	1945	12,438,352
1920	2,081,200	1946	12,008,614
1921	2,399,400	1947	13,466,645
1922	2,399,400	1948	13,750,384
1923	2,399,400	1949	14,042,198
1924	2,399,400	1950	14,656,673
1925	3,345,407		

* Office space only.

Year	Capital and Surplus	Bonds and Debentures	Sales	Profits	Dividends Common	Dividends Preferred
	$	$	$	$	$	$
1901	50,000		110,000			
1902	200,000		150,000			
1903	200,000		230,000	8,503		
1904	200,000		456,773	71,043		
1905	313,758		769,982	122,361	7,700	
1906	429,395		1,045,172	112,174	12,000	
1907	532,510		1,681,191	214,287	18,000	
1908	767,129		2,128,354	355,801	6,000	
1909	1,117,620		3,017,958	538,177	44,187	
1910	4,047,879		5,271,040	1,394,835	55,638	8,801
1911	4,478,841		7,462,581	616,912	135,791	50,159
1912	5,831,899		11,688,188	1,189,927	190,500	63,016
1913	7,089,959		15,720,907	1,628,060	300,000	70,000
1914	9,947,678		19,250,109	3,227,719	300,000	70,000
1915	13,974,972		25,319,475	4,517,272	419,978	70,000
1916	27,456,847		44,135,325	5,926,568	869,971	89,547
1917	39,507,821		61,587,219	5,819,727	1,302,903	432,500
1918	43,712,999		75,801,506	8,356,230	2,100,000	510,000
1919	60,826,708		91,078,513	9,306,978	2,052,908	544,880
1920	58,469,387		114,980,969	9,396,912*	3,607,685	1,214,385
1921	39,374,928		66,372,938	949,354*	543,860	1,299,683
1922	44,784,034		64,507,301	7,348,421		1,293,182
1923	47,830,709	2,000,000	77,583,149	6,104,992		1,224,302
1924	53,587,430	2,000,000	85,610,004	8,116,689	1,396,028	1,188,334
1925	60,680,641	3,754,000	125,597,998	12,800,412	2,132,583	1,137,935

1926	70,766,038	3,507,600	144,397,626	7,622,339	2,483,382	1,555,593
1927	78,452,477	13,137,500	127,696,759	13,780,966	2,472,833	1,683,833
1928	80,754,853	23,016,800	125,664,666	7,072,014	3,690,280	1,646,545
1929	²29,892,508	22,717,800	144,585,804	7,726,870	2,948,280	1,589,116
1930	121,424,659	21,679,800	120,015,663	1,541,034	3,176,076	2,935,147
1931	110,503,838	20,630,800	113,797,283	6,028,631	2,136,521	3,371,904
1932	103,276,428	19,430,300	84,337,173	5,151,978	2,041,123	3,024,233
1933	100,214,015	18,962,800	75,402,268	2,397,060	1,037,340	2,814,966
1934	100,003,216	17,350,000	99,130,244	4,154,656	772,588	2,799,605
1935	101,602,066	16,000,000	121,670,572	5,649,146	751,575	2,796,309
1936	106,451,712	14,650,000	135,701,916	9,142,654	1,725,083	2,796,776
1937	108,346,054	13,300,000	156,823,095	9,269,177	4,831,713	2,796,804
1938	107,362,744	50,000,000	141,882,682	5,258,041	2,392,403	2,796,354
1939	108,742,740	48,500,000	160,119,022	6,722,046	1,926,282	2,795,604
1940	112,687,091	45,800,000	187,209,292	8,652,608	1,929,403	2,795,604
1941	117,793,555	50,000,000	268,091,826	11,262,428	2,403,279	2,795,604
1942	123,452,151	48,000,000	352,693,500	12,481,130	2,895,725	2,753,897
1943	132,592,981	46,000,000	545,389,601	15,183,383	3,872,829	2,724,774
1944	136,647,147	44,000,000	651,410,411	16,310,846	3,892,741	2,433,944
1945	145,094,933	42,000,000	681,744,073	16,446,735	4,869,302	1,957,532
1946	161,339,131	40,000,000	577,833,423	27,682,878	8,290,745	1,903,530
1947	151,972,789	63,000,000	638,447,166	26,977,877	7,803,336	724,516
1948	169,947,184	60,250,000	633,858,425	27,674,344	7,804,336	670,514
1949	178,113,856	57,500,000	579,606,107	17,823,621	7,805,336	616,512
1950	199,832,407	54,750,000	690,571,555	33,267,561	9,757,870	562,512

*Before depreciating inventories.

Index